# THE
# THIRD✠REICH
## IN 100 OBJECTS

# THE
# THIRD✠REICH
## IN 100 OBJECTS
### A MATERIAL HISTORY OF NAZI GERMANY

ROGER MOORHOUSE

FOREWORD BY RICHARD OVERY

Greenhill Books

Greenhill Books

*The Third Reich in 100 Objects*
This edition published in 2017 by
Greenhill Books,
c/o Pen & Sword Books Ltd,
47 Church Street, Barnsley,
S. Yorkshire, s70 2as

www.greenhillbooks.com
contact@greenhillbooks.com

ISBN: 978–1–78438–180–6

© Roger Moorhouse, 2017
Foreword © Richard Overy, 2017

The right of Roger Moorhouse to be identified as author of this work
has been asserted in accordance with Section 77 of the
Copyrights Designs and Patents Act 1988.

CIP data records for this title are available from the British Library

Designed by Jem Butcher

Printed and bound in India by Replika Press Pvt. Ltd.

For Nic & Eve
with love

# CONTENTS

# FOREWORD

*Hitler's Third Reich lasted only twelve years*, yet it continues to exert a macabre fascination long after its violent demise. There is no other modern political movement and no other modern dictator that can compete with the instant recognition of the images, symbols and propaganda surrounding Hitler and his regime. The swastika, adapted by Hitler himself from the traditional Hindu symbol of good fortune, is still daubed on walls by anti-fascists and neo-fascists because it enjoys such a powerful resonance even today. When the British comedy actor John Cleese chose to poke fun at the Germans in an episode of *Fawlty Towers* in the 1970s, his raised arm was all he needed to evoke in his audience an instant reminder of the hundreds of thousands of Germans in newsreel footage with their arms stretched out as far as they could go towards their adored *Führer*. The image of Hitler himself, with the neat black moustache and the limp forelock, has been superimposed on hundreds of election posters and advertising hoardings, or exploited in political cartooning. He enjoys as bizarre a celebrity status in death as he did in life.

Hitler with an excited young admirer at his Berghof retreat in happy prewar days.

The Messerschmitt Bf 109 fighter, one of the crucial elements in Germany's early-war military successes.

Image was all-important to Hitler and the National Socialist Party that he led. Visibility was one of the key explanations for their electoral success in the early 1930s, a quality that almost all other German political parties ignored. The image of Hitler himself was massaged all the time to show him alternately as the stern, unyielding messiah of the German people, or as the genial, unpretentious leader happy to pat small children and play with his dog. Hitler was completely absorbed by the image he presented as his political persona; no photograph of the leader wearing glasses was allowed to be published. The Party was also image-conscious. Its public face depended on the showy marches, the torchlight processions, the flags and symbols – a carefully staged and choreographed political drama to make the movement distinctive. The Nuremberg rallies became orchestrated and disciplined expressions of the 'national revolution', impressive even by today's standards. The high point of this political artistry was reached in the Leni Riefenstahl film, *Triumph of the Will*, which conveys simply through image the powerful message of national revival and a single 'people's community'. The imagery itself encourages participation and belonging. The *'Heil Hitler!'* greeting and the Swastika flag draped from the bedroom window were as often as not spontaneous expressions of affirmation. Symbolism replaced the need to think very seriously about what it all meant.

The regime also generated a darker symbolism, evident in the choice of objects presented here. If there is no rubber truncheon, there are concentration camp relics, and the slogan *'Arbeit macht frei'* – 'work makes you free' – which greeted prisoners at Auschwitz and other camps where work was usually a physical torture, or in many cases a prelude to early death. The name of the dreaded Gestapo, the political secret police, is still a byword for vicious oppression, though unlike the SS organisation with its black uniforms, silver badges and ornate daggers, the Gestapo is not immediately recognisable by any external trappings. The secret police were policemen, doing political detective work, or later pursuing Jews in hiding, and remain even today a more anonymous element in the history of the Hitler dictatorship than they should be. The SS, on the other hand, were designed to be seen, admired or feared. The black uniform and death's head badge were an inspiration, a menacing fashion statement that the manure-coloured uniform of the SA could never match. The SS as a result features in the 100 objects a good deal.

Some of the symbols exploited by the regime were fatal in their consequences. In autumn 1941 Hitler finally ordered all German Jews to wear a yellow star sewn onto their clothing. The yellow star, first used in medieval Europe to distinguish Jews, was adapted by the regime for its policy of racial exclusion. Jews in all of German-occupied Europe were made to wear the star, which eventually made it easier to collect and deport them to their deaths in the extermination camps. The Jewish Star of David was visible from the start of the dictatorship when it was daubed on shop windows or the houses of Jewish attorneys and doctors to warn Germans not to buy goods or services from Jews. The caricature of the Jew was used widely in all party newspapers, a familiar narrow-eyed, hook-nosed figure clutching money-bags or menacing German womanhood.

The heart of evil: the rail tracks and gate at the Auschwitz-Birkenau extermination camp.

The *Reichsadler* or 'Imperial Eagle', chosen by Hitler to be emblematic of the Third Reich.

Of course, choosing 100 objects to define the Third Reich can never be an easy task, and there will be things here that readers think should be included, just as there are many objects that will be reassuringly familiar. The selection below shows many different aspects of the story of Hitler, his rise to power and the dictatorship that followed. Taken together they provide a broad approach to the complex history of the period, and a set of images that give the history a firm material texture. The commentaries on each object are a reminder, however, that nothing is ever as simple as it seems. The objects need interpretation and context, whether they are as mundane as the brush Hitler used for his moustache, or as momentous as the volumes of *Mein Kampf*, Hitler's personal account of his brief life and the philosophy that informed it. The Third Reich was both ordinary and extraordinary, both daily life and malign drama. The 100 objects give a sense of those contrasts and of the way leaders and led experienced them.

Richard Overy,

April 2017

# THE
# OBJECTS

# 1 Hitler's Paint Box

*This battered, enamelled box* of well-used watercolour paints – made in 1910 by the Nuremberg firm of Redeker & Hennis – once belonged to Adolf Hitler. Looted by Belgian war correspondent Robert Francotte from Hitler's office desk in his Munich apartment, on Prinzregentenstrasse, in May 1945, it is evidence of an aspect of Hitler's life and career that rarely receives scrutiny – his artistic pretensions.

If his account in *Mein Kampf* is to be believed, Hitler decided to become an artist at the age of twelve. Indulged by his adoring, widowed mother, he insisted that he would one day be a famous painter and dropped out of school in 1905 to pursue his dream. Two years later, he travelled to Vienna to enrol in the Academy of Fine Arts. Armed with a portfolio of his sketches, he was convinced, he later wrote, that he would 'pass the examination quite easily'.[1]

Though his paintings are often derided, Hitler was certainly a competent artist. Even before he arrived in Vienna, he was scarcely without his sketchbook, and was constantly scribbling aspects of buildings that pleased him or designs for the stage sets of operas he wanted to write. As his youthful friend, August Kubizek, remembered:

A watercolour paint set that once belonged to Adolf Hitler.

On fine days, he used to frequent a bench on the Turmleitenweg [in Linz] where he established a kind of open-air study. There he would read his books, sketch and paint in watercolours.[2]

By the time he left Linz to live in Vienna, therefore, Hitler was confident of success in applying to the Academy, recalling that he had been 'by far the best student' in his school drawing class and that, since that time, he had made 'more than ordinary progress'.[3] He was to be frustrated, however. Though he qualified to sit the examination for the Vienna Academy, his drawings were deemed 'unsatisfactory' by the examiners,

---

### 'Hitler decided to become an artist at the age of twelve.'

---

who gave the lapidary explanation that he had included 'too few heads'.[4] Crestfallen, Hitler doggedly pursued his dream, and the following year applied again, though this time without even qualifying to sit the examination. It was a rejection that would torment him until the end of his life.

In the years that followed, Hitler would scrape a meagre living as an artist, selling his paintings and postcards, first in Vienna and later in Munich. During this period, he claimed to have painted as many as 700 or 800 pictures, asking around five marks for each. His style was straightforward, simple and naturalistic, using as his subjects mainly buildings, flowers and sweeping landscapes: 'I paint what people want,' he once said. He showed a fascination for detail, particularly architectural, but included very few human figures – an echo of his earlier failing.

With the outbreak of war in 1914, Hitler took his watercolours with him to the Western Front, where he painted and sketched his surroundings. The example opposite of his wartime work was painted in December 1914 and depicts a monastery ruined by shellfire at Messines, south of Ypres. It is unclear whether Hitler was still dreaming of a career as an artist by this point, or merely exercising his hobby, but it is notable that he spent his first period of leave in Berlin, visiting the city's galleries.

Though he idly dreamed of once again applying for an art academy after the war, politics would soon take over his life. Thereafter, painting would be relegated to a few doodles and marginal sketches, not least among them some of the architectural sketches that would later resurface in the Germania plan to rebuild Berlin (see 'Hitler's Germania Sketch', pages 101–2). In addition, Hitler's tastes would dictate the artistic tone and cultural style of the Third Reich. He overruled Goebbels's liking for modern art, and decreed that a dull classical style, presenting ideal Aryan families in mawkishly sentimental terms, should be the 'official' art of the Reich. He patronised such traditional artists as the neo-classical sculptor Arno Breker, while those more avant-garde artists who had flourished under the Weimar Republic, such as the Bauhaus designers, were forced into exile.

Hitler's own paintings, meanwhile, were suppressed, with tame buyers dispatched to acquire those that could be located. Only a handful were ever published, and in

1937 exhibiting them was prohibited.[5] By the later years of the twentieth century, they would become quite sought after by collectors, with some examples fetching over €100,000 at auction. Hitler's watercolour set made a rather more modest €8,000, when it was sold in 2010.

Hitler claimed that his failure to be accepted into the Vienna Academy had made him 'tough', but it also rankled. More seriously, it marked a fork in his life; a point at which his dreams of becoming an artist receded, and his frustrations with the world grew. It is impossible to say for sure, of course, but perhaps that rejection contributed to Germany's later catastrophe.

Aquarelle of a ruined monastery painted by Adolf Hitler in December 1914 while he was serving in the German Army.

1   A. Hitler, *Mein Kampf* (London, 1939), p. 30.

2   A. Kubizek, *The Young Hitler I Knew* (London, 2006), p. 40.

3   Hitler, *Mein Kampf*, p. 30.

4   F. Spotts, *Hitler and the Power of Aesthetics* (London, 2003), p. 124.

5   Spotts, p. 140.

# 2 Hitler's German Workers' Party Card

*On 12 September 1919, Adolf Hitler* attended a meeting of a small nationalist political party in a Munich beer hall. The Deutsche Arbeiter-Partei (DAP or 'German Workers' Party') had been founded earlier that year, during the chaos of the German revolution, by a Munich rail worker, Anton Drexler, in the hope of combining nationalism with a mass appeal. Hitler, who was still a serving soldier, was there to observe proceedings on behalf of the Army.

The precise process by which Hitler ended up joining the organisation he was supposed to observe is rather unclear, obscured by Hitler's own self-aggrandising account and later Nazi mythology. Yet it appears that Drexler was sufficiently impressed when the shabby-looking Hitler stood up to interject that he later thrust a pamphlet into his hand. According to legend, he said of the newcomer: 'That one's got something. We could use him.'[1]

Hitler's DAP membership card, number 555.

> *'The card gives Hitler's membership number as "555", a blatant attempt to make the party seem larger than it was.'*

In the days that followed, after Hitler perused the pamphlet, he was surprised to receive a postcard from Drexler informing him that he had been accepted as a member of the DAP and was duly invited to attend the next meeting. The party that Hitler joined was – according to his own account – a somewhat ramshackle outfit; with a tiny membership of barely fifty, it had no fixed political programme or basic organisation. At the meeting Hitler attended, the party's total funds were reported to amount to 7 marks 50 pfennigs.[2]

It was only in January 1920 that the DAP issued formal membership cards. Hitler's card, shown here, was dated 1 January. It gives his address at the army barracks, Lothstrasse 29, and was signed both by Drexler and the party's record keeper, Rudolf Schüssler. It also shows Hitler's name spelt with two 't's, one of which has been crudely crossed out. Most curiously, the card gives Hitler's membership number as '555', a blatant attempt to make the party seem larger than it was. In truth, the membership list began at 501 and Hitler was the 55th member.[3]

By the time that Hitler received this membership card, he was already a rising star in the DAP. After making his speaking debut in October 1919, he began drawing sizeable audiences – larger than the party's events had previously attracted – thereby swelling the party coffers and generating increased publicity. The DAP, it seemed, was on the move.

The breakthrough would come on 24 February 1920, when the party organised its biggest event yet – at the cavernous Hofbräuhaus in central Munich. There, before some 2,000 people, Hitler gave the DAP the direction that he believed it had lacked by promulgating a manifesto – the Twenty-Five-Point Programme – a curious mixture of anti-Semitic, anti-Marxist and anti-capitalist positions. That same evening, Hitler announced that the party had changed its name to express its political principles better; the German Workers' Party was thereby transformed into the National Socialist German Workers' Party (Nazionalsozialistische Deutsche Arbeiterpartei – NSDAP). The Nazi Party was born and, barely six months after his first appearance, Hitler was already its primary motive force.

1   Various versions of the statement exist – see, for instance, Ian Kershaw, *Hitler: Hubris 1889–1936* (London, 1998), p. 126, and Volker Ullrich, *Hitler: Ascent 1889–1939* (London, 2016), p. 87.

2   Alan Bullock, *Hitler: A Study in Tyranny* (London, 1962), p. 65.

3   Ullrich, *Hitler: Ascent 1889–1939*, p. 87

# 3 The Blood Flag

*If Nazism is best understood as a political religion*, then the *Blutfahne* or 'Blood Flag' was one of its most sacred artefacts. Originally, it was an ordinary swastika banner belonging to the 5th Sturm of the Munich Sturmabteilung or SA, Hitler's 'Brownshirts'. However, during the Nazis' abortive attempt to seize power in Munich in November 1923, it was soaked with the blood of three of the dead, Anton Hechenberger, Lorenz Ritter von Stransky-Grippenfeld and Andreas Bauriedl, killed when the Bavarian police opened fire on the marchers.

---

*'The Blood Flag was essentially accorded the status of a holy relic.'*

---

Restored to Hitler after his release from prison in December 1924, the Blood Flag quickly became the centrepiece of Nazi ceremonial. A new swastika finial was added to the tip of the pole, and a silver collar was inserted beneath it bearing the names of three of the sixteen Nazis – Hechenberger, Stransky-Grippenfeld and Bauriedl – who had been 'martyred' in the 1923 *Putsch*. After that, the flag was not only ceremonially presented at all major Nazi events, its touch was used by Hitler to 'sanctify' other Nazi flags and standards and to seal the oath of newly enlisted SS men.

The Blood Flag was essentially accorded the status of a holy relic. When not in use, it was given pride of place in the foyer of the Nazi Party Headquarters – the so-called 'Brown House' – in Munich. It was considered so important to the Nazi movement that it was allocated its own attendant – an otherwise unremarkable, toothbrush-moustached SS man by the name of Jakob Grimminger – whose sole task it was to accompany the flag on its ceremonial peregrinations around the country.

Grimminger can be seen in this propaganda postcard from 1937, lowering the Blood Flag before one of the burning pyres in front of the Feldherrnhalle in Munich, the focus of the annual commemoration of the Beer Hall *Putsch*. The text beneath reads: 'In memory of 9 November 1923'.

The Blood Flag was last seen in public in Berlin in October 1944, when it was used for the swearing in of the first cadres of the Volkssturm, Nazi Germany's last line of defence, consisting largely of boys and old men. After that, the flag disappeared. It is, of course, possible that it has survived, perhaps folded up in a suburban American attic, having been unwittingly looted by a GI in 1945 and since forgotten. But, it is most likely that the flag was destroyed when the Brown House was severely damaged in an Allied air raid in January 1945, or that it subsequently disappeared in the chaos of post-war Germany. Grimminger survived the war and died in obscurity in 1969.

Zum Gedenken des 9. November 1923

The Blood Flag: Nazi Germany's most sacred relic.

# 4 Hyperinflation Banknote

*This banknote – for a mind-boggling 100 trillion marks –* is a reminder of a dark period in Germany's inter-war politics, a period that arguably contained the seeds of even darker days to come.

After Germany was defeated in World War I, the country not only faced a political crisis of revolution and collapse, but also an economic one. As well as the problems of economic dislocation and the cost of reparations payable to the Allies, it faced the looming catastrophe of hyperinflation. Germany's war effort before 1918 had been largely funded by printing money, in the expectation that – after Germany's victory – their enemies could be made to pay. However, with defeat, those hopes were dashed, and huge inflationary pressure had been built up within the German economy. Already, by the spring of 1920, one US dollar was worth over 83 marks; in August 1914, it had been worth 4 marks.[1]

As if to compound such difficulties, many of Germany's economic experts – including the president of the Reichsbank, Rudolf Havenstein – appeared not only not to know how to deal with the crisis, but also to have only a vague idea of what was causing it. And Havenstein's response to the devaluation was to print more money, thereby causing the currency to devalue still further.[2] Consequently, by February 1922, one US dollar was already worth over 200 marks.

> *'This 100 trillion mark note would be the largest denomination banknote ever issued in Germany.'*

By the summer of the crisis year of 1923, the background hum of inflation had become a roar. That January, French and Belgian troops had occupied Germany's industrial heartland, the Ruhr district, as a punishment for the non-payment of reparations. In response, the German government had espoused a policy of 'passive resistance', calling for Ruhr workers to withhold their labour, while Berlin continued paying them. This, along with the ongoing political crisis, finally provoked a runaway economic collapse. By July, the dollar exchange rate topped 100,000 marks for the first time; by the following month, it had trebled; a month after that, it had increased tenfold. The German currency was soon in free-fall. It would peak, on 1 December, with one US dollar standing at 6.7 trillion marks: $1 = 6,700,000,000,000.[3]

Barely worth the paper it was printed on: a 100 trillion mark banknote.

Of course this collapse had a huge effect on German society. With a loaf of bread or a humble postage stamp costing anything upwards of a trillion marks that autumn, the middle classes saw any savings they had wiped out. Workers meanwhile, were often paid twice a day – to offset the effects of inflation – and were known to take their wages home in wheelbarrows. Bartering goods and services once again became commonplace. Children played with worthless bundles of money; their parents burnt money in the grate for heat, and beggars refused to accept any note below a million.[4]

Inevitably, the galloping chaos had a political echo, and for a time, Germany itself appeared to be on the brink of falling apart. Communist risings broke out in Hamburg and Thuringia that summer and, in November 1923, Hitler launched his own abortive attempt to seize power in Bavaria, the Munich *Putsch*.

The crisis was finally brought to an end over the winter of 1923–4, when the hapless Havenstein died and Hjalmar Schacht succeeded him as president of the Reichsbank. Under Schacht, the currency was reformed, with the introduction of the 'Rentenmark', which effectively lopped twelve zeros off the old 'Papiermark', and stability gradually returned. This 100 trillion mark note,[5] first issued in November 1923 and bearing a pen portrait by Albrecht Dürer, would be the largest denomination banknote ever issued in Germany. It was emblematic of the country's inter-war fragility.

In the years that followed, normality was restored and Hitler retreated once again to the political fringes. But memories were long, and when economic crisis struck again in 1929 – albeit a deflationary crisis this time – the experiences of six years earlier were still raw for many people; the toxic sentiment that 'the system' was simply broken gained credence, and those with the most radical solutions to Germany's problems suddenly moved to centre stage. From taking 2.6 per cent of the national vote in the Reichstag election of 1928, Hitler's Nazis polled 18 per cent in 1930.[6] From there they would not look back.

It is a truism that Hitler was brought to prominence in Germany – if not necessarily to power – by the corrosive effects of the Wall Street Crash of 1929. Yet, even though economics is central to the story, there is more to Hitler's rise than 1929 alone. This banknote is a reminder that the economic collapse of 1923 should also be considered as a major contributory factor, weakening still further popular faith in the economic and political status quo. It is worth remembering that, less than a decade after this note was issued, Hitler was already Chancellor of Germany.

German children play with bundles of worthless banknotes during the great inflation.

1   F. Taylor, *The Downfall of Money* (London, 2013), pp. 361–2.

2   A. Fergusson, *When Money Dies* (London, 2010), p. 75.

3   Statistics quoted in Taylor, pp. 366–7, 370.

4   Fergusson, p. 188.

5   The note is marked as '*Hundert Billionen Mark*' but the German word *Billion* means a million million (a trillion), rather than a thousand million, the usual modern meaning of 'billion' in English.

6   Volker Berghahn, *Modern Germany* (Cambridge, 1982), p. 284.

# 5 Hitler's Moustache Brush

*In 1923, Hitler's friend and confidant Ernst 'Putzi' Hanfstaengl* tried to persuade him to shave off his moustache. Long bothered by the meagre toothbrush moustache on Hitler's upper lip, which he dismissed as 'puny' and 'an invitation to the caricaturists', Hanfstaengl suggested that Hitler should instead grow a goatee beard, as a demonstration of 'manliness'. Shocked, Hitler replied that Hanfstaengl was kidding himself: 'My moustache will one day be all the rage,' he said, 'You can rely on that!'[1] He was not entirely mistaken.

Aside from the dubious question of manliness, a second part of Hanfstaengl's argument was that Hitler could ill afford the time required constantly to trim and preen his moustache. Yet, as this item shows, Hitler was quite prepared to put in the work. This 7 cm horn-backed 'moustache brush' was Hitler's own and was taken from the bedroom of his Munich apartment after his death, by his housekeeper Anni Winter. According to the recollections of Hitler's entourage, it was an integral part of Hitler's toiletry bag, which travelled with him wherever he went.[2]

The grooming of an icon – Hitler's moustache brush.

It is not clear precisely when Hitler adopted the toothbrush style moustache that would become his trademark. During World War I, he sported a rather fuller 'Kaiser-style' moustache, and it is sometimes suggested that he first trimmed it in order to ensure a better seal on his gas mask. This seems plausible, except that pictures of Hitler recuperating at the military hospital at Pasewalk in October 1918 show him still wearing the 'Kaiser-style', so the change must have come after the end of the war.

---

*"'My moustache will one day be all the rage,"*
*Hitler said. "You can rely on that!"'*

---

The toothbrush moustache was certainly en vogue in the 1920s, made popular most notably by Charlie Chaplin. It may seem surprising to modern readers but Hitler was extremely image-conscious and worked hard, with his photographer Heinrich Hoffmann, to hone his public image in the 1920s, to create a 'look' that would appeal to his audience. It may well be, then, that his choice of moustache was a part of that process. However, Hitler's adoption of the style was perhaps as much practical as fashionable; as he confessed to a friend in Munich: 'Imagine my face without the moustache! My nose is much too big.'[3]

Whatever his motivation, Hitler was right about the style catching on, at least amongst his followers. By 1923, when Hanfstaengl was trying to persuade Hitler to abandon the 'toothbrush', both Heinrich Himmler and Ernst Röhm were already following suit. In later years, the numbers would multiply. Alongside countless ordinary Germans, a host of Nazi bigwigs all adopted what had become known as the 'Hitler moustache', including Gauleiters Julius Streicher, Erich Koch and Josef Wagner, Generals Lothar Rendulic, Gotthard Heinrici and Heinrich von Vietinghoff, as well as senior SS men such as Irmfried Eberl, Christian Wirth, and Hitler's long-time friend Sepp Dietrich. For many of them, certainly, wearing a Hitler moustache was much more than a fashion statement; it was an act of political fealty, a personal homage to their *Führer*.

1  Ernst Hanfstaengl, *15 Jahre mit Hitler* (Munich, 1980), pp. 82–3.

2  Henry Picker, *Tischgespräche im Führerhauptquartier: 1941–1942* (Bonn, 1951), p. 239.

3  Erich Kempka, *I was Hitler's Chauffeur* (London, 2010), p. 174.

# 6 *Der Stürmer* Front Page

*Der Stürmer was a notorious weekly tabloid newspaper* expressing virulently anti-Semitic Nazi propaganda within the Third Reich. Published in Nuremberg by Julius Streicher, a leading early member of the Nazi Party, it ran from 1923 until close to the end of World War II, and at its peak was selling almost half a million copies per week. Rife with salacious and obscene anti-Semitic material and caricatures, it made no secret of its desire to see the Jewish population of Germany removed. The regular front-page strap-line – seen at the bottom of this issue from 1940 – proclaimed: 'The Jews are our misfortune!' – a phrase coined by German politician Heinrich von Treitschke in 1880.

Front page of *Der Sturmer* – 'The Attacker' – a weekly tabloid newspaper devoted to anti-Semitic Nazi propaganda within the Third Reich.

> *'Der Stürmer was self-consciously scurrilous, deliberately libellous, revelling in its own notoriety.'*

Anti-Semitism was at the very heart of Hitler's 'philosophy'. It was not a political tactic, it was a core article of faith, running like a red thread all the way from the Nazi Twenty-Five-Point Programme of 1920 to his regime's bloody demise in 1945. Yet, the biological, racial anti-Semitism of the Nazis was not necessarily shared by the wider German population; it had to be actively propagated, encouraged by the use of propaganda. And in this process, multiple voices and multiple messages were required, to appeal to different sectors of society. With its crude stereotypes and simplistic messaging, *Der Stürmer* unashamedly targeted the German working class.

Unlike the other newspapers of Nazi Germany, *Der Stürmer* made little attempt to present itself as a serious publication, rather it was self-consciously scurrilous, deliberately libellous, revelling in its own notoriety. Scandal and sensationalism were its stock in trade, combining personal smears on prominent Jewish personalities with preposterous stories of Jewish sexual perversion. Indeed, apart from titillating its audience, its sexual content – particularly its obsession with racial miscegenation – was a base expression of the so-called 'Impregnation Theory', the idea that Germany was being genetically undermined, biologically threatened, by the systematic admixture of 'alien' (Jewish) blood. *Der Stürmer* was not just a vile tabloid for consumption of the masses, it carried a central message of Nazi philosophy.

Given its notoriety, *Der Stürmer* divided opinion, even among senior Nazis. Göring loathed it, not least as he had found himself the subject of some of its 'revelations', and forbade its presence in any of his departments. Goebbels, meanwhile, was concerned by the effect that it might have on foreign opinion about Germany, and periodically suspended publication. Streicher, too, was widely considered by the Nazi leadership (probably rightly) to be less than entirely sane; Goebbels described him as 'perhaps a bit pathological'.[1] However, he was largely protected by the patronage of Hitler himself, who praised Streicher's 'moderation', stating that:

> Streicher is reproached for his *Stürmer*. The truth is the opposite of what people say: he idealised the Jew. The Jew is baser, fiercer, more diabolical than Streicher depicted him.[2]

Even Hitler could not protect Streicher for ever, though, and in 1940 he was removed from the position of *Gauleiter* after being implicated in a financial scandal. Tried with other leading Nazis at the end of the war in his native Nuremberg, he was convicted of crimes against humanity and sentenced to death. As he went to the gallows, he was still raving against the Jews.

---

1 Quoted in T. Thacker, *Joseph Goebbels: Life and Death* (London, 2009), p. 40.

2 Quoted in Hugh Trevor-Roper (ed.), *Hitler's Table Talk: 1941–1944* (New York, 2000), p. 154.

# 7 *Mein Kampf*

*When, on April Fools' Day 1924*, Adolf Hitler sat down to write the first lines of *Mein Kampf*, he would scarcely have believed the significance – and the notoriety – that the book would one day have.

Languishing in Landsberg Jail, where he had just been sent to serve a five-year sentence of 'fortress detention' for his part in the Beer Hall *Putsch* of the previous autumn, Hitler had some time on his hands. Surrounded by his Nazi acolytes, and enjoying comfortable conditions, he began penning his magnum opus on an old Remington typewriter, tapping away, two-fingered, into the small hours.[1]

There are conflicting accounts of the book's origins. The most common story is that it was commissioned by Hitler's publisher – and former superior officer – Max Amann, who was evidently expecting a racy, sensational account of the Munich *Putsch*. Others suggest that Hitler was motivated to put pen to paper by an overwhelming desire to justify his actions and damn his political opponents.[2] It is also possible that he was seeking to address his intellectual inferiority complex, by joining those of his fellows – including Alfred Rosenberg and Dietrich Eckart – who had already committed their Nazi principles to print.

Whatever the precise reason, after a few false starts Hitler set to work with an unusual determination, getting properly under way in June 1924. After his release from Landsberg that December, he continued work on the book, delivering his first volume in June 1925, for publication the following month. Thereafter, he retired to the Obersalzberg in the summer of 1926, where he wrote the second volume, which duly appeared that December.

The result was not immediately successful. Part Nazi manifesto, part rose-tinted autobiography, *Mein Kampf* expounded Hitler's theories on race, anti-Semitism, anti-capitalism, anti-Bolshevism and current affairs, from the use of propaganda to the idea of *Lebensraum*, the failings of the German revolution to the perils of democracy. It was verbose, pretentious and overblown, reflecting the author's intellectual insecurities as much as his prejudices. It was the work of someone so desperate to be taken seriously that he appeared to cram every argument, every supporting piece of evidence, every clumsy metaphor possible, into his text, in the hope that by sheer weight of words alone he would convince his reader.

Review after review criticised the book, attacking not only its content and its glutinous style, but even questioning the mental stability of its author. The Catholic *Bayerische Vaterland* even resorted to ridicule, referring to the book as *Sein Krampf*, or 'His Cramp'.[3] According to the later dissident Otto Strasser, the reception amongst Nazi circles was

> 'It was verbose, pretentious and overblown, reflecting the author's intellectual insecurities as much as his prejudices.'

Two volumes of *Mein Kampf*.

scarcely more enthusiastic, with many Party members privately confessing that they had never read the book. He claimed they even played a game whereby the first person to admit to reading *Mein Kampf* would have to pay the bar bill for the rest. The first to enter, Strasser claimed, was his brother Gregor, who 'answered with a sonorous "No". Goebbels shook his head. Göring broke out in a loud laugh.'[4] Even Italian dictator Benito Mussolini was unimpressed with it; it was, he said, 'a boring tome that I have never been able to read'.[5]

Sales were understandably rather sluggish, but by the end of 1925, the 10,000 print run of that first edition had all but sold out.[6] In the half dozen years that followed, spurred by Hitler's political rise, the book sold nearly 300,000 copies. In 1933, the year of his appointment as chancellor, it then sold over a million more.[7] In total, *Mein Kampf* would sell a remarkable 12,450,000 copies over its author's lifetime.[8] It was even gifted by the Nazi state to newlyweds, a perverse dowry intended to speed the happy couple's indoctrination.

Even after Hitler's death and Nazism's demise, *Mein Kampf* was still casting its shadow. With publication in Germany restricted by the Bavarian state – to which the rights had passed – the prospect of the book's copyright lapsing in 2016 (allowing anyone to reprint it) prompted a new, annotated edition, which took the original 700 pages up to a whopping 2,000, but included a thorough academic commentary to inoculate incautious readers against any possible seduction by Hitler's words.[9] Naturally, the new edition's editors were horrified when the book – once again – became a bestseller in Germany, thereby prompting another round of soul-searching and agonising in the German media about the perceived contemporary resonance of Hitler and his odious ideology.[10]

Nonetheless, it is doubtful that many of Hitler's readers – now or during the Third Reich – ever actually read much of *Mein Kampf*. In its day, it was a potent symbol of loyalty to the regime, a 'must-have' addition to the faithful Nazi's bookshelf and a useful demonstration of bona fides for the less convinced. To modern readers, it is a historical curiosity, a toxic relic, but surely little more. *Mein Kampf* is, perhaps, the most talked about, but least read book in history.

1   Volker Ullrich, *Adolf Hitler* (Frankfurt am Main, 2013), p. 199.

2   Christian Hartmann et al. (eds), *Hitler, Mein Kampf: Eine kritische Edition*, Vol. 1 (Munich, 2016), p. 13.

3   Quoted in Timothy Ryback, *Hitler's Private Library* (London, 2009), p. 77.

4   Strasser, quoted in ibid., p. 77.

5   Denis Mack Smith, *Mussolini* (London, 1981), p. 200.

6   Ullrich, *Adolf Hitler*, p. 200.

7   Othmar Plöckinger, *Geschichte eines Buches: Adolf Hitlers 'Mein Kampf': 1922–1945* (Munich, 2006), p. 185 *fn*.

8   Ullrich, *Adolf Hitler*, p. 200.

9   See Hartmann et al., *Hitler, Mein Kampf*.

10  See, for instance, www.theguardian.com/world/2016/jan/01/mein-kampf-book-adolf-hitler-copyright-expires.

# 8 The Hitler Greeting

*The use of the 'Heil Hitler' or 'German Greeting'*, with the right arm outstretched, was one of the most iconic and ubiquitous features of everyday life during the Third Reich.

Though the origins of the salute were widely thought to be Roman, there is no contemporary evidence of its use in antiquity and it came to prominence through its adoption by Mussolini's Fascists in the early 1920s, from whom the practice was borrowed by the Nazis. Despite some early concerns that the arm salute was rather too Italianate, and thereby 'un-German', it was nonetheless taken up in Nazi circles and in 1926 became the compulsory form of greeting used between Party members.

After the Nazi seizure of power in 1933, the 'German Greeting' was gradually rolled out to encompass ever larger sectors of German society. In July of that year, all state employees were ordered to use it, and it was stipulated to be used by all those present during the playing of the German national anthem and the Horst Wessel Song.

> *'The use of the "German Greeting" became a test, a public show of loyalty to the Nazi regime.'*

Soon, elaborate guidelines were published, explaining when the greeting was to be employed and the circumstances in which it could be excused: amputees who had lost their right arm, for instance, could use the left, as could gentlemen who were escorting a lady on their right arm. Beyond such exceptions, the instruction given was 'to raise the right arm at an angle so that the palm of the hand becomes visible'. The appropriate phrase to go with it was decreed as *'Heil Hitler'* or at least *'Heil'*. Similarly, official letters were to end with the valediction *'Heil Hitler'* – with the notable exception of dismissal notices.[1]

By way of spreading the use of the greeting, enamelled signs such as this one began to appear by the mid-1930s. Bearing the text 'Our greeting is "*Heil Hitler*"', alongside a swastika – or the more poetic '*Volksgenosse, trittst du ein, soll dein Gruss "Heil Hitler" sein*', or 'Comrade, when you're meeting, you should use the Hitler Greeting' – they would commonly be placed in factories, workplaces and public areas to encourage the faithful and admonish the recalcitrant.

Other methods were less passive. Children would be taught the greeting in *Kindergarten*, with the words *'Heil Hitler'* being included in basic writing exercises. Dutiful parents would encourage their charges to *'mach dein Hitlerchen'* – 'do your little Hitler-kins' – at appropriate moments.[2] Jews, incidentally, were forbidden to use the greeting in 1937.

A constant reminder.

One of the most sensitive sites where the 'German Greeting' was demanded of all passers-by, was the Feldherrnhalle in Munich, where the Nazi *Putsch* had been stopped amid a hail of gunfire in 1923. There, a permanent SS picket ensured total compliance, even from cyclists, who were obliged to wobble past one-handed. Those who wished to avoid a confrontation could duck down the nearby Viscardigasse, which soon earned the nickname of 'Shirkers' Alley'.[3]

One surprising bastion of resistance to such conformity was the German Army, which managed for a long time to exempt itself from the Nazi Party's diktats on the issue. The change came in the summer of 1944, when – in the wake of the July Bomb Plot on Hitler's life, carried out by Colonel Claus von Stauffenberg – the 'German Greeting' was finally adopted as a visible and public demonstration of the Army's subordination.

Ironically, Hitler himself used the greeting only intermittently. In most situations he acknowledged it simply by raising his right hand with the elbow bent and the palm facing forwards. Usually, he employed the German Greeting only on formal public occasions, such as for the military parade for his fiftieth birthday in 1939, during which he stood to attention, arm outstretched, for hours on end, to the astonishment of his entourage. His secretary, Christa Schroeder, swooned: 'It is simply amazing to me where he gets his strength from.'[4]

Increasingly, then, the use of the 'German Greeting' became a test, a public show of loyalty to the Nazi regime – like displaying a copy of *Mein Kampf*, or a photograph of Hitler – which many Germans dared not fail, whatever their political convictions.

21

Pressure to conform, and the ever-present peril of denunciation, could make for an oppressive atmosphere. This was illustrated by the perhaps apocryphal tale of a music hall performer, who strode onto the stage and made what appeared to be the 'German Greeting'. As he stood in silence, with a serious expression and his right arm outstretched, his audience were increasingly unsure of how to react, and many duly stood and responded in kind, with even the reluctant amongst them finally joining in for fear of being seen as disloyal. Only then, with his entire audience standing and saluting, did the performer break the silence to deliver the punch line: 'Last year, the snow in my village was *this* high.' It is highly doubtful that the Gestapo would have seen the funny side.

Hitler's public perform the 'German Greeting'.

1   Richard Grunberger, *A Social History of the Third Reich* (London, 1970), pp. 114–15.

2   Ibid., p. 114.

3   Maik Kopleck, *München, 1933–1945* (Berlin, 2005), p. 5.

4   Christa Schroeder, *He Was My Chief* (London, 2009), p. 70.

# 9 Horst Wessel Song Original Score

*In 1929, a young Berliner wrote a marching song.* Horst Wessel was the 21-year-old son of a Lutheran pastor, a student of jurisprudence at Berlin University, and the leader of his local *Sturm* of the SA, the Nazi 'Brownshirts'. By many accounts, he was unusually ambitious and proactive, and – dreaming of a career in the brave new world of Nazi politics[1] – proved adept at provoking the communists in their Berlin strongholds.

To that end, Wessel penned a song – entitled '*Die Fahne hoch!*' or 'The Flag on High!' – with a rousing, marching melody cobbled together from old folk tunes. The words were classic fascist fare, including the flag and the massed ranks marching in unison; it even proclaimed – somewhat darkly – that the spirits of SA men murdered by communists and reactionaries were marching in lock-step with the living.

> Die Fahne hoch! Die Reihen fest geschlossen!
> SA marschiert mit ruhig festem Schritt.
> Kam'raden, die Rotfront und Reaktion erschossen,
> Marschier'n im Geist in unser'n Reihen mit.
> Kam'raden, die Rotfront und Reaktion erschossen,
> Marschier'n im Geist in unser'n Reihen mit.
>
> The flag on high! The ranks tightly closed!
> The SA marches with quiet, steady step.
> Comrades shot by the Red Front and reactionaries
> March in spirit within our ranks.
> Comrades shot by the Red Front and reactionaries
> March in spirit within our ranks.

The song was first sung publicly, in Berlin, on 26 May 1929, and in September of that year its words appeared anonymously in Goebbels's newspaper *Der Angriff*, shortly after Wessel had led his *Sturm* in a parade at the Nuremberg Rally.[2]

That winter, Wessel evidently decided to spur his rise further by writing directly to Hitler. As a New Year gift, he put together a package of items, including a photograph of himself in SA uniform, a covering note addressed to '*Mein Führer*', and this hand-written score of his song, with lyrics to the first verse, which he signed beneath. It would have been one of numerous gifts that were sent to Hitler, and the recipient's

The signed score of 'Die Fahne hoch!' that Horst Wessel sent to Hitler.

response is not recorded. Nonetheless, Wessel must have hoped that the gesture would raise him from the comparative obscurity of Berlin SA circles.

Within a few weeks, Wessel would become a household name in Germany, but not because of his gift to his *Führer*. On the evening of 14 January 1930, he was shot point-blank in the face by an assailant, and as he hovered between life and death for the next five weeks, he would be raised to the status of a Nazi martyr.

The circumstances of Wessel's shooting have long been disputed. In the autumn of the previous year, he had begun a relationship with an eighteen-year-old prostitute, Erna Jänichen, and moved in with her in the Berlin suburb of Friedrichshain. By January, the two were in dispute with their landlady, Elisabeth Salm, over unpaid rent, and Salm, resolving to have the couple removed, turned to the local communist underworld for help. Of course, when the latter heard the name Horst Wessel, they responded with alacrity, and what might otherwise have been a forced eviction became a deadly assault.[3]

In the aftermath, as Wessel languished in his hospital bed missing most of his palate and upper jaw, before finally succumbing to blood poisoning on 23 February, Goebbels expertly transformed the young SA man into a martyr to the Nazi cause. Though the communists desperately sought to muddy the waters, portraying the shooting as a squabble over Jänichen and so making a politically motivated attack into a tawdry quarrel between pimps, Goebbels was undeterred. Mindful of the political power of martyrdom, he set out to glorify Wessel as a fallen hero, a bright star brought low by his dastardly communist opponents, a young man whose death could be an inspiration. 'A quiet, heroic bleeding has entered our ranks,' he would write, 'and yet our eyes have never shone with such joy and warmth.'[4] Crowning the apotheosis was the curious prescience of Wessel's lyrics, which spoke of the comrades 'shot by the Red Front and reactionaries, marching in spirit in our ranks'. On 7 February 1930, while Wessel was still alive, some 15,000 sang his hymn at a Nazi rally at the Berlin Sportpalast. The Horst Wessel Song had arrived.

---

*'The words were classic fascist fare, including the flag and the massed ranks marching in unison.'*

---

In time, Wessel would be immortalised by the Nazis. After 1933, the district in which he had lived – Friedrichshain – would be named after him, as would the hospital in which he died. His name would later be appended to a Waffen-SS division, a Luftwaffe squadron, a navy training ship and countless streets and squares. His story would inspire a hagiographic film, *Hans Westmar*, as well as numerous novels and biographies. Most famously, his song would be elevated to the status of a secondary national anthem – played after the *Deutschlandlied* – with all Germans obliged to give the Hitler salute as they sang.

The Nazis would have their revenge on Wessel's killers. Albrecht Höhler – who had pulled the trigger, and had already been sentenced to six years for the killing – disappeared in September 1933, murdered by an SA detachment which, bizarrely, included a former Prussian prince, August-Wilhelm.[5] Two of Höhler's accomplices were later sentenced to death and executed.

After 1945, Wessel – once lauded as a blameless Nazi martyr – would be damned. His grave in the Nikolai cemetery in Berlin was destroyed, and the song that bore his name was banned in Germany – a ban that still holds to this day.

1   See Daniel Siemens, *The Making of a Nazi Hero: The Murder and Myth of Horst Wessel* (London, 2013), p. 57.

2   Ibid., p. 62.

3   Michael Burleigh, *The Third Reich: A New History* (London, 2000), p. 118.

4   Quoted in Siemens, p. 60.

5   See Nigel Jones, 'A Song for Hitler', *History Today*, October 2007.

# 10 Runes

*A common aspect of the public face of the Third Reich* was its extensive use of runic symbols. Runes were a primitive Nordic script, the earliest dating from around AD 150, which were used to write the proto-Germanic languages of Scandinavia.

Falling out of use with the adoption of the Latin alphabet, runes were confined largely to academic study until revived (in part) by the Austrian occultist and pan-German nationalist Guido von List, who claimed in 1906 that their sacred power was revealed to him during a period of blindness following a cataract operation. From their resulting popularity amongst German nationalists in the early twentieth century, they then came into widespread use within the Nazi movement, with Heinrich Himmler and the SS in the vanguard. By 1939, the understanding of runic symbolism formed an essential part of SS training.[1]

A German Army parade assembled around a runic symbol during a Nuremberg Rally.

The badge of the Nazi Women's Organisation – Deutsches Frauenwerk – incorporating the 'life-rune'.

The most common – and widely recognised – rune used by the Nazis was the so-called *sig*-rune, denoting 'victory'. Two of these were used as the symbol of the SS from 1930 and were shown on flags, on the collar tabs of SS men, and even as a modified key on German typewriters. However, the SS runes were only one of many such adoptions. The Hitler Youth, for instance, adopted a single *sig*-rune as its symbol, while the National Socialist Women's Movement (Das Deutsche Frauenwerk) used an *algiz*-rune (denoting 'life') as its marker – as shown in the movement's badge– topped with a 'sunwheel' swastika. The Nazi People's Welfare Organisation (Volkswohlfahrt), meanwhile, incorporated both the *eif*-rune (denoting 'enthusiasm') and the *algiz*-rune in a device that cleverly resembled its initials – NSV.

Numerous SS military formations also adopted runes as their divisional symbols, including the 6th SS Mountain Division *Nord* – which used the *hagal*-rune, denoting 'faith' – and the 7th SS Division *Prinz Eugen* – which used the *odal*-rune, signifying 'kinship'. The *tyr*-rune (representing 'leadership') was used by the 32nd SS Division *30 Januar*. In addition, 'life' and 'death' runes were used by the SS for its obituary notices, and were often included on gravestones, in place of the conventional markers for birth and death.

Runes were very commonplace in Nazi Germany, so much so that many, perhaps, took them for granted and so were unaware of their deeper significance. But, for Himmler at least, they were not just simple markers; they signified a reconnection with an older, pre-Christian, Germanic past, and thereby a rejection of corrupt 'Jewish' concepts, such as democracy and liberalism. Runes were themselves symbols of the Nazi revolution.

An officer of 7th SS *Prinz Eugen* Division,
showing the *odal* rune on his collar.

1   Robin Lumsden, *SS: Himmler's Black Order, 1923–45* (Stroud, 1997), p. 145.

# 11 Geli Raubal Bust

*This bronze bust of Hitler's niece*, Geli Raubal, was made for Hitler by the renowned Munich sculptor Ferdinand Liebermann. Completed in 1932, it was placed in the bedroom of Hitler's Munich apartment, where Raubal had committed suicide the year before.

Born in Linz in 1908, Angela 'Geli' Raubal was the second child of Leo Raubal and Hitler's elder half-sister, Angela. A lively child, she first met her uncle in the early 1920s, with regular contact following from 1927, when she enrolled as a medical student at Munich University. In 1929, Raubal decided to give up medicine, declaring that she wanted to train as a singer. Soon after, she moved into a spare room in Hitler's Munich apartment on Prinzregentenplatz. With her mother installed as Hitler's housekeeper on the Obersalzberg, the 21-year-old Geli found herself growing closer to Hitler.

Geli Raubal – the focus of Hitler's affections.

The relationship between the two was not kept secret and seems – despite countless rumours to the contrary – to have been purely platonic and familial; Geli referred to Hitler as 'Uncle Alf' and she became an integral part of his entourage. She was his regular companion to cultural and political events, even attending the Nuremberg Rally in 1927. Geli was a bright, quick-witted young woman, whose simple, unaffected nature drew many compliments. Hitler's photographer Heinrich Hoffmann, for instance, said that she was 'an enchantress, whose very presence would transform the mood of the group. Everybody loved her.'[1]

However, the relationship between Geli and Hitler came under strain when she began courting Hitler's chauffeur, Emil Maurice. Hitler, it seems, became protective and domineering over his niece, and – insisting that she concentrate on her studies – ended the affair by dismissing Maurice from his service. Soon after, as the carefree young girl grew increasingly introverted and melancholy, she asked permission to travel to Vienna to continue her singing training there. Hitler bluntly refused.

Geli Raubal shot herself on the afternoon of 18 September 1931 in Hitler's Munich apartment. The post mortem suggested that she had aimed for her heart, but had instead perforated her lung and had subsequently suffocated after losing consciousness.[2] She left no suicide note and so her motive remained unclear. She was twenty-three.

Hitler, who was in Nuremberg at the time, was distraught when he heard of her death, and though he rushed back to Munich – getting a speeding ticket en route – he did not attend her funeral, five days later in Vienna. Soon, lurid rumours began circulating, spurred by Hitler's political opponents, speculating about the nature of the relationship between the two and questioning the precise circumstances of Geli's death. According to the various tabloids of the day, Hitler was a masochist engaged in an incestuous affair with his niece; Geli had been pregnant; or she had been murdered on his orders. No credible evidence has ever emerged to back up such wild theories.

Geli and her 'Uncle Alf'.

In the febrile politics of 1930s Germany, Geli's suicide forced the Nazis into a frenzied damage-limitation exercise. Hitler issued a formal rebuttal of the rumours and demanded a retraction from the press. Moreover, the widespread and damning publicity surrounding the death caused a seismic shift in the Nazis' presentation of Hitler's public image. The man pilloried in the press as a deviant and a morally dubious extremist would be repackaged as a chaste, cultured aesthete and a would-be statesman.[3]

---

*'Hitler demonstrated an affection for his niece that he rarely showed even to his later wife, Eva Braun.'*

---

On a personal level, meanwhile, Hitler was inconsolable and shut himself away for a week in Geli's room in Haus Wachenfeld, on the Obersalzberg, during which time he allegedly contemplated suicide.[4] Once he recovered his equilibrium, he ordered that the room – like her room in Munich – should be preserved untouched, as a shrine to her memory. In addition, his entourage was instructed never again to mention her name.

Hitler also ordered this bust of Geli. A first prototype by the sculptor showed the subject smiling, but Hitler decided on a more serious expression. The completed bronze, standing 40 cm high on a marble plinth, was presented to him the year after its subject's death and took pride of place in his bedroom in Munich.

Whatever the precise nature of the relationship between Hitler and Geli – which will probably never be known for sure – it was nonetheless remarkable. In creating a shrine to her on the Obersalzberg and ordering the creation of the bust, Hitler demonstrated an affection for his niece, after her death, that he rarely showed even to his later wife, Eva Braun. Contemporaries were perhaps right to have described Geli Raubal as the only woman that Hitler ever loved.[5]

Some suggest that Geli's death had political as well as personal consequences. Hermann Göring would later claim that after Geli died Hitler's 'relationship to everyone else'[6] changed; in short, he hardened his heart. Hitler might well have concurred. In the aftermath, he described himself as 'completely free'. 'Now', he said, 'I belong only to the German people and my mission.'[7]

1   Quoted in Anna Maria Sigmund, *Die Frauen der Nazis* (Vienna, 1998), p. 142.

2   Ibid., p. 149.

3   Despina Stratigakos, *Hitler at Home* (New Haven & London, 2015), p. 23.

4   Herbert Döhring, *Hitlers Hausverwalter* (Bochum, 2013), p. 53.

5   William Shirer, *The Rise and Fall of the Third Reich* (London, 1959), p. 132.

6   Ron Rosenbaum, *Explaining Hitler* (New York, 1998), p. 192.

7   Quoted in Ullrich, *Hitler: Ascent 1889–1939*, p. 284.

# 12 Junkers Ju 52

*The Junkers Ju 52 was the durable aerial workhorse of the Third Reich.* In its most common configuration, powered by three, nine-cylinder BMW radial engines, it served in both civilian and military roles from 1932 through to 1945.

Originally designed by Ernst Zindel at the Junkers factory at Dessau in 1930, the Ju 52 was robustly built, with a fixed undercarriage, low cantilever wings, and a corrugated all-metal skin made from aluminium alloy. Quickly proving its worth, it served as a seventeen-seat passenger airliner for Deutsche Lufthansa in the 1930s, flying routes within Germany, and around Europe and beyond.

Already, before he came to power, Hitler had had his eyes opened to the potential of air travel by a Ju 52. He had used the aircraft, very successfully, for the 1932 presidential election campaign, flying in to speak in forty-six locations across the country, in a campaign dubbed 'Hitler over Germany'. In the aftermath, he had been keen to buy a Ju 52 for his personal use, but despite his royalties from *Mein Kampf*, the 270,000 mark cost was beyond him. Nonetheless, he promised his pilot, Hans Baur, that once he was 'master of the Third Reich', he would establish a government squadron, and Baur would be its commander.[1]

'Auntie Ju' – an aviation icon.

## 'Hitler had his eyes opened to the potential of air travel by a Ju 52.'

Hitler was true to his word, and in February 1933 he took delivery of his first Junkers Ju 52 – registration number D-2600 – and engaged Hans Baur as his personal pilot. By 1939, when Hitler switched to using the more modern Focke-Wulf Fw 200 Condor for his flight, the Ju 52 provided the backbone of the VIP squadron with some seventeen aircraft, including two for Hitler's personal use, three for Göring – one with extra wide seats – and the remainder for other senior figures.[2]

The Ju 52 also played a significant military role, being first employed during the Spanish Civil War, when it was used to transport Franco's Army of Africa to the Spanish mainland on the outbreak of the conflict, and took part in the infamous bombing of Guernica in April 1937. Thereafter, and following the outbreak of World War II, over 3,000 examples were supplied to the Luftwaffe, for which it served as a reliable transport aircraft, moving soldiers or functioning as an air ambulance. Paratroopers jumped from it and it could even tow two gliders at a time. *Tante Ju* – or 'Auntie Ju', as it was affectionately nicknamed – was crucial to all German airborne operations in the war: from the Scandinavian campaign of 1940 and the seizure of Crete in the spring of 1941, to the failed attempt to supply the surrounded Sixth Army in Stalingrad in the winter of 1942–3.

A flight of Ju 52s over a North African town, bringing supplies to the *Afrika Korps*.

The Ju 52 served until the end of the war and beyond. Though it was technologically obsolete well before 1945, its characteristic corrugated fuselage and trimotor configuration had already earned it the status of an aviation icon.

1   H. Baur, *Hitler at my Side* (Houston, 1986), p. 59.

2   C. G. Sweeting, *Hitler's Squadron* (Dulles, 2001), pp. 25 & 29.

# 13 Nazi Party Election Poster, 1932

*'Work, Freedom and Bread!' promises this poster* encouraging Germans to vote for the Nazi Party. It was one of a series drawn in 1932 by graphic artist Felix Albrecht to appeal to working-class voters, who had been hit hard by unemployment and economic turbulence, and were now the target electorate for the Nazis. It marked a turning point in Nazi fortunes that would bring Hitler to the very threshold of power.

Four years earlier, in 1928, the political situation had not been promising for Hitler and his Nazi Party. Under the conservative statesman Gustav Stresemann, the German economy had recovered from the ruinous hyperinflation of 1923, and the return of relative prosperity had weakened the appeal of the extremist parties. In the Reichstag elections of 1928 the Nazis had been confined to the political fringes, winning only twelve seats and taking a paltry 2.6 per cent of the national vote.

A year later, however, the political picture in Germany changed dramatically when the Wall Street Crash plunged the USA and then Europe into the Great Depression. The new downturn hit Weimar Germany hard in 1930, with American banks withdrawing the loans upon which the German economy had been rebuilt, causing businesses to fail and sending unemployment rocketing to nearly six million – fully 30 per cent of the working population – by 1932.[1]

President von Hindenburg with Chancellor Adolf Hitler, shortly after Hindenburg had appointed Hitler to office.

In such circumstances, with popular faith in the political and economic status quo failing, Hitler was well placed to garner increased support. In the election of 1930 the Nazis gained over six million votes, 18 per cent of the total, and sent 107 delegates to the Reichstag, becoming the second-largest party in Germany after the socialist SPD.

By the spring of 1932, with German politics deadlocked, and the government forced increasingly to rule by presidential decree, Hitler had another chance to test the political mood of the country. In March 1932, he ran for the presidency against the aged monarchist and World War I field marshal Paul von Hindenburg and, despite taking more than 30 per cent of the vote, lost to his opponent in the second round.

Promising the earth: a Nazi Party campaign poster of 1932.

Despite his defeat, Hitler had enjoyed great exposure for himself and his party, not least by the then-revolutionary strategy of criss-crossing Germany by air, speaking at several meetings in one day, thereby identifying himself with the forces of progress and modernity. The following month another opportunity presented itself, with regional parliamentary elections in a number of German states, including the largest, Prussia, which together held nearly two-thirds of the total population.

It was for this election that Albrecht's poster was deployed, hoping to chime with the desperate *Zeitgeist* in the predominantly rural areas of the north and east by depicting a bluff Aryan farmworker broadcasting seeds from a sling over his shoulder. Beside him stands the simple slogan 'Work, Freedom and Bread', text which aped the wording employed in the same election by the Communist KPD – 'Prussia Red: for Work, Freedom, Bread'.

The tactics paid off handsomely. In Prussia, the Nazis emerged – for the first time – as the largest party, with 36 per cent of the vote and 162 seats in parliament. Similar results were posted in Hamburg (31 per cent) and Württemberg (26 per cent), with Bavaria also posting a 32 per cent return for the Nazis, despite the Bavarian People's Party beating them into second place. Those elections were to prove a watershed. Not only were the Nazis established across vast swathes of the country as the largest party, in concert with the Communists they now also commanded a 'negative majority' and so were able effectively to paralyse parliamentary government. The death knell for Germany democracy was beginning to chime.

In the national parliamentary elections that followed – in July and November 1932 – the trend of the April elections accelerated, with the Nazis winning first 230, then 196 seats in the Reichstag, and emerging nationally as the single largest party. Thus hamstrung, the Weimar Republic stumbled towards its anguished end, as chancellors desperate to break the impasse succeeded each other in a political game of musical chairs. Heinrich Brüning of the Catholic Centre Party was forced to rule by decree for lack of a Reichstag majority. Unpopular because of his austerity policies, he was succeeded by Franz von Papen, a reactionary favourite of Hindenburg. But Papen, too, lacked a parliamentary majority, and was soon brought down by the former friend who had elevated him to power, Interior Minister General Kurt von Schleicher, an inveterate intriguer who hoped in vain to split the Nazis and win over the party's left-wing faction headed by Gregor Strasser.

---

*'The death knell for Germany democracy was beginning to chime.'*

---

Schleicher's rule would also be brief. Papen, burning for revenge, made a pact with Hitler under which the Nazi leader would become chancellor in a coalition government, most of whose members would be Papen's conservative allies. Confused and senile, Hindenburg agreed to the deal and appointed Hitler as Germany's chancellor on 30 January 1933.

Papen had hoped to contain and marginalise the Nazis – as he colourfully put it, to 'push Hitler so far into the corner that he'll squeal'[2] – but he would be rapidly out-manoeuvred. Hitler would not be squeezed and, once in office, he moved swiftly to strengthen his grip on government and destroy his opponents. He would make good on his private promise to his cronies that, once in power, he would never voluntarily give it up.

1   Berghahn, *Modern Germany*, p. 266.

2   Quoted in Frank McDonough, *Hitler and the Rise of the Nazi Party* (London, 2003), p. 100.

# 14 Last *Vorwärts* Newspaper, 1933

*Founded in 1876*, Vorwärts *had become the official newspaper* of the German Social Democratic Party – the SPD. It boasted a rich tradition, having published articles by Friedrich Engels and Leon Trotsky, and having been edited for nearly a decade by the party's founder, Wilhelm Liebknecht. By 1933, however, that tradition of left-wing journalism was nearing its end.

The front page overleaf, dated Tuesday 28 February 1933, was from the final pre-war edition of *Vorwärts* to be published in Germany.[1] That same day, it was banned by the Nazis, along with many other newspapers and magazines. Freedom of the press – previously enshrined in the constitution of the German Republic – was suspended, along with numerous other civil rights, such as freedom of expression, freedom of assembly and *habeas corpus*. With that, Germany took a large step towards dictatorship.

The reason for this step-change was given in the paper's headline: '*Riesenbrand im Reichstag*' – 'Huge Fire in the Reichstag'. The previous evening, shortly after 9 p.m., the German parliament building in Berlin – the Reichstag – had been reported to be on fire. By the time that fire crews arrived, the building was well ablaze, with tongues of flame licking the inside of its grand glass dome. Entering the Reichstag, policemen discovered a 23-year-old Dutch communist – Marinus van der Lubbe – running amok, half-dressed, having used his shirt to help set the fire. When asked what he had done, van der Lubbe replied: 'Protest! Protest!'[2]

---

*'Germany took a large step towards dictatorship.'*

---

When Hitler arrived at the building some time later to survey the damage, he already had an idea of who was to blame. 'God grant that this be the work of the communists,' he said, 'This fire is just the beginning . . . If the communist spirit takes hold of Europe, everything will be destroyed by fire.' He added: 'There will be no mercy. Anyone who stands in our way will be crushed . . . Each communist official we come across will be shot . . . Everyone associated with the communists must be arrested . . . Social democrats will also no longer be spared.'[3] Hitler was declaring war on Germany's political left.

The following day, Hitler made good on the hot-headed threats of the previous evening. Invoking the power of the German president to protect public safety against 'communist acts of violence', the Decree for the Protection of People and State was

The last pre-war issue of *Vorwärts* from 28 February 1933, reporting on the Reichstag fire.

promulgated: suspending civil liberties, allowing the Reich government to intervene in the provinces and establishing the death penalty for arson. Even as it came into force, dozens of communists and socialists across Germany were being arrested, their institutions and publications being closed down. Known to history as the 'Reichstag Fire Decree', it represented a key step towards the establishment of a one-party state, a legal key-stone of the Third Reich.

With the decree in force, there was no obstacle in law to the Nazi persecution of their political enemies. Within days, some 10,000 had been arrested, including 100 Communist (KPD) members of the Reichstag, along with their leaders Ernst Thälmann and Ernst Torgler, as well as trade unionists and Social Democrats. Some 25,000 of the Nazis' political opponents ended up in prison, or incarcerated in a sinister new phenomenon – the 'concentration camp'.

A week after the fire, on 5 March, Germany went to the polls in an election that Hitler had called five weeks earlier, in an effort to strengthen his position. Unsurprisingly, with the political left violently suppressed, and propaganda labelling them as traitors to Germany, the Nazi vote rose by nearly 11 per cent, while that of the SPD and KPD fell by 2.1 and 4.6 per cent respectively. Though Hitler was denied an outright majority, he was nonetheless able to free himself of his coalition partners and form a Nazi government. It would be the last election held in a united Germany until 1990.

Within weeks of the 1933 election, Hitler's power was already well established. The KPD and SPD were formally banned, their assets confiscated, their leadership and members arrested or forced into exile. In due course, the Nazis would be decreed the only permissible political party. At the end of March, the so-called 'Enabling Act' was passed by a cowed Reichstag – now meeting in the nearby Kroll Opera House – giving Hitler the power to rule without the involvement of the German parliament, for a period of four years. Hitler had effectively been granted dictatorial authority.

Fire rips through the Reichstag on the night of 27 February 1933.

Given the magnitude of what followed, the Reichstag fire is still controversial, not in the fact of van der Lubbe's authorship of it – he confessed to the crime, and persistently claimed to have worked alone[4] – but in the question of whether he may have been the tool of unseen forces, a 'cat's paw' of the Nazis. Some hold the view that Hitler's swift and expert political exploitation of the Reichstag fire must point to Nazi complicity in its origin; others rebut that argument, pointing out that Nazi plans for a clampdown on the German left were already prepared before the fire, and its outbreak merely provided a serendipitous opportunity for action. The truth of the matter will probably never be known for sure.

In the aftermath, Hitler's power was secured and his opposition silenced. Van der Lubbe was tried for arson and high treason. Found guilty, he was guillotined in January 1934, three days before his twenty-fifth birthday. *Vorwärts* would rise again after World War II, but this was its last pre-war issue to be published in Germany. It marks a key moment in the process by which German democracy was dismantled – a process that was completed in less than two months.

1   *Vorwärts* was published in exile after 1933, and was re-established in Germany in 1948.

2   Quoted in Sven Felix Kellerhoff, *The Reichstag Fire* (Stroud, 2016), p. 28.

3   Ibid., pp. 39–40.

4   Ibid., p. 46.

# 15 Winter Aid Collection Tins

*Among the features of civilian life* during the Third Reich were the apparently interminable street collections for 'Winter Aid'. Established in 1933, drawing on earlier local initiatives, the Winter Aid Programme – Winterhilfswerk – was a coordinated, nationwide charity action to raise money for the needy.

Every year, in October, the Winter Aid collection drive would begin with a speech by Hitler, usually extolling the virtues of the German 'national community', the *Volksgemeinschaft*, and its allegedly boundless willingness to help the less fortunate within its ranks. Thereafter, for six months, until the March of the following year, local Party organisations across the country would be mobilised to collect donations, with the young people of the Hitler Youth and the League of German Girls (Bund deutscher Mädel) in the forefront.

With that, collection tins such as these ones – often marked with the region, or *Gau* in which they were used – would be rattled across the country to encourage donors to part with their money. In Berlin alone, in one year, 75,000 helpers were involved in the

'Organised highway robbery' – Winter Aid collection tins from Vienna and other locations.

Winter Aid collection drive. No surprise then that the Nazis' opponents complained that the collections took on the character of 'organised highway robbery'.[1]

To sweeten the pill, perhaps, collection drives might feature celebrities or senior Nazi figures as tin shakers, or trinkets could be offered in return for a donation – often pin badges of different animals or city coats of arms – with donors encouraged to give every week so as to complete the set.

> *'Winter Aid was trumpeted by the Nazi regime as an expression of the "pure" socialism supposedly at the heart of National Socialism.'*

In fact, though they certainly represented the public face of the enterprise, street collections made up less than 10 per cent of Winter Aid donations. The majority came from material donations of food and clothing, large-scale gifts from businesses and organisations, and obligatory deductions levied on larger firms through taxation. Another source of revenue was the *Eintopfsonntag*, or 'One-Pot Sunday' initiative, whereby restaurants would serve a single stew at a fixed price to all customers, one Sunday in the month, with the resulting savings being donated to the Winter Aid.[2]

Winter Aid was trumpeted by the Nazi regime as an expression of solidarity and of the 'pure' socialism supposedly at the heart of National Socialism. In reality, it was rather more sinister. Donations were often less than entirely voluntary, with many – especially state employees – pressured to give more, and more often, than they might have wished. There could even be consequences for the recalcitrant: denunciations were common, and one civil servant was prosecuted for refusing to donate – his defence that he thought the donations were voluntary was laughed out of court.[3]

In addition, Winter Aid provided a substantial source of revenue for the government – rising from 300 million Reichsmarks in 1933/4 to 1.6 billion in 1942/3 – which could be used to replace, or at least supplement, existing welfare and social spending, and thus free up monies for other government expenditure, such as on armaments. During the war, for instance, some Winter Aid initiatives took the form of clothing collections for the troops on the Eastern Front. Unsurprisingly, then, some Germans joked darkly that Winter Aid's initials, WHW stood, in reality, for *Waffen Hilfswerk* – 'Weapons Aid'.[4]

---

1   Quoted in *Deutschland-Berichte der Sozialdemokratischen Partei Deutschlands (SOPADE), 1934–1940* (Salzhausen 1980), p. 1422 (December 1935).

2   Grunberger, *Social History*, p. 45.

3   Cited in Mark Mazower, *Dark Continent* (London, 1998), p. 35.

4   Herwart Vorländer, 'NS-Volkswohlfahrt und Winterhilfswerk des Deutschen Volkes', *Vierteljahrshefte für Zeitgeschichte*, No. 34 (1986), p. 53.

# 16 Golden Nazi Party Badge

*All totalitarian regimes demand some outward show* of loyalty from their citizens, and Nazi Germany was no different. For many Germans, a carefully placed photograph of Hitler, or copy of *Mein Kampf*, would suffice to demonstrate their Nazi bona fides.

Nazi Party membership could also be used to the same effect. From the small numbers registered in the party's early years in Munich, NSDAP membership grew substantially after the electoral breakthrough of 1930, reaching some 900,000 by the time of the seizure of power in January 1933, and increasing hugely thereafter. By 1939, there were some 5.3 million Nazi Party members in Germany.[1] Many of them chose to advertise their allegiance by wearing an NSDAP badge – colloquially known as the *Bonbon*, or 'sweetie' – on their left lapel.

Hubert Klausner's *Bonbon*.

*'Hitler could issue Golden Party Badges at his discretion, to those whose service to the Nazi Party merited special recognition.'*

Party membership – which peaked at 7.7 million in 1943, less than 10 per cent of the total population – was not obligatory, but could bring with it considerable personal and professional benefits. For this reason, many of the new members after January 1933 were viewed by older members as opportunists, rather than convinced National Socialists. They came to be known, derisively, as the 'March Violets'.[2]

Some Nazi Party members, therefore, were granted the elevated status of the 'Golden Party Badge'. Established in 1933, featuring a gold-plated wreath surrounding the usual design, these badges were only available to those who fell within the first 100,000 party members, and could demonstrate uninterrupted service from 1925 – a category usually referred to as the *alte Kämpfer*, or 'Old Fighters'. In such cases, the badge would have the recipient's party membership number engraved on the reverse.

In addition, Hitler could issue Golden Party Badges at his discretion, to those whose service to the Nazi Party merited special recognition, yet fell outside the existing award criteria. These badges, given annually on the anniversary of the Nazi seizure of power, 30 January, were engraved with 'A.H.' and the date of the award. Recipients of the Golden Party Badge – across the two categories – included Reinhard Heydrich, Hitler's doctor Theodor Morell, Reichsmarschall Hermann Göring, and Albert Speer. In total, it is thought that fewer than 25,000 Golden Party Badges were issued.

The badge shown here is one of Hitler's discretionary awards. It was issued on 30 January 1939 to the Party *Gauleiter* of Carinthia in Austria, Hubert Klausner – a veteran Nazi, who had been instrumental in engineering the *Anschluss* of 1938 and had even coined the propaganda phrase *Ein Volk, Ein Reich, Ein Führer*. Klausner died, apparently of a stroke, two weeks after receiving the award.

The most famous of the Golden Party Badges, of course, was Hitler's own, mendaciously numbered '1'. He wore it constantly, alongside his Iron Cross (First Class) and Wound Badge from World War I, and famously gave it to Magda Goebbels as a parting gift shortly before his suicide in 1945.[3] Unlike its new owner, the badge survived the war and surfaced in Moscow in 1996, in the possession of the Russian security service, the FSB. Put on display as part of the commemorations of the sixtieth anniversary of the end of the war in 2005, it was stolen by an unknown burglar. It has not yet been recovered.[4]

---

1 Figures from Michael Grüttner, *Das Dritte Reich. 1933–1939* (Stuttgart, 2014), p. 101.

2 Grunberger, *A Social History of the Third Reich*, p. 82.

3 Joachim Fest, *Inside Hitler's Bunker* (London, 2004), p. 144.

4 www.spiegel.de/panorama/justiz/moskau-hitlers-goldenes-parteiabzeichen-gestohlen-a-385807.html.

# 17 Volksempfänger Radio Set

*Uniquely perhaps among the regimes of the 1930s*, the Nazis well understood the propaganda potential of radio broadcasting. From its origins in the bleak years following World War I, German radio had already made great strides before the Nazis came to power in 1933, but it was the Third Reich that propelled it to the status of a genuine mass medium. Joseph Goebbels said that the Nazi revolution would have been 'impossible' without radio.[1] For once, he was telling the truth.

The *Volksempfänger* – or 'People's Receiver'.

In the summer of 1933, the Nazis were already making strides to extend radio ownership radically, and so achieve their goal of having a mouthpiece of the regime in every home and workplace. At the tenth annual German Radio Exhibition that August, the *Volksempfänger* – or 'People's Receiver' – radio set was launched. Selling at just 76 Reichsmarks – equivalent to a little more than two weeks' average wages – it was competitively priced, at around half the cost of a traditional radio set. Its smart, brown Bakelite case, with a large speaker and tuning dial on the face, contained a simple three-valve, two-band receiver, too weak – in most locations – to pick up any but German broadcasts. Its link to the new Nazi regime was explicit; its formal designation – VE301 – even referred to the date of Hitler's seizure of power: 30 January.

---

*'Joseph Goebbels said that the Nazi revolution would have been "impossible" without radio.'*

---

So it was that the most influential radio set in history – and the most important propaganda tool of the Nazi regime – was born. Already during the exhibition, the first 100,000 *Volksempfänger* sets were sold, dispelling the makers' concerns that the product would not find a ready market. Further models – including a *Kleinempfänger* 'Small Receiver' priced at 35 RM, and a portable suitcase model – would push sales up into the millions. By the outbreak of war, Reich radio chief Eugen Hadamovsky would boast: 'There was scarcely a single German who did not possess a radio.'[2]

Of course, having so assiduously promoted radio ownership, the regime was most anxious to prevent its listeners from switching the set off. To this end, Goebbels ordered a diverse schedule of programming, from light entertainment and poetry to sport and public information, all in an effort to make the radio an essential part of the German people's daily life. To be truly effective, he knew that propaganda had to be subtle; it had to seduce rather than bludgeon the listener.

By their skilful exploitation of the new technology of radio, the Nazis seized a vital advantage in the propaganda wars of the 1930s and 1940s. And it was an advantage that they would fight hard to maintain, outlawing listening to foreign broadcasts on the outbreak of war. In this battle, a cheap, reliable radio set such as the humble *Volksempfänger* was essential. It brought radio – Nazi radio – to the masses.

---

1   Quoted in Joseph Goebbels, 'Der Rundfunk als achte Großmacht', in *Signale der neuen Zeit: 25 ausgewählte Reden von Dr. Joseph Goebbels* (Munich, 1938).

2   'Wie Adolf Hitler in jedes Wohnzimmer drang', *Die Zeit*, 18 August, 2008, accessible at http://www.welt.de/kultur/article2320561/Wie-Adolf-Hitler-in-jedes-Wohnzimmer-drang.html.

# 18 Hitler Youth Uniform

*The Hitlerjugend – Hitler Youth – was the only* official organisation for young people in the Third Reich from 1933 to 1945. First established as the Nazi Jugendbund or 'Youth League' in 1922, it was originally viewed as a junior branch of the SA, training boys for a future role in the Brownshirts. By 1930 it had recruited over 25,000 boys aged between fourteen and eighteen, and had a number of ancillary organisations, such as the Deutsches Jungvolk, 'German Youth', for boys aged ten to fourteen, the Bund Deutscher Mädel – BDM, 'League of German Girls', for girls from fifteen to eighteen, and the Jungmädelbund 'Young Girls' League' for those between ten and fourteen. While the boys' organisations taught a variety of sporting and paramilitary skills – including camping, hiking and rudimentary weapons training – the girls' units put their emphasis on domestic science, health and racial purity. All members were fully exposed to Nazi ideology and propaganda.

---

*'This uniform was an essential part of the appeal of joining the Hitler Youth, bringing with it a precious sense of camaraderie and belonging.'*

---

In 1933, with the Nazis in power, the Hitler Youth was finally granted state recognition and the youthful 26-year-old Baldur von Schirach became the first Reich Youth Leader. Soon all other German youth organisations – from rowing clubs to poetry circles, Boy Scouts to football teams – were forcibly absorbed into the Hitler Youth, boosting membership to over two million. Rival organisations were banned, and children came under enormous pressure from their peers and schoolteachers to join up, facing bullying and extra homework if they refused. In 1936, membership became mandatory for all those who were German citizens or ethnic Germans and free from hereditary diseases. By the outbreak of war in 1939, over seven million young people had joined its ranks. To resist was to court ostracism, or worse.

The Hitler Youth uniform, as shown here, clearly shows both the organisation's origins and its political and social rationale. The brown shirt, for instance, was shared with the SA, which led to some difficulties in the early years, with Hitler Youth boys sometimes being attacked by the SA's political opponents. In response, a redesigned armband was introduced, showing a swastika over three red and white bars. In addition, other parts of the uniform mimic that of the scouting movement, particularly the neckerchief and woggle. The military component is shown by the Sam Browne belt, and the addition

Hitler Youth uniform: scouting with a Nazi twist.

of a dagger (not shown here) which was designed to resemble a bayonet. The belt buckle carried the Nazi slogan '*Blut und Ehre*', 'Blood and Honour'.

One should not underestimate the extent to which this uniform – rather than any ideological content – was an essential part of the appeal of joining the Hitler Youth, bringing with it a precious sense of camaraderie and belonging. In addition, the activities that the Hitler Youth engaged in – camping, hiking, sport and military training – were hugely popular. For many young working-class people, these outings in the German countryside were their first holidays, and they often revelled in a new-found sense of freedom and responsibility. A typical Hitler Youth activity was wargaming. In this, typically, one unit would hold a

Hitler Youth members during a summer camp. On the surface a scene little different from the camps of youth organisations in other countries.

strongpoint while another would try to capture it. As one boy wrote home, the results could be brutal brawls and fistfights:

> We attacked in two groups. The first group was to provide a diversion. Then the second group was to attack. The first attack failed. Then the second attempt began. Of course, it was chaotic. Some of them were bleeding, one was half-unconscious. The battle was a draw. How did you spend Easter?[1]

Clearly, roughness and toughness were positively encouraged, as a precursor to formal military training. As one former Hitler Youth member recalled:

> In the beginning I hated this kind of fighting but with time I got used to it. Human beings, given enough time, seem to get used to anything and then accept it as something natural. In any case, it developed the latent aggressiveness in us which, I am sure, had something to do with the Wehrmacht's early successes in the coming war.[2]

Aside from such wargaming, the training also included contributions by Wehrmacht officers, who would lecture the boys on the wonders of Germany's new military technology – its tanks, fighter planes and U-boats, and veterans of World War I, who spoke about their experiences on the Western Front. It was all designed to impart a hunger for all things military, to inculcate Nazi values and to prime the next generation of German soldiers.

When war broke out, the Hitler Youth was duly deployed as an auxiliary force on the home front, helping the postal and fire services as well as assisting anti-aircraft crews. Inevitably, members were propelled towards military service, and when the

German Army faced a crisis in manpower in 1943, Hitler Youth cadres were directly recruited, forming the 12th SS Panzer Division *Hitlerjugend*, comprised of seventeen and eighteen-year-olds. The division took part in the fighting following the Normandy invasion and its soldiers became notorious for their fanaticism, committing a number of atrocities against captured Allied troops.

Younger Hitler Youth boys would not escape the carnage either. In 1945, as Germany itself was invaded from the east and west, youths as young as twelve were enlisted into the Volkssturm and instructed in how to use the Panzerfaust recoilless gun against enemy tanks. They remained among the most fanatical of Nazis even as the Third Reich crumbled, and many of them would die fighting in a war already long lost.

Hitler with some of the Hitler Youth who fought in the final battle for Berlin.

1    Quoted in Roger Moorhouse, *Berlin at War: Life and Death in Hitler's Capital, 1939–1945* (London, 2010), p. 194

2    H. Metelmann, *A Hitler Youth* (Staplehurst, 2004), p. 91

# 19 Nazi Party *Haustafel*

*The Nazi Party penetrated German society* from top to bottom. Just as Hitler and his acolytes controlled the levers of political power at a state level, so their underlings sought to exercise control at a local level. Their primary tool in that latter struggle was the *Blockleiter* or 'Block Leader', colloquially known as the *Blockwart*, or 'Block Warden'.

The Party speaks – and watches . . .

The *Blockwart* stood at the lowest level of the Nazi Party hierarchy and was usually responsible for the political supervision of between forty and sixty households, perhaps 150–200 individuals. Despite being a rather lowly figure, often someone of limited ambition or intelligence, he – and it was almost always a man – wielded considerable power and played a vital dual role in the propagation of Nazi propaganda and the maintenance of order.

First of all, the *Blockwart* served as the primary point of contact for all those within his area who required assistance from the state, such as those in need of ration cards or requiring any contact with the Party or its organisations. That contact was maintained, most usually, via a *Haustafel* or 'House Board' such as this, which would ordinarily be mounted in the lower hallway of each apartment block, or in an otherwise accessible location.

> 'One party functionary described the House Board as "the visiting card of the Nazi movement".'

Headed with '*Hier spricht die NSDAP*' – 'Here speaks the Nazi Party' – it proclaimed: 'Comrades: If you require advice or help, turn to the NSDAP' and then provided contact details and office hours for responsible individuals. Beneath, it allowed space for chalk messages to be added, which might give details of meetings, deadlines and other public information. One Party functionary described the House Board as 'the visiting card of the Nazi movement'.[1]

And yet it was more than that. Just as the *Blockwart* was the conduit through which the Party and the individual communicated, he was also the eyes and ears of the Nazi regime. And, if he suspected that an individual within his block was politically dubious – left-leaning, opposition-minded or sympathetic towards the Jews – he might use a note on his House Board to deliver a coded warning. In 'helping' backsliders, one Nazi official recalled, 'a message on the House Board could work wonders'.[2] If subtle measures failed, then the *Blockwart* would report his suspicions to his superiors and in due course the suspect could expect a visit from the Gestapo.

It is, perhaps, unsurprising that the lowly *Blockwart* was generally a despised figure. Burdened with a raft of petty orders and decrees from an ever-watchful government, he was rarely able to exercise sufficient tact in enforcing their implementation amongst a sometimes apathetic or recalcitrant population. As a result, his dealings with local inhabitants could be fraught with latent conflict; he would often be given a wide berth by 'his' people. The role earned a number of derogatory nicknames, including 'the stair terrier' or 'the snooper'. The House Board was as much a source of irritation as a source of information, but it was the public face of the regime.

1  Detlef Schmiechen-Ackermann: '"Der Blockwart". Die unteren Parteifunktionäre im nationalsozialistischen Terror- und Überwachungsapparat', *Vierteljahrshefte für Zeitgeschichte*, No. 48 (2000), p. 590 n. 79.

2  Sven Felix Kellerhoff, *Berlin im Krieg: Eine Generation erinnert sich* (Berlin, 2011), p. 65.

# 20 Leibstandarte Cuff Band

*Established in 1933 as Hitler's personal bodyguard*, the SS *Leibstandarte* would grow to become one of the most renowned – and most feared – units of the Waffen-SS.

At the beginning of his political career, Hitler's personal security had been the responsibility of the *Stabswache*, a group of eight trusted individuals, drawn from the ranks of the SA. However, as Hitler's prominence grew, and the empires of his underlings expanded, a number of additional bodyguard units were established. Once Hitler came to power that expansion continued and the *Leibstandarte* was created as an elite group of SS bodyguards to protect Hitler's residences and his person. Its members were required to belong to the German 'master race'; be Nordic in appearance, over 1.8 metres (5 feet 11 inches) tall, with no criminal record and proven Aryan ancestry.

Because of its special role, the SS *Leibstandarte* was also marked out with a few distinctive touches to its uniform. It was the first unit, for instance, to use the SS runes, which would eventually become the symbol for the entire organisation.[1] In addition, only the *Leibstandarte* wore the striking white leather gloves and belts with their dress uniforms. They also sported hand-embroidered cuff bands – as in this example – carrying Hitler's name in elaborate Sütterlin script. Cuff bands would become very common in Nazi Germany, used as identifiers for various units from the Afrika Korps to the parachute divisions, but this was the most coveted cuff band of all. It marked the *Leibstandarte* out as belonging to the very elite of the Third Reich.

> *'All members of the Leibstandarte were required to give an oath of personal allegiance to the Führer.'*

The first commander of the unit was Josef 'Sepp' Dietrich, a jovial Bavarian thug, who had been one of Hitler's earliest followers. After service in World War I, in which he had fought in one of Germany's first tank units, Dietrich had worked as a policeman, then as a garage manager, before joining the SS in 1928, when he was made responsible for Hitler's personal security at political meetings. Rising through the SS ranks – he would end the war as an SS *Oberstgruppenführer* (four-star general) – Dietrich was unquestioningly loyal to Hitler, and was a central figure in his entourage.

Under Dietrich's leadership, loyalty was absolute. As with the rest of the SS, all members of the *Leibstandarte* were required to give an oath of personal allegiance to the *Führer*, making no mention of the constitution, or even the German people:

'I swear to you, Adolf Hitler, as *Führer* and Chancellor of the German Reich, loyalty and bravery. I vow to you and my superiors designated by you, obedience unto death. So help me God.'[2] In addition, however, the peculiar role of the *Leibstandarte* as Hitler's bodyguard gave it a certain autonomy from the remainder of the SS. It was very close to being Hitler's private army.[3]

Of course, the *Leibstandarte* was not just a corps of bodyguards. To the German public, it served the primary ceremonial function for the Third Reich, parading for special events – such as Hitler's birthday – and providing the guard of honour for visiting dignitaries. It also participated in every military parade as the Third Reich expanded: the Saar in 1935, Rhineland in 1936, Vienna in 1938, Prague and Warsaw in 1939 and Paris in 1940. Away from the public's gaze, however, its functions were more sinister, as in June 1934, when its men played a central role in the Röhm purge against the leadership of the SA. As well as performing ceremonial and security roles, as it expanded the *Leibstandarte* also developed as a fighting formation, being formed into a combat regiment in 1939 and a full Waffen-SS division later in the war.

Political indoctrination was predictably thorough. The SS as a whole was intended to be ideologically 'on message', but this was applied most rigorously to the *Leibstandarte*, whose men were subjected to weekly indoctrination sessions to school them in Nazi racial theory, and the dangers supposedly posed to the German nation by Jews, Freemasons and Marxists. The intention, as one SS memo proclaimed, was to forge the *Leibstandarte* into the 'shock troops of the regime . . . a stout tool in the hands of the Führer.'[4]

*Leibstandarte SS Adolf Hitler* cuff band.

Unsurprisingly, then, with the outbreak of war, the unit swiftly gained a reputation for committing atrocities, burning countless villages and slaughtering civilians. At Błonie, west of Warsaw, for instance, the *Leibstandarte* executed fifty Jews in September 1939. Most infamously, during the British retreat to Dunkirk the following summer, its soldiers massacred some eighty British and French prisoners of war at Wormhout in Flanders.

The unit went on to fight across Europe's battlefields: in Greece, Italy and on the Eastern Front, where it played a pivotal role in the recapture of Kharkov and the Battle of Kursk in 1943. In Normandy, the following year, some of the *Leibstandarte*'s Tiger tanks, under the command of Michael Wittmann, cut a swathe through the British 7th Armoured Division, at the Battle of Villers-Bocage.

Fanatical to the last, the *Leibstandarte* would take a leading role in the bitter fighting in the last-ditch Ardennes Offensive in December 1944. Equipped with Panther and Tiger tanks, it smashed into the American lines, until a lack of fuel stemmed the advance. True to form, however, it added one final atrocity to their black record when its men shot dead eighty-four surrendered US soldiers at Malmedy. As a result, by the end of the war, this cuff band, which had once inspired respect, provoked little more than revulsion.

The SS *Leibstandarte* parading before Hitler on 30 January 1937, the anniversary of the Nazi accession to power.

1   S. Cook & J. Bender, *Leibstandarte SS Adolf Hitler: Uniforms, Organization, & History* (San Jose, 1994), p. 288.

2   P. Hoffmann, *Hitler's Personal Security* (Boston, 2000), p. 38.

3   J. Weingartner, *Hitler's Guard* (Nashville, 1974), p. ix.

4   Quoted in Weingartner, p. 26.

# 21 *Autobahn*

*The German motorway system* – or *Autobahn* – was once symbolic of the bright, technocratic future that the Third Reich appeared to promise. It was not a Nazi invention; Italy under Mussolini had the *Autostrada* from 1925 and within Germany a few local, toll-financed schemes, such as a road between Cologne and Düsseldorf, had already been begun prior to Hitler's accession to power. However, with Hitler's appointment as Chancellor in 1933, motorway-building met with the approval of central government in Germany for the first time.

The attraction for Hitler was primarily economic. The *Autobahn* project was a classic piece of Keynesianism: the state intervening with a large-scale, labour-intensive, public works programme, thereby providing employment and stimulating a stalled economy. In addition, it is often thought that the motorways had a military rationale. Hitler's planners suggested, for instance, that by the end of the project, 300,000 German troops could be shifted from one side of the Reich to the other in just two days of driving. The strategic advantages were therefore obvious.

Hitler exchanges salutes with a group of construction workers at the opening of a stretch of *Autobahn*.

So it was that the *Autobahn* was born. Soon after coming to power, Hitler commissioned loyal Nazi (and civil engineer) Fritz Todt to oversee the project. Todt was given a budget of five billion Reichsmarks, spread over five years, to build 6,000 kilometres of modern motorway. Later that year – on 23 September 1933 – Hitler dug the first sod on the construction site for the road that would link Frankfurt and Darmstadt. Within a year 1,500 km of the *Autobahn* were already in construction; within two years the first 100 km had been opened; within three years another 1,000 km. By the outbreak of war in 1939, over 3,000 km had been completed.

Hitler's *Autobahn* was a propaganda triumph, exploited by the Nazi regime to propagate the image of the Third Reich as a technologically advanced, forward-looking state, with economic centres linked by high-speed roads. Aside from that, the wider expected benefits of the programme were rather more limited. The contribution to the easing of unemployment, for instance, was meagre, with a maximum of some 130,000 employed on the motorways. The expected strategic advantage also failed to materialise,

A 1942 photograph of the Draackensteiner Hang viaduct built for the *Reichsautobahn*.

as most supplies and troops were still moved more easily around the country by train, and because, for much of the war, the fighting took place far from Germany's frontiers.

Nonetheless, the *Autobahn* appealed to Hitler, not just on a technological level, but also on a social one. In a late night conversation in July 1941, he mused about German roads that he foresaw one day stretching into conquered Russia:

> The beauties of the Crimea, which we will make accessible by means of an *Autobahn* – for us Germans, that will be our Riviera . . . Better than the railway, which has something impersonal about it, it's the road that will bring peoples together. What progress in the direction of New Europe! Just as the *Autobahn* has caused the inner frontiers of Germany to disappear, so it will abolish the frontiers of the countries of Europe.[1]

This was Hitler's vision behind the building of the *Autobahn* – motorways as the very arteries of the Nazi Empire.

1  Trevor-Roper, *Hitler's Table-Talk* (Oxford, 1988), pp. 4–5.

# 22 SA Dagger

*This dagger, one of the most ubiquitous in Nazi Germany,* was presented from 1934 to members of Hitler's SA – popularly known as the Brownshirts – the street-fighting thugs who had helped to bring the Nazis to power.

The SA had its origin in the political turmoil of the 1920s, when Hitler recruited 'Assault Units' – '*Sturmabteilungen*', SA for short – to keep order at his own speeches and disrupt those of his rivals. Under the able leadership of its chief of staff, Ernst Röhm, the organisation grew, numbering over half a million members by the end of 1932. The SA caught the spirit of the age. With rising unemployment, many young German men were looking for a new source of pride and a new sense of community and purpose – the SA gave it to them. Renowned for their penchant for violence, and their fondness for fists, cudgels and knuckledusters, SA cadres would fight numerous street battles against the Communists as the Nazis rose to prominence.

When Hitler became German Chancellor in 1933, the SA continued to serve as the defenders of his regime, and indeed helped consolidate his grip on power by serving as auxiliary policemen. They also enforced the Nazi boycott of Jewish businesses in April 1933, one of the first anti-Semitic outrages committed by the new regime.

However, power brought with it new tensions between Hitler and his erstwhile confederates. Hitler now had what he wanted, but Röhm – who by this time led a force of some two million men and dreamed of arming the SA and transforming it into a radical revolutionary movement – was frustrated. More importantly for Hitler, Germany's generals

Dagger presented to members of Hitler's SA, known popularly as the Brownshirts.

57

were beginning to express their concerns about the SA's possible role as a parallel army. It seemed that a showdown was in the offing.

It was against this political backdrop that the SA dagger was instituted in the spring of 1934. A simple, elegant design, it featured a runic SA roundel on its hilt, a Nazi eagle and swastika on the handle, and an acid-etched inscription on the blade, reading *Alles für Deutschland*: 'Everything for Germany'. The initial order – which would be fulfilled by a variety of manufacturers – was for a million pieces, the first 100,000 of which were to be issued to SA members of long-standing and etched with a facsimile of Röhm's signature and the message *In herzlicher Kameradschaft*: 'In heartfelt comradeship'. The irony was that, by the time this ceremonial weapon had been issued, the SA's street-fighting days were very much behind it.

An SA man proudly grips his dagger as he greets his *Führer*.

A few months after those first daggers were distributed, the 'problem' of the SA was solved in bloody style, when Hitler had Röhm shot, along with his senior lieutenants, in the 'Night of the Long Knives' in June 1934. With that, the SA was brought to heel and reduced to a mainly ceremonial role, and those members whose daggers bore Röhm's signature sent them away to have the offending inscription ground off.

# 23 Heinrich Hoffmann's Leica

*This rather unassuming looking camera* – a Leica IIIa from 1935 – sparked something of a revolution.

The 1930s was a time of enormous, ground-breaking developments in camera technology, when much of what we take for granted today was introduced. Around 1930, most professional photographers were still using plate cameras, cumbersome contraptions on wood and brass tripods. The Leica changed all that.

Using 35-mm camera film instead of glass plates, adding a rangefinder for sharper focusing and benefiting from the development of colour film, the Leica – from 'Leitz Camera' – was easily portable, robust and reliable. Effectively the first 'point and shoot' camera, it revolutionised photography and even made a new career possible, that of the photojournalist.

Heinrich Hoffmann's Leica IIIa – serial number 178859 – from 1935.

This was an opportunity that was not to be missed by Munich photographer Heinrich Hoffmann. Already established with his own studio, Hoffmann developed a close professional relationship with Adolf Hitler through the 1920s, and, by 1933, was a fixture in Hitler's entourage.

*'Hoffmann's pictures would prove to be essential components of the Nazi propaganda campaign.'*

But Hoffmann was much more than just the *Führer*'s tame photographer; he had helped Hitler to develop his 'style' through the 1920s, working with him to ascertain which poses worked best, and which styles of dress flattered him most – *Lederhosen* and SA uniform were out, sober suits were in. Together, Hitler and Hoffmann were consciously creating a public image, at a time when few politicians gave such apparently frivolous things a second thought.

But, in addition to his studio work, the development of the Leica gave Hoffmann the opportunity to use his photography more immediately as a weapon of Nazi propaganda. This Leica IIIa – one of Hoffmann's own examples – was purchased in November 1935 and is engraved with 'Presse Hoffmann, Berlin' beneath the viewfinder. In the decade that followed, it captured some of the most seminal moments of Hitler's odious career, many of which would be presented to the German public in handsome picture books.

Such volumes, promising a glimpse of the 'real Hitler' or celebrating the victorious advance of German forces, were hugely successful. Including 'Hitler in His Home' (1938), 'The Face of the *Führer*' (1939) and 'With Hitler in the West' (1940), they helped to bolster not only Hitler's personal popularity, but also the perception – once war had broken out – that German forces

Perfecting the public image: Hitler and Hoffmann examining one of the photographer's prints.

were marching inexorably to success after success. Gracing many a wartime coffee table, their pictures brought an up-close immediacy to the reader and reinforced the identification felt between the citizen and the Nazi regime.

Heinrich Hoffmann was not the only photographer to serve the Nazi regime, but he was certainly the most influential, and he was the only one to be granted access to Hitler's close-knit inner circle. His pictures, taken with this Leica IIIa camera, would prove to be essential components of the Nazi propaganda campaign; reproduced in countless newspapers, books, magazines, placards and postcards, they were the images that Hitler's regime showed to the world.

Hoffmann survived the war and died in Munich in 1957. His camera, looted by Allied soldiers in 1945, resurfaced in France in the 1980s.

*Mit Hitler im Westen* – 'With Hitler in the West' –
one of Hoffmann's successful picture books.

# 24 *Stahlhelm*

*The Stahlhelm – meaning 'steel helmet'* was the iconic and effective German anti-shrapnel helmet. First introduced midway through World War I and replacing the spiked leather *Pickelhaube*; it became synonymous with the German Army during the Third Reich. Frequently described as a 'coal-scuttle helmet', it was more directly inspired by the fifteenth-century sallet, with its peaked visor and flared neck guard.

The French were first to introduce steel helmets for trench warfare, and their 'Adrian' design was quickly followed by British and German types in 1916. The *Stahlhelm* was developed by Dr Friedrich Schwerd of the Technical Institute of Hanover, and first entered service at the Battle of Verdun, where it was worn by stormtrooper units. Officially known as the M1916, it had a chinstrap and a leather lining to cushion it against the skull, as well as the distinctive side lugs, which provided ventilation and fixing points for a reinforced brow-guard.

The M1935 *Stahlhelm*.

By the end of World War I the *Stahlhelm* had become so closely identified with German militarism that the word was adopted as the name of what was for a time the largest nationalist paramilitary organisation in the Weimar Republic. Composed largely of World War I veterans, it became the paramilitary arm of the German National People's Party (DNVP), until it was forcibly merged with parallel Nazi organisations after Hitler came to power.

*'Hitler was unwilling to undermine the symbolic significance of the Stahlhelm.'*

When the militarisation of the Third Reich began in earnest in 1933, a new variant of the *Stahlhelm* was tested and introduced, with Schwerd again offering advice. The M1935 was smaller and lighter, with a shorter visor and neckguard, and the side lugs were replaced by shallow ventilator holes. Over one million of these helmets were produced as the size of the Third Reich's army increased. In 1940, with the country at war, the design was slightly modified to make it easier and cheaper to manufacture, with the ventilator holes stamped directly into the helmet rather than being separate rivets. As the war continued, further production economies were made. A less flared version of the helmet was worn by Luftwaffe paratroopers.

Interestingly, a new, more conical helmet design was drawn up by German engineers in 1942. Intended to be easier to make and offer improved protection for the wearer, it was nonetheless rejected by Hitler, who was unwilling to undermine the symbolic significance of the *Stahlhelm*. That new design went on to be adopted by the East German Volksarmee in 1956.[1]

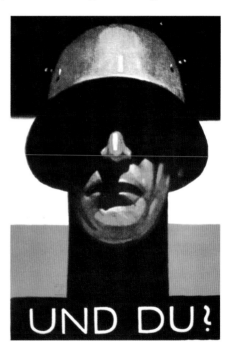

Emblematic of the power of the *Stahlhelm* image is this 1932 poster for Der Stahlhelm, Bund der Frontsoldaten – 'Steel Helmet, League of Front Soldiers'. The Nazis merged this group with the SA and disbanded the remnants in 1935.

1   F. Tubbs & R. Clawson, *Stahlhelm: Evolution of the German Steel Helmet* (Kent, Ohio, 2000), pp. 80–1.

# 25 Honour Temples

*In the political religion of National Socialism*, Hitler was the movement's prophet, the Blood Flag was its holiest relic, and its most significant martyrs were the dead from the Munich *Putsch* attempt of November 1923.

Fifteen Nazi supporters died that day; thirteen were shot in a brief firefight with the Bavarian police on the Odeonsplatz, and a further two were killed in an exchange at the nearby War Ministry. A sixteenth victim, Karl Kuhn, was an inncent bystander, caught in the crossfire. All but one were ordinary Germans: students, ex-soldiers and shopkeepers. The exception was Max Erwin von Scheubner-Richter, a 39-year-old former vice-consul, who was marching alongside Hitler when he was shot in the chest. In death, all of them would be honoured as the Nazis' first 'blood martyrs'.

After the Nazis came to power in 1933, plans were made for a redesign of the Königsplatz district of Munich, under the supervision of Hitler's first tame architect, Paul Ludwig Troost. As well as some new office buildings – amongst them the *Führerbau* – Troost included two 'Honour Temples' to house the mortal remains of the Nazi martyrs.

One of the two Honour Temples in Munich *c.* 1937: the holiest of Nazi holies.

*'It was the holiest of Nazi holies and would be the scene of elaborate ceremonial.'*

Completed in 1935, the year after Troost's death, the Honour Temples were neo-classical in style, using limestone facings over reinforced concrete, and stood around ten metres tall with elegant square pillars supporting a partial roof, leaving the central section open to the elements. That November, they were formally consecrated when the remains of the martyrs were reinterred in the temples – eight in each – in cast-iron sarcophagi, each one bearing a relief of the Nazi eagle, along with the name of the deceased and the words *'Der letzte Appell'* ('The last roll call') and *'Hier'* ('Here'). There, before a permanent SS guard, visitors were obliged to give the Hitler salute upon entering; silence was to be observed and headwear removed.

As the holiest of Nazi holies it would be the scene of elaborate ceremonial throughout the Third Reich, not least as the end-point of the annual commemoration of the *Putsch*, when thousands of Hitler's *Alte Kämpfer* – 'Old Fighters' – would march through the streets of Munich, culminating in a solemn wreath-laying on the Königsplatz.

By 1945, however, Hitler had been defeated, the political religion of Nazism had lost its allure, and the Honour Temples and sarcophagi of the martyrs were merely an embarrassing reminder of a faded fervour. At the command of the American occupying authorities, the sarcophagi were melted down, and their contents given back to the families of the deceased or buried in unmarked graves. In January 1947 the temples themselves were demolished; the rubble was used for reconstruction elsewhere in the city or else disposed of, and the interiors were filled with earth. Now, only the two concrete bases are left, dilapidated and overgrown. Few of those bustling by on Munich's streets know or care about the profound significance that they once had.

# 26 Swastika Flag of Nazi Germany

*The swastika – or Hakenkreuz* ('hooked cross') in German – is a symbol that was common throughout the ancient world and was most closely associated with India, where it is sacred to the Hindu, Jain and Buddhist faiths. However, embraced by German nationalist movements, it would acquire far more sinister connotations.

Around the start of the twentieth century, mystically-minded German nationalists – most notably the Thule Society – began to claim the swastika as a symbol of the Aryan race, a group they believed to have migrated to Europe from India in prehistory to become the forefathers of the Nordic and Germanic people. It was most likely in this context that the swastika would have first come to the attention of Adolf Hitler.

Nazi swastika flags in the museum at Oskar Schindler's Factory in Kraków, Poland.

In the early days of the Nazi Party, Hitler was keen to match the impact that flags had for his political opponents. Impressed by the sea of red at Communist rallies, for instance, he wrote that he could 'feel and understand how easily a man of the people succumbs to the suggestive charm of such a grand and massive spectacle'. He knew that the Nazis also needed a distinctive visual identity. As he wrote in *Mein Kampf* 'the party members lacked every outward sign of their belonging together'.[1]

> ## 'Hitler wanted the swastika to unify the Nazi movement and symbolise its principles.'

According to his later account, Hitler set about designing his own flag. He was not alone in that task, and confessed that the issue occupied the Nazi leadership 'intensely' in that period. An important contribution was made by a Starnberg dentist, Friedrich Krohn, who submitted a design incorporating the swastika and the red, white and black colours, which was 'very similar' to Hitler's own.[2]

Hitler's idea copied the red of the Communists but also took inspiration from the old Imperial German flag with its red, white and black colours, and – importantly – incorporated the swastika. The resulting flag, Hitler declared, expressed the Nazi movement perfectly: 'In red we see the social idea of the movement,' he wrote, 'in white the nationalistic idea, in the swastika the victory of the Aryan man, and, by the same token, the victory of creative work, which as such has always been and will always be anti-Semitic.'[3]

SA Brownshirts parade with swastika-adorned flags at the fifth Nazi Party Congress in Nuremberg in September 1933. Dubbed the 'Rally of Victory', it celebrated the Nazi seizure of power.

The question of the flag design was no trifling matter for Hitler, as evidenced by his lengthy discussion of the subject in *Mein Kampf*. He wanted the swastika to unify the Nazi movement and symbolise its principles, but he also knew that a striking emblem could in itself prove a very effective recruiting tool. When the new flag first appeared at Tegernsee in 1920, he wrote that its effect was 'akin to that of a blazing torch'.[4]

By the time it was adopted as the national flag in 1935, the swastika had already come to dominate the Third Reich. Thereafter, it would become Nazi Germany's face to the world.

1   S. Heller, *The Swastika: Symbol Beyond Redemption?* (New York, 2000), pp. 62–3

2   Hitler, *Mein Kampf*, p. 410

3   Spotts, *Hitler and the Power of Aesthetics*, p. 51

4   Hitler, *Mein Kampf*, p. 411

# 27 *Arbeit Macht Frei* Gate

*Of all the slogans employed by the Nazis, 'Arbeit macht Frei' –* or 'Work sets you free' – was perhaps the most infamous. A common inscription on the gates of the concentration camps, the slogan was apparently first used in 1873 as the title for a novel, in which the book's criminal protagonists find redemption through honest hard work.

It is unclear how it came to the attention of the Nazis, though it may have been via Theodor Eicke, an early commandant of the regime's first concentration camp, Dachau, and the first SS Inspector of Concentration Camps. Following the brutal and arbitrary excesses of his predecessor at Dachau, Hilmar Wäckerle, Eicke presided over a wholesale reorganisation of the concentration camp system, bringing in strict discipline, uniforms, and the idea that prisoners might repay their perceived 'debt' to society by hard labour.

The first '*Arbeit macht Frei*' concentration camp gate – here in its original form – at Dachau.

It was a concept that also put a positive propagande gloss on the concentration camps, portraying them as instruments of mass re-education (at least for those who could be reformed), where – redeemed by their labour – prisoners might ultimately become fit to rejoin the 'national community'.[1] Consequently hard labour became an essential component of concentration camp life. Many camps were located close to quarries, for instance, such as Mauthausen, Flossenbürg and Gross Rosen, while others – like Neuengamme and Sachsenhausen – were sited next to vast brickworks. All of them spawned a bewildering myriad of sub-camps, established to provide labour to the SS and to German businesses large and small, from huge industrial concerns to local butchers and bakers.

It is perhaps unsurprising, then, that the slogan '*Arbeit macht Frei*' would be employed by many camps. First used at Dachau in 1936, it would even be incorporated into a prisoner song – the *Dachaulied* – which urged the prisoners to 'remain human' but to do their work, as only 'work would set them free'.[2] Later the slogan would also be used on the entrance gates at Auschwitz, Sachsenhausen and to the ghetto at Theresienstadt, as a reminder to the unfortunate inmates. The concentration camp at Buchenwald, by contrast, used a different motto: there, the main gate proclaimed '*Jedem das Seine*', which can be translated either as 'To each his own', or the rather more sinister 'You get what you deserve'.

Those camp gates, with their inscriptions, would become darkly iconic. Those at Auschwitz I, for instance, are said to have incorporated an upside-down B as an act of resistance by the prisoner-blacksmith, Jan Liwacz, who forged them. They were stolen in 2009, on behalf of Swedish neo-Nazis, and – though swiftly recovered – were badly damaged in the process.[3] In 2014, the gate at Dachau was also stolen. It was recovered in December 2016 in Bergen, Norway.[4]

---

*'Hard labour was an essential component of concentration camp life.'*

---

Of course the idea that a concentration camp inmate might find 'liberation' through his or her labour was utterly fanciful. Prisoners were often released from the camps – before the outbreak of war at least – but the decision was entirely on the whim of the SS or Gestapo, and thus entirely independent of the amount, or the quality, of an inmate's work. '*Arbeit macht Frei*', therefore, was nothing but a cynical, empty promise.

1   Nikolaus Wachsmann, *KL: A History of the Nazi Concentration Camps* (London, 2015), pp. 100–1.

2   See https://de.wikipedia.org/wiki/Dachaulied.

3   Jan Puhl, 'Eine bizarre Tat', in *Der Spiegel*, No.48, 29 November 2010, pp. 121–2.

4   See http://www.bbc.co.uk/news/world-europe-38187597.

# 28 Messerschmitt Bf 109

*The Bf 109, commonly called the Me 109*, was arguably the most impressive of all German fighter planes in the Third Reich. Designed by renowned aircraft engineer Willy Messerschmitt, and developed at Bayerische Flugzeugwerke (BFW: Bavarian Aircraft Works) in Augsburg, it served the Luftwaffe from the Spanish Civil War right through World War II, being supplanted only by the Focke-Wulf Fw 190 in the later years of the conflict. In the skies over England during the Battle of Britain in 1940 it was the only German fighter plane to equal the legendary Supermarine Spitfire in quality and performance.

In 1933, as the Third Reich began to shake off the constraints of the Versailles Treaty and prepare its armed forces for a future war, the Reich Aviation Ministry requested designs for its new air force. One of the companies invited to develop a single-seat fighter was BFW, and its prototype was ready in 1935. Impressive from the outset, the Bf 109 soon became the front-runner for development, with its lightweight framework, superior control and smoothly efficient retractable undercarriage proving popular with pilots. Spurred by news of the British development of the Hawker Hurricane and Supermarine Spitfire, the prototype was put into production and it made its public debut at the 1936 Berlin Olympics.

The Messerschmitt Bf 109 on display in the Smithsonian Air and Space Museum.

> *'It is thought that the Bf 109 destroyed more aircraft than any other in World War II.'*

Powered (in its most numerous variants) by the formidable Daimler-Benz DB601 (33-litre V-12) engine, which produced over 1,000 bhp, the Bf 109 was certainly fast, with a maximum speed of just under 400 mph (640 kmh) in early-war versions. Armed initially with two 7.92 mm machine guns firing through its propeller arc and soon with added wing-mounted 20 mm cannons, it also proved to be a ferocious adversary in aerial combat.

But, while it had dominated the skies in the first year of the war, the Bf 109 met its match during the Battle of Britain in the late summer of 1940, when it was opposed by the Spitfires and Hurricanes of the RAF. Though performance indicators for the Bf 109 and Spitfire were broadly similar, the German aircraft – which was employed as a bomber escort – was operating at the very limits of its range and so was exposed to the twin threats of enemy action and fuel starvation. The cost, therefore, was comparatively high, with some 600 Bf 109s

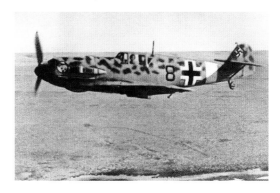

A Messerschmitt Bf 109 in flight over the North African desert.

being destroyed during that campaign, around a third of the Luftwaffe's total losses.[1]

After that chastening experience, the Bf 109 was able to return to its traditional role as a fighter, and with the introduction of the 'F' variant in late 1940, which boasted many improvements, including enhanced aerodynamics, its fortunes began to be restored. In the Balkans, Mediterranean and North African theatres, it once again proved its worth, before action on the Eastern Front – often against poorly trained and poorly equipped Soviet forces – propelled the aircraft once more towards legendary status. There, Bf 109 pilots enjoyed a field-day, with many of them being credited with shooting down 100 or more enemy aircraft. Overall, it is thought that the Bf 109 destroyed more aircraft than any other in World War II.[2]

---

1   Cited in R. T. Bickers, *The Battle of Britain* (London, 1990).

2   U. Feist, *The Fighting Me 109* (London, 1993), p. 50.

# 29 Jackboots

*The Wehrmacht's characteristic marching boots – Marschstiefel*, commonly known as jackboots in the English-speaking world – became synonymous with tyranny in the World War II era. Serried ranks of jackboot-wearing German troops strutting in their stiff-legged 'goose-step' march became a familiar image in the 1930s and 1940s and seemed to define the era, symbolising the machine-like power of totalitarianism.

The name jackboot is said to derive from knee-high British cavalry boots of the seventeenth century that were reinforced with mail 'jack' armour sewn into the leather. Calf-high pull-on marching boots had been worn by German soldiers since the nineteenth century and were used throughout World War I. Made of brown leather which was usually polished black in the field, they had hobnailed soles, with between thirty-five and forty-five hobnails hammered into each. A horseshoe-shaped iron was fitted to the heel and an iron plate to the toe. They were known to German soldiers as *Knobelbecher* – or 'dice-shakers' – because of their inevitably poor fit.

As the German Army grew rapidly in size through the late 1930s, the height of the boot was reduced to save leather, and as the war progressed they were gradually replaced by laced ankle boots. By 1943, marching boots were no longer being produced and their issue was tightly controlled, limited to infantry, pioneers and other special categories. Officers, meanwhile, wore taller knee-high boots – *Reitstiefel* or 'riding boots' – many of which were privately purchased and of higher quality.

During the war, German marching boots served their purpose well, with the only major shortcoming being

Wehrmacht marching boots – *Marschstiefel* – commonly known as jackboots.

> *'Serried ranks of jackboot-wearing German troops strutting in their stiff-legged "goose-step" march became a familiar image in the 1930s and 1940s.'*

their performance in the cold of the Russian winter. While the nails and metalwork in the sole of the boots were intended to reduce wear, in extremely cold temperatures they had the added effect of speeding the transfer of the cold in, towards the foot. For this reason, German troops on the Eastern Front often looted thick *valenki* overboots – usually made of felt or straw – from Red Army corpses. Nonetheless, frostbite cut a swathe through German ranks each winter of the war. In the winter of 1941, for instance, the Wehrmacht recorded over 100,000 cases of frostbite, more than 14,000 of which required one or more amputations.[1]

Jackboot-wearing, goose-stepping troops of 1st Division, VIII Army Corps, march through Vienna in March 1938.

Away from the front, the primary symbolic significance of the German jackboot lay in its close connection to the characteristic goose-step march, known to the soldiers as the *Stechschritt* – 'piercing step'. Originated in Prussian drill in the eighteenth century, the goose-step was part of a general European desire in that era to impose greater discipline and cohesion on the movement of soldiers on the battlefield, yet found its greatest expression in Hitler's Germany. There, the image of soldiers marching in lock-step was somehow symbolic of the wicked, controlling ambition of totalitarianism. As George Orwell wrote:

> The goose-step is one of the most horrible sights in the world, far more terrifying than a dive-bomber. It is simply an affirmation of naked power; contained in it, quite consciously and intentionally, is the vision of a boot crashing down on a face.[2]

1   A. Clark, *Barbarossa: The Russian–German Conflict, 1941–1945* (London, 1995), p. 181.

2   G. Orwell, *The Orwell Reader* (London, 1956), p. 254.

# 30 Concentration Camp Badges

*To the untrained eye, the unfortunates consigned* to the Nazi concentration camps during the Third Reich must have looked like an undifferentiated mass of suffering humanity. Yet, as their SS guards well knew, there were ways and means of telling them apart, even of seeing – at a glance – what perceived misdemeanour had brought them to the camp.

After the lawless chaos of the early 'wild' concentration camps – those established after the Nazi seizure of power in January 1933 – the setting of rules and regulations for the camp system soon became necessary, especially after the reorganisation of the camps from 1934. Key to that process was SS-Gruppenführer Theodor Eicke, who – as Inspector of Concentration Camps – had already devised new guarding provisions and protocols for camps like Dachau. Eicke was no woolly liberal, though; he was a vicious, psychopathic martinet, with a visceral loathing of Marxists and Jews. His 'system' would provide the guiding principles of the entire Nazi camp network.

---

*'The badges served the SS's goal of dividing and dehumanising the prisoners.'*

---

A part of the wider reorganisation of the camps was the differentiation of prisoners, and, to that end, a system of coloured badges was introduced in 1936, by which SS guards could visually ascertain a prisoner's status and background. The system was illustrated with tables, such as that shown here, which would be displayed in the various camp administration offices and SS guard rooms to increase familiarity.

Each prisoner was registered and given a number, which would be sewn on to their prison uniform on the left breast and on the seam of the trousers. Beneath it, a coloured triangle was added, which denoted the nominal reason for the prisoner's incarceration – red for political offenders, green for habitual criminals, blue for 'emigrants' (those who had been expelled from Germany and had returned), purple for Jehovah's Witnesses, pink for homosexuals and black for 'asocials'. Those prisoners who were Jewish had an inverted yellow triangle added to their designation, thereby forming a Star of David.

In addition to these badges, bars and circles could be added to denote repeat offenders, would-be escapers and those on punishment details. After 1939, initials would also be used to denote nationality: F for French, B for Belgians, P for Poles, T for Czechs (*Tschechen* in German) and so on.

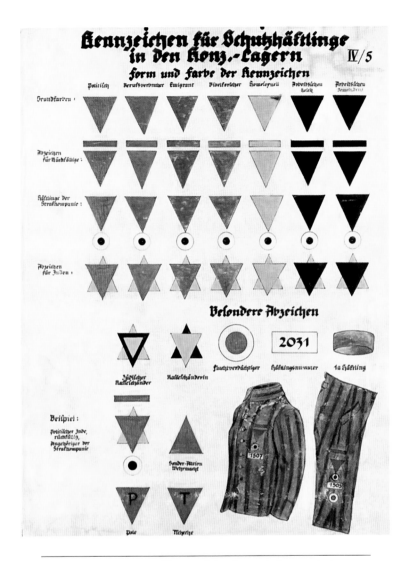

A poster explaining the different varieties of concentration camp badge.

In this way, all the various categories of miscreant – in Nazi eyes – could be visually marked. Socialist and communist agitators would receive a red triangle, for instance; poachers, thieves and burglars would receive green, and beggars, prostitutes and the 'workshy' would receive a black triangle. Proportions, across the concentration camp system, are very difficult to ascertain, but it is clear that political prisoners made up the largest single category, in large part because it served as a catch-all for most opposition activity. Elsewhere, particular camps could have a larger proportion of a particular category at certain times: 38 per cent of the prisoner population of Buchenwald, for instance, were listed as 'criminals' in early 1938, while Sachsenhausen, outside Berlin, held a larger proportion of homosexual prisoners than most other camps.[1]

Far from being merely administrative in function, such identifications could dictate how a prisoner was treated, and thereby decide their fate. Jewish prisoners, obviously, could always expect harsh treatment from the guards, but 'politicals' were also prone to random persecution, as were homosexuals and repeat offenders, who were much more likely to be consigned to a punishment detail, with predictable results. At Dachau, for instance, the death rate among homosexual prisoners was consistently higher than among their heterosexual follows.[2] Those with green triangles, meanwhile – criminals – were often favoured by the camp authorities to serve as *Kapos*; the trusty prisoners who took charge of each barrack block, in return for improved conditions.[3] The fact that they were merely 'criminal' and not 'political' or 'asocial', evidently elevated them in the eyes of some of their SS overlords.

Auschwitz inmate Czesława Kwoka, showing her uniform and badge.

In practice, most of the more complex additional symbols remained rather theoretical, and the reality for the vast majority of prisoners was far more pedestrian, as shown in the image of Czesława Kwoka, a fourteen-year-old prisoner in Auschwitz in 1942, the red triangle denoting a 'political', P for Polish, and the number 26947. Nonetheless, the badges were an integral part of the concentration camp system, serving the SS's goal of dividing and dehumanising the prisoners, reducing each of them simply to a number and a perceived crime.

The badges also featured strongly in the post-war commemoration of the victims of the camps, particularly in the former East Germany. There, the red triangle was a frequent addition to concentration camp memorials, with the best example being at Sachsenhausen, outside Berlin, where a communist-era obelisk, erected in 1961, features an array of fifty-four red triangles. It neatly conveys the fiction, propagated by the communists, that all of the camp's inmates had been 'politicals'.

1   See Wachsmann, *KL*, p. 145; Moorhouse, *Berlin at War*, p. 242.

2   Stanislav Zámečník, *That was Dachau: 1933–1945* (Brussels, 2003), p. 219.

3   See Wachsmann, *KL*, pp. 125–8, 521–5. Zámečník, *That was Dachau*.

# 31 Berghof Plate

*It is perhaps ironic that, when Hitler first came* to the Obersalzberg, he came seeking a retreat. In time, that retreat – and the building that he had constructed there – would become one of the most famous addresses in the Third Reich.

Hitler had first discovered the Obersalzberg in 1923 when his ideological mentor, the nationalist writer Dietrich Eckart, came to the area while on the run from the police. Hitler joined Eckart at a small guesthouse, staying under the false name of Herr Wolf, and immediately fell in love with the dramatic landscape. In 1925, he rented a small country house there, the Haus Wachenfeld. Later, funded in part with the growing royalties from the sales of *Mein Kampf*, he bought the house, which he would transform into the Berghof. As he would afterwards recall, the place was very important to him:

Porcelain souvenir wall plate showing the 'Haus Wachenfeld', from 1934.

When I go to Obersalzberg, I'm not drawn there merely by the beauty of the landscape. I feel myself far from petty things, and my imagination is stimulated. When I study a problem elsewhere, I see it less clearly, I'm submerged by the details. By night, at the Berghof, I often remain for hours with my eyes open, contemplating from my bed the mountains lit up by the moon. It's at such moments that brightness enters my mind.[1]

After Hitler was appointed Chancellor in 1933, the house slowly became something like a place of pilgrimage, with many Germans – first from the surrounding area, and then from further afield – flocking there to try to catch a glimpse of their new hero. Security in those early days was rather lax. Up until 1936, Hitler would wander the wooded trails quite informally, with only a few guests in tow, or a cursory guard detail. Sometimes, hiking tourists would greet him and he'd wave back. In time – as the site became the epicentre of the Hitler cult – security was ramped up, and the area surrounding the house was fenced off and patrolled, while SS guards marshalled the crowds of well-wishers.

*'After Hitler was appointed Chancellor in 1933, the house slowly became something like a place of pilgrimage.'*

For many of those visitors, their trip to the Obersalzberg would not be complete without a memento such as the porcelain wall plate on the previous page. Made by Rosenthal in Munich, it was hand-painted and glazed and depicted 'Haus Wachenfeld' in the form that it took in 1934, after Hitler's first round of expansion had added a garage and small terrace. In the distance, the peaks of the Reiter Alpe can be seen, and to the right, the foothills of the Untersberg, beneath which German Emperor Frederick Barbarossa was said to wait for resurrection.

While the Haus Wachenfeld was thus immortalised in porcelain, the real building barely stood still. In 1935, Hitler ordered a programme of expansion, which would transform the simple Alpine house into the huge 'Berghof' complex, which he believed would be a more appropriate residence for the leader of the German nation. Initially completed in 1936, with a further extension in 1939, it impressed its guests – among them Prime Minister Neville Chamberlain, the Duke and Duchess of Windsor, and Britain's former Premier David Lloyd George – with its magnificent, opulent rooms, its wide terrace with spectacular mountain views, and especially its panoramic picture window, which overlooked the valley and could be raised or lowered electronically.

By the time it was completed, the Berghof stood at the heart of a Nazi enclave, including a barracks for over 2,000 troops and residences for senior Nazis, including Martin Bormann, Hermann Göring and Albert Speer. The relaxed atmosphere of earlier days was totally transformed, and the building was ringed with a two-metre-high barbed-wire and chain-link fence, with anyone approaching having to pass through inner and outer security pickets policed by the SS. Local residents had even been removed by Bormann, Hitler's ruthlessly ambitious secretary, who used dubious methods to acquire the land around the building, often forcing residents out of their homes with bribes, compulsory purchases, or the threat of a spell in a concentration camp. With that, Hitler became a virtual recluse when he was at the Berghof, and the heady days of smiling crowds and kitsch souvenirs were consigned to memory.

Given that Hitler's entourage and much of the apparatus of government would move with him when he stayed at the Berghof, building on the Obersalzberg continued at a furious pace, and a branch of the Reich Chancellery was even established in the valley at Stanggass. Hitler spent much of his time 'on the mountain', surrounded by his most senior cohorts, as well as visiting VIPs. It was there that he made some of his most important decisions, including for the signing of the Nazi–Soviet Pact in 1939, and the invasion of the USSR two years later. Such was the importance of the Obersalzberg as the informal second capital of the Third Reich that, by the later stages of the war, vast underground bunkers and a labyrinth of tunnels were dug and fortified against bombing raids. What had once been a peaceful alpine retreat became a major construction site and the reflexive loyalty of the locals began to waver. For his part, Hitler remarked that when it was all over he would buy himself a nice little chalet.

Hitler on the terrace at his Berghof mountain retreat, with members of his entourage and pets.

Hitler had little chance of a peaceful retirement, however, and in April 1945, only a week before his suicide in Berlin, an RAF bombing raid on the Obersalzberg, damaged part of the Berghof and destroyed much of the wider complex. Thereafter, in the chaos of defeat, the building was set on fire by the SS, before being captured and thoroughly looted by the American 101st Airborne Division. In 1952, its charred remains were then dynamited by the Bavarian government to prevent them becoming a neo-Nazi shrine. Now, all that remains of the building is a moss-covered concrete retaining wall, deep in a rubble-strewn wood.

The famous picture window and view from the Berghof.

1   Trevor-Roper, *Hitler's Table-Talk*, pp. 164–5.

# 32 Elastolin Toy Figure

*Like any regime with totalitarian ambitions*, the Third Reich sought to bring Germany's children under its nefarious influence as early as was possible. To this end, toys were a useful weapon in the battle for hearts and minds, particularly those with a military or political theme – such as this Hitler figure.

Produced by the Ludwigsburg firm O. & M. Hausser, figures such as this one were highly sought-after by German children during the Nazi period. Standing 7 cm high, they are made from 'Elastolin', Hausser's trademark composite material consisting of sawdust and resin, which was cast over a wire frame and then painted. Hausser offered a selection of Hitler figures, including him seated, standing or speaking at a podium hung with a swastika. Some of them had a hand-painted porcelain head; others – as in this example – even had a movable right arm, so that he could be made to salute.

They were part of a huge range of figures which included Mussolini, Hermann Göring, Francisco Franco and Rudolf Hess, as well as all manner of military vehicles and personnel, from the Hitler Youth to the SS. More elaborate models included artillery guns that fired a small projectile and rifles that released a puff of smoke. They would originally have sold for around 5 Reichsmarks each, and with the average weekly wage in 1938 at around 30 Reichsmarks, they were certainly not cheap.

> 'Some of the Hitler figures even had a movable right arm,
> so that he could be made to salute.'

Elastolin toys thrilled a generation of German children with the prospect of re-enacting Hitler's speeches or playing war games on their bedroom floors. Of course, they were never intended to be politically neutral; they were an integral part of Nazi propaganda. Not only did they serve to inculcate in young minds a fascination with all things military, they also sowed the seeds of political indoctrination, fostering a hero-worship of the Nazi Party leadership. For this reason, the Nazi regime kept a very close eye on the business and Hitler even intervened to make the cast of his own head look more realistic.

Ironically, the sale of Elastolin figures was halted in 1943, when the shift to a 'total war' economy in Germany put an end to almost all non-military production. By that time, of course, many of those Germans who had been raised playing with toy soldiers in the 1930s were already fighting for real on the battlefields of Europe.

Playtime with Hitler. Hitler figure, in Elastolin (*c.* 1938).

# 33 A 'Protective Custody Order'

*The Nazi complex of prisons and concentration camps* is rightly a well-known aspect of our understanding of the Third Reich. However, the method by which individuals might find themselves incarcerated in that terror network is often only imperfectly understood. Central to it was the use of this document, the *Schutzhaftbefehl* – or 'Protective Custody Order'.

Contrary to popular belief, Nazi Germany was not an entirely lawless place; its legal system – though swiftly 'coordinated' to Nazi norms – continued to function throughout. Yet, even so, the Gestapo and police authorities were unwilling to be restricted by such niceties, and so developed a way of by-passing the entire legal framework: the concept of 'protective custody'.

Drawing on an earlier precedent, used during World War I, Nazi 'protective custody' helpfully dispensed with the bothersome concept of evidence. This did not mean, of course, that the Gestapo would not investigate misdemeanours – their investigations were often exhaustive[1] – but it did mean that the threshold of proof could be reassuringly low. A 'miscreant' need not have committed any actual crime – indeed the majority had not, otherwise they would likely be dealt with via the traditional legal route; instead 'protective custody' allowed for Gestapo suspicion merely of an anti-Nazi attitude to be punished with a spell of incarceration.

The protective custody order was a single sheet of paper – usually pink – pre-typed with spaces for the suspect's name, address and personal details to be entered, along with a larger space for the grounds upon which the order was based, most commonly membership of a socialist or communist organisation, anti-Nazi sentiment, or that the suspect in some way posed a 'threat to public order'.

All that was required was for the relevant sections to be filled in and then stamped and signed at the bottom of the page by a Gestapo officer, after an authorisation from the relevant Gestapo department. The grounds for detention would be read to the prisoner and then he or she would be taken away – either to a Gestapo prison or to a concentration camp – accompanied by a copy of the protective custody order, which would be used to classify the new arrival.

This example – which is signed by Reinhard Heydrich himself – was issued in April 1936 for a 25-year-old socialist, Eberhard Hesse, who was suspected of taking part in meetings of a 'revolutionary organisation' in Berlin. In the 'interests of public security' it was requested that he should remain in custody for three months, during which time

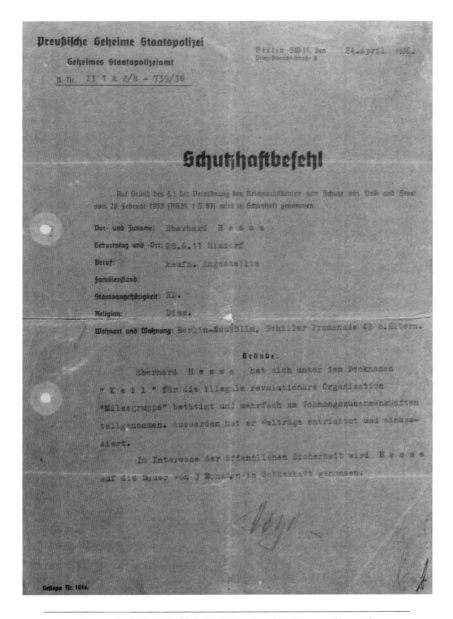

An example of a *Schutzhaftbefehl* – 'kidnapping with a bureaucratic veneer'.

his activities could be thoroughly investigated by the Gestapo. In the event, Hesse remained in custody for nine months.[2]

As this example shows, this single piece of paper was sufficient for an individual to be imprisoned. Though Hesse would later be tried in court and sentenced to eighteen months hard labour for his 'crimes', at the time of his initial arrest and interrogation, no judge was involved, no court was convened, and no lawyer was present. He had no right of appeal. Though the authorities promised a review of each protective custody case every three months, in practice release was down solely to the whim of the Gestapo case officer or the concentration camp commander. It was, as one historian has aptly put it, 'little more than kidnapping with a bureaucratic veneer'.[3]

Given its ease of use, 'protective custody' was rapidly extended to become the Gestapo's most significant method of combatting its opponents. After the early months of 1933, when it was used primarily against communist and socialist party members, after 1936 it was rolled out and used to target ever wider circles of genuine and perceived resistance, as well as those who defied the Nazis' social norms: Jehovah's Witnesses, Gypsies, prostitutes, beggars, alcoholics and the workshy.[4] Petty criminals could also be dealt with under its aegis, particularly re-offenders who appeared impervious to conventional punishment. The total number of protective custody orders issued cannot be known for sure, but must be well into the hundreds of thousands.

---

*'A "miscreant" need not have committed any actual crime – indeed the majority had not.'*

---

The humble *Schutzhaftbefehl* is something that rarely receives any examination in the conventional narrative of the Third Reich. But it was profoundly emblematic, not only of the Nazi mania for bureaucracy, but also of the oddly extra-legal methods by which the Gestapo by-passed its own legal system. For these aspects alone, it deserves notice. But, above all, it should be remembered for the countless thousands of lives that it altered, diverting them to an uncertain fate in the prisons and concentration camps – with barely a signature and a few hurriedly typed lines.

1   Frank McDonough, *The Gestapo: The Myth and Reality of Hitler's Secret Police* (London, 2015), pp. 55–6.

2   Stiftung Topographie des Terrors (ed.), *Topography of Terror – Documentation* (Berlin, 2014), p. 148.

3   Wachsmann, *KL*, p. 32.

4   See Lothar Gruchmann, *Justiz im Dritten Reich 1933–40* (Munich, 1988).

# 34 Olympic Stadium

*Berlin's Olympic Stadium* – alongside Tempelhof Airport and Göring's former Air Ministry – is one of the German capital's most impressive Nazi-era buildings. Constructed for the 1936 Olympics, it was designed by local Berlin architect Werner March.

The award of the hosting of the 1936 Olympics predated Hitler's rise to power in Germany, but he exploited the event masterfully for the purposes of Nazi propaganda, presenting Germany as a united, positive, forward-looking country. Aside from the politics, the Berlin Olympics also marked something of a watershed in Olympic history, being the first Games to be televised and the first to be prefaced by the (now conventional) torch relay from Olympia in Greece to the host site. With its overwhelming sense of spectacle and its shameless commercialisation, the Berlin Olympics arguably set the tone for the Olympiads that were to follow.

The Berlin Olympic Park in 1936: nearest the camera is the Dietrich Eckart amphitheatre, then the vast May Field and the main stadium.

Aside from the sailing, which was held on the Baltic at Kiel, the remainder of the events in 1936 were held in Berlin, with most being located in the complex of venues surrounding the Olympic Stadium, in the western suburbs. The stadium itself was built on the site of the earlier Deutsches Stadion, which had been constructed for the cancelled 1916 Olympics. Hitler had a hand in the design and, after declaring himself dissatisfied with the original concept, had brought Albert Speer in to assist. Rather than the suggested renovation of the old site, he demanded a completely new stadium – a grand showpiece for the regime – which could accommodate 110,000 spectators.

---

*'All future Olympic Games were to be held in Germany and were to be a showcase for the natural superiority of the Aryan race.'*

---

The result bore many of the hallmarks of Nazi architecture: uniformity, monumentalism, and the liberal use of shell-limestone veneers to cover the reinforced-concrete skeleton. Cleverly, like the original stadium on the site, the Olympic Stadium was built into the ground, with the running track and sports field being some twelve metres lower than the ground level outside, thereby saving the high cost of an extensive superstructure and giving it an elegant, almost modest profile.

And yet money-saving was never the intention, as was amply demonstrated by the array of buildings that surrounded the site. The Olympic Stadium was only the centrepiece of a vast 300-acre complex – including an open-air swimming and diving pool, indoor and outdoor arenas, a hockey stadium, an equestrian arena, and an open-air amphitheatre, named after Hitler's political mentor, Dietrich Eckart.

Indeed, though sport was the primary purpose, politics was never far from the surface. The stadium complex was littered with limestone statues of men, horses and athletes, by the renowned sculptors Karl Albiker, Willy Meller and Joseph Wackerle. These sought to echo classical Greek styles, albeit with a newer fascistic aesthetic – all rippling muscles and jutting chins.

In addition, the vast Maifeld ('May Field') to the west of the stadium – with its capacity for 250,000 participants – was used for dressage and polo, but was clearly intended as much for political rallies as for sporting activity.[1] Indeed the layout of the complex betrayed a profound political significance. The stadium approach, stadium, and Maifeld were all arranged along an axis, running approximately east–west, aligning also with the 'Marathon Gate', which breaks the perfect oval of the stadium. At the western end of that axis – at the focus of the stadium's stony gaze – was the main grandstand of the Maifeld, beneath which is the 'Langemarck Hall', a memorial to the German dead of Langemarck, an engagement of the First Battle of Ypres in 1914 that was considered to be especially symbolic of the patriotic sacrifice of the wartime generation. For those alive to them, the references were very clear: the sporting heroes of the present had one eye on the military heroes of the past.

Hitler was clearly hoping for a new crop of heroes to grace 'his' Olympics. He was not disappointed. Germany topped the medal table and its presentation of the Games was a critical and commercial success. However, it was a very different symbolism for which the Berlin Games would be best remembered. Hitler once told Albert Speer that all future Olympic Games were to be held in Germany and were to be a showcase for the natural superiority of the Aryan race.[2] Yet, at his own Games, in 1936, the limelight was stolen by an outstanding athlete winning four gold medals in Berlin's Olympic Stadium – someone whom Hitler considered to be racially inferior – African-American Jesse Owens.

The Olympic Stadium, packed for some of the track and field events.

1   Wolfgang Schäche, Norbert Szymanski, *Das Reichssportfeld. Architektur im Spannungsfeld von Sport und Macht* (Berlin, 2001), p. 57.

2   Albert Speer, *Inside the Third Reich* (London, 1970), p. 116.

# 35 The 88 mm Gun

*Unquestionably the most famous – and infamous –* German artillery weapon of World War II, the 88 mm began life as an anti-aircraft gun. Drawing on a design produced at the very end of World War I, the 'eighty-eight' – or '*Acht-Acht*', as it was known in German – was first produced in 1932 as an anti-aircraft or 'Flak' gun. (The term Flak is a contraction of *Fliegerabwehrkanone* – 'aircraft defence gun'.)

In an age of great fear of the destructive potential of aerial warfare, the 88 offered a highly effective response; its semi-automatic loading mechanism was able – in concert with a well-trained crew – to fire up to fifteen high explosive shells per minute, to an operational ceiling of 8,000 metres. Unsurprisingly, perhaps, once Hitler came to power in 1933, the 88 was swiftly approved and put into production. With various subsequent versions that improved range and provided updated firing instruments, it would become the Third Reich's most effective anti-aircraft gun.

However, it was in its ground role that the 88 would perhaps gain the most notoriety. It was first battle-tested in that capacity during the Spanish Civil War, when the 88s sent to the Spanish Nationalists cut a swathe through the light tanks of the Republicans. Indeed, in the last great offensive of that conflict, in Catalonia, fully 93 per cent of 88 ammunition used, was fired against ground targets.[1]

An 88 on display in the Overloon War Museum in the Netherlands.

That pattern persisted with the outbreak of war in 1939, and – though 88s continued to provide the backbone of Germany's air defence network – they would also be used increasingly in an anti-tank capacity. General Erwin Rommel was a particular fan, and employed the guns to devastating effect in his campaigns, especially in North Africa. Sometimes emplaced so deeply in the sand that only their barrels showed, they ripped apart Allied armour. At the battle for Halfaya Pass on 15 June 1941, the British had high hopes for their Matilda tanks but, as they rumbled forward, the 88s snapped into action and of the eighteen Allied tanks destroyed on that day, fifteen had fallen victim to them. As one captured German colonel boasted to US Army intelligence: the 88 was a crucial weapon in North Africa, as it 'was able to pierce the armour of even heavy enemy tanks at long range'.[2]

In its many versions and variants, the German 88 was ubiquitous during World War II. At their most numerous, in the summer of 1944, nearly 11,000 examples were in action,[3] firing in total over 100,000 shells per day. Yet, alongside those used for anti-aircraft defence, or in an anti-tank role, the 88 also found service – in modified form – in heavy tanks such as the Tiger I and Tiger II, as well as a range of heavy tank-destroyers, such as the Elefant and the Nashorn. Thanks to this ubiquity, and the devastating effect that it wrought, the 88 – uniquely among artillery guns – wrote itself a page in history.

An eighty-eight in action in North Africa, in the general artillery role rather than its specialities of anti-tank or anti-aircraft operations.

1   J. Norris, *88 mm Flak 18/36/37/41 & PaK 43, 1936–45* (Oxford, 2002), p. 8.

2   R. Kriebel, *Inside the Afrika Korps* (London, 1999), p. 45.

3   T. Gander, *German 88: The Most Famous Gun of the Second World War* (Barnsley, 2009), p. 57.

# 36 Eva Braun's Lipstick Case

*Eva Braun was an essential part* of the history of the Third Reich. Hitler's lover and companion for over a decade, she first met him in 1929, while she was working in Heinrich Hoffmann's Munich studio; three years later the two had begun the relationship that would define her life. Ultimately, she would share his fate, committing suicide with her husband in the Reich Chancellery bunker on 30 April 1945.

Braun's early life was very conventional. Born in 1912, to a middle-class Munich family, she was educated in a Catholic school, where she scored average grades, before finding work as an assistant to Heinrich Hoffmann, Hitler's photographer. Blonde and blue-eyed, she was certainly attractive – Hoffmann described her as 'doll-like'[1] – and possessed an easy charm. She was young, fun-loving and somewhat flighty, but otherwise very normal – one might even say unremarkable. Albert Speer would later predict that she would prove 'a disappointment' to writers of history.[2]

> *'She struggled with this frustrating and ambiguous existence – acknowledged neither as a wife nor a mistress.'*

Her relationship with Hitler was certainly remarkable, if only for its secrecy. Though it began around the end of 1932, Braun was kept very much in the background, and – in marked contrast to Geli Raubal – was not permitted to be seen with Hitler in public. On the rare occasions when she was allowed to accompany him – such as to Italy in 1938 – she was hidden in the entourage as one of Heinrich Hoffmann's photographers. Such caution was thought essential because of the stark focus on Hitler's private life that had followed Raubal's suicide in 1931, and the resulting need for him to be rebranded as an ascetic, statesman-like figure, with no life (or potential embarrassments) outside politics. It was to this end that Hitler famously declared that he was 'married to the German people'.[3]

So, for the next twelve years, Eva Braun remained confined to the shadows, an important member of Hitler's entourage on the Obersalzberg, certainly, but unknown to the ordinary German public. Initially, it seems, she struggled with this frustrating and ambiguous existence – acknowledged neither as a wife nor a mistress – and her feelings were perhaps expressed by her two apparent suicide attempts, in 1932 and 1935. On her birthday in 1935, she confided to her diary: 'I turned 23 today, but that does not necessarily mean I'm a happy 23. At the moment, I'm definitely not.'[4]

Eva Braun's lipstick case: a gift from Hitler, *c.* 1938.

Yet, in time, she seems to have grown accustomed to Hitler's gilded cage. Though she had to retreat into the background whenever he had official visitors to the Berghof, otherwise she lived there as the 'lady of the house', bringing a welcome feminine touch to proceedings.[5]

The staff on the Obersalzberg would later comment on her life of luxury there. She would change outfits a couple of times a day, and received regular visits from her hairdresser.[6] Beyond that, she enjoyed walking her two dogs – Negus and Stasi – or relaxing with novels. She wanted for nothing, waited upon by a coterie of household staff who were forbidden to mention her name beyond the building.[7] She was always immaculately dressed and often sported the latest gifts from Hitler: gold watches, jewellery or trinkets. Albert Speer even designed a monogram for her, combining her initials 'EB' into an elegant four-leaf clover, which would subsequently adorn many of her possessions. It can be seen on the inside of this elaborately engraved lipstick case, made from Italian silver, which – like many of her possessions – was most likely given away to a member of the Berghof household.

Ironically, Hitler was rather unimpressed by Eva's glamorous lifestyle. He disliked variety in her wardrobe and was bemused by her regular costume changes. He was also rather puritanical in matters of beauty, preferring that women should embrace modesty with a minimum of artifice. On one occasion, seeing Eva's lipstick marks on a napkin, he shocked his secretaries by explaining to them his bizarre theory that French lipstick was made using the fat from the Paris sewers.[8]

As if that were not enough, Hitler's patronising and patriarchal views on women – though certainly not unusual for the 1930s – would probably not have pleased Eva either. Hitler once told an acolyte that 'a woman must be a cute, cuddly, naïve little thing – tender, sweet and stupid'. On another occasion, he boasted that, though he enjoyed the company of beautiful women, he saw no need for them to be intelligent: 'I have enough ideas for us both,' he claimed.[9] In Eva Braun, perhaps, he found what he wanted: a pretty, affectionate companion, who did not challenge his prejudices.

The precise nature of Hitler's relationship with Eva Braun remains the subject of occasional scrutiny from historians, with some luridly speculating about its sexual component or vaguely suggesting that Braun may have had some political influence over the *Führer*.[10] Yet, the most credible conclusion is perhaps the most obvious, that Eva Braun played no political role and exerted little influence, that she was – as Speer suggested – a disappointment to future generations of historians. Whether she liked it or not, she was, it seems, little more than an adornment.

After Eva Braun's death in April 1945, Hitler's secretary Traudl Junge went down to the room in the Reich Chancellery bunker where the couple had committed suicide. She smelt the bitter almonds from the cyanide, and saw Hitler's blood on the sofa where he had been sitting. Then she noticed the brass case of the poison capsule that Eva had used lying on the floor. It looked, she recalled, 'like an empty lipstick'.[11]

Eva Braun in 1939.

1  Quoted in Ullrich, *Hitler: Ascent 1889–1936*, p. 286.

2  Quoted in Shirer, *The Rise and Fall of the Third Reich*, p. 1319.

3  Quoted in Ullrich, *Hitler: Ascent 1889–1936*, p. 287.

4  Ibid., p. 615.

5  Traudl Junge, *Until the Final Hour* (London, 2003), p. 64.

6  Schroeder, *He Was My Chief*, p. 143.

7  Anna Plaim, *Bei Hitlers* (Munich, 2005), p. 53.

8  Quoted in Junge, *Until the Final Hour*, p. 74.

9  Quoted in Robert G. L. Waite, *The Psychopathic God: Adolf Hitler* (New York, 1993), p. 51.

10  See for instance Heike Görtemaker, *Eva Braun: Life with Hitler* (London, 2011).

11  Quoted in Junge, *Until the Final Hour*, p. 188.

# 37 Great German Art Exhibition Catalogue

*The Great German Art Exhibition* – Grosse Deutsche Kunstausstellung – was an annual display of Nazi art in the Third Reich, which ran from 1937 to 1944. Held in the Haus der Deutschen Kunst – 'House of German Art' – in Munich, a stark neo-classical exhibition hall, purpose-built by Hitler's favoured architect Paul Ludwig Troost, it was the most important cultural event under the Third Reich, and was a vital part of Hitler's totalitarian determination to dominate the intellectual and artistic climate of the day.

The exhibition was organised under the auspices of the Reichskultur-kammer – 'Reich Chamber of Culture' – which effectively controlled Nazi Germany's cultural output. Its primary purpose was to establish a style of art appropriate for the Third Reich, expressing its Aryan racial vision, and drawing a stark contrast to those supposedly 'decadent' tendencies that the Nazis believed were prevalent in modern art and sculpture.

Hitler made his preferences on the issue very clear in his opening speech to the first exhibition, on 18 July 1937. What he wanted to encourage, he said, was a 'new, vigorous flowering . . . of German art', of art based on ability, representing the 'new human type', which was healthier, stronger, and more beautiful than before. He went on to damn modern art – with its 'clique of chatterers, dilettantes and frauds' – declaring that 'there really are men who can see in our people only decayed cretins, who feel that the meadows are blue, the

Cover of the Grosse Deutsche Kunstausstellung catalogue of 1940.

heavens green, clouds sulphur-yellow'. If they really saw things in this way, he said, it was 'a matter for the Ministry of the Interior', if not, it was 'a matter for the criminal court'. In response to such 'smearings' and 'bespatterings', he promised a 'purification of art', and a 'relentless war' against the 'cultural destruction' that modernism represented.[1]

Those permitted to exhibit in the Nazi-approved art exhibition, therefore, included sculptor Josef Thorak, whose oversized, muscle-bound figures closely followed the Aryan aesthetic; Hubert Lanzinger, who – in 'The Standard Bearer' – painted Hitler as a medieval knight in armour; and Sepp Hilz, whose bucolic, rural themes placed him among Hitler's favourite artists.

Those who failed to meet with official approval had their own space. The 'Degenerate Art Exhibition' was

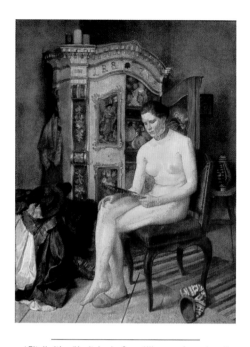

*'Eitelkeit'* – 'Vanity' – by Sepp Hilz, one of a series of idealised commentaries on life in the Third Reich by the artist, exhibited at the Grosse Deutsche Kunstausstellung in Munich in 1940.

housed across the road from the House of German Art, in the Hofgarten, and opened the following day. It showed some 600 works by many well-known artists, including Marc Chagall, Paul Klee and Emil Nolde, albeit displayed with derogatory or mocking slogans. It was made very clear what opinion the visitor should form of the art on show.

*'It was a vital part of Hitler's totalitarian determination to dominate the intellectual and artistic climate of the day.'*

Hitler wanted his 'Great German Art Exhibition' to show art that was 'for the people', which found 'ready inner agreement' with the masses. He would doubtless have been dismayed to discover that it attracted barely a third as many visitors as the derided 'degenerate' exhibition across the road.

---

1   Hitler speech on 18 July 1937, quoted in B. Sax & D. Kuntz (eds), *Inside Hitler's Germany: A Documentary History of Life in the Third Reich* (Lexington, 1992), pp. 224–32.

# 38 Nuremberg Rally Beer Stein

*The Nazi Party rallies, held every September* in Nuremberg, Bavaria, were one of the highlights of the Third Reich's calendar. Attracting the regime's most senior personnel, as well as notable guests from home and abroad, they provided a memorable spectacle for visitors, and a crucial reaffirmation of their faith in the Nazi cause.

The first Nazi Party rally had been held in the movement's birthplace of Munich, but from 1927 they were held only in Nuremberg. This move was partly due to the strong party network in the city, led by the odious *Gauleiter*, Julius Streicher, which benefited from a compliant local police force. It was also a conscious effort to co-opt Nuremberg's rich medieval history, suggesting a clear continuity between the 'First Reich' of the Holy Roman Empire, of which Nuremberg had been a Free City and an imperial residence, and Hitler's 'Third Reich'.

Souvenir beer stein from a Nazi Party rally in Nuremberg.

The rallies grew rapidly in size after the Nazi seizure of power in 1933, spilling beyond the main sites: the Zeppelinfeld, the Luitpoldhain and the Luitpold Hall, and into the centre of the city itself. Each rally had a central theme. That of 1934, for instance, was dubbed the 'Rally of Unity and Power' and featured Albert Speer's spectacular 'cathedral of light' on the Zeppelinfeld, where 152 searchlights were set up, shining their beams vertically into the night sky. It was also the subject of German film director Leni Riefenstahl's famous documentary film, *Triumph of the Will*, the perfect expression of Nazi propaganda.

The following year, 1935's 'Rally of Freedom', saw Hitler announce the Nuremberg Laws, a raft of anti-Semitic legislation that sought to marginalise German Jews. It was named to mark the country's 'liberation' from the humiliation of Versailles said to be represented by the reintroduction of conscription. Subsequent rallies celebrated other 'achievements' in the Third Reich, including the 'Rally of Labour' of 1937, which marked the dramatic reduction in unemployment, and the 'Rally of Greater Germany' in 1938 that celebrated the annexation of Austria earlier that year. The 'Rally of Peace', due to be held in September 1939, was cancelled at the last moment when Germany invaded Poland.

*'Nuremberg was an act of political pilgrimage, but it was also something like a scout jamboree.'*

Though they grew progressively larger and more grandiose, the routine of the rallies followed an established pattern; each branch of the Nazi movement and German state – from the SS and the Reich Labour Sevice, to the Wehrmacht and the Hitler Youth – was allocated a day in the programme for speeches, march-pasts and 'exercises', all carried out before huge enthusiastic crowds. Alongside the elaborate ceremonial, the highlight would be one of Hitler's many set-piece speeches: in 1937, he delivered nine. 'For us zealous National Socialists', he said in one, 'these days are the most splendid celebration of the whole year.'[1]

Of course, with over 500,000 visitors to Nuremberg for the rallies, only a tiny minority could find space in the city's guest houses and hotels; the remainder had to bed down in the vast marquee city that was erected beyond the southern suburbs. This was all part of the appeal for the Party Rally attendee. Visiting Nuremberg was – on one level, certainly – an act of political pilgrimage, but it was also something like a scout jamboree, where Nazi Party, Hitler Youth or SS members from across the country would rub shoulders, share meals, make music and drink together, reinforcing their common identity as Germans and members of the *Volksgemeinschaft* – the 'national community'. As one participant wrote home in 1938:

> I can hardly describe how wonderful this communal experience has been. You don't really get the same sense of it from the radio. Nuremberg has been a real source of strength for us . . . All of Germany stood represented in the mass before the *Führer*.[2]

Yet this object reminds us that, beyond the politics, Nuremberg also represented something much more mundane. This humble stoneware beer jug, featuring the spires of Nuremberg's medieval old town and bearing the words 'City of the Reich Party Rallies', was one of many sold in the city as souvenirs to visitors. It shows another side to the Nuremberg rallies, their significance to the countless thousands of ordinary Germans for whom the high politics on show was perhaps just a little too arid, for whom Nuremberg was little more than somewhere to see and be seen, a story to tell friends and neighbours, an experience to be remembered with a simple souvenir.

Hitler greeting a march-past of the SA during a 1933 rally.

1   M. Domarus (ed.), *Adolf Hitler: Speeches and Proclamations, 1932–1945*, Vol. 2 (London, 1992), p. 930.

2   Quoted in A. Schmidt & M. Urban, *Das Reichsparteitagsgelände* (Nuremberg, 2009), p. 35.

# 39 Gestapo Warrant Disc

*Officers of the Gestapo were not required* to give their names when dealing with the public; being in plain clothes, their identity was established by the presentation of their Warrant Disc or *Dienstmarke*. It was all part of the mystique, the whiff of menace, that was cultivated around the Secret State Police in the Third Reich.

After the reorganisation of German police forces in 1937, the various earlier warrant discs were replaced by a disc such as this one – die-struck in a silver-coloured metal, it bore the eagle with a swastika on the front, while the reverse carried the inscription 'Geheime Staatspolizei' and the officer's identification number. Similar discs in bronze were carried by the Kripo, the state criminal police. Both would normally be carried on a chain, and worn like a pocket-watch.

The Gestapo Warrant Disc or *Dienstmarke* was their principal means of identification.

Along with the SS, the Gestapo was the most notorious organisation of the Third Reich, but it is also one of the least well understood. The persistent stereotype of the Gestapo, propagated by a generation of *noir* films and novels, is that of an omniscient and omnipotent force, spreading fear throughout Germany, terrorising the population into unquestioning compliance with the Nazi regime. According to this image, plain-clothes Gestapo officers – bearing their warrant discs – had the power to arrest anyone and do whatever was needed to extract information from a suspect, a power that was used unsparingly in the interrogation cells of their national headquarters: Berlin's Prinz-Albrecht-Strasse, the very epicentre of terror in the Third Reich. It is a stereotype that requires some clarification.

Typically of the squalid internal politics of the Third Reich, the Gestapo was initially something of a plaything for the Nazi elite. Established by Hermann Göring in 1933, only weeks after the Nazis had came to power, it passed the following year under the control of Heinrich Himmler, and his sinister placeman Reinhard Heydrich, before a former Bavarian policeman, Heinrich Müller, took over in 1939, thereby earning himself the nickname 'Gestapo Müller'.

The primary purpose of the Gestapo was to hunt down and punish any opposition to the Nazi regime. Even the most minor anti-Hitler joke was sufficient to warrant a warning and an intimidating interview with the Gestapo, and further misbehaviour could mean the miscreant's confinement in a concentration camp. The authority of the Gestapo was absolute, with officers able to bypass the established legal system, and imprison suspects merely on suspicion of an oppositional attitude. Torture, though technically illegal in Germany, was not uncommon in Gestapo interrogations, with various brutal methods employed including beatings, sleep deprivation and electric shocks.

*'It was all part of the mystique, the whiff of menace, that was cultivated around the Gestapo.'*

So the Gestapo was very much a law unto itself, given free rein to pursue Nazism's opponents, but the degree to which it had full oversight and control over German society is often overstated. It was never as large a force as the SS, employing at its height some 30,000 people in Germany and occupied Europe, including office and administrative staff.[1] Indeed, the number employed at its national headquarters in Berlin never exceeded 800, even at the very height of the Third Reich.[2]

Instead of numbers, then, the Gestapo relied on a consciously propagated air of mystery and menace – the idea that it was tapping every telephone and listening to every conversation – and a widespread network of informers, who supplied it with information on all and sundry, from genuine anti-Nazis to unfaithful spouses. From that information, the Gestapo sifted those who it believed warranted its closer attention: Jews, communists, Gypsies, priests, trade unionists, Jehovah's Witnesses and sexual minorities.

Despite the later mythology, therefore, the Gestapo's terror, within Germany at least, was a very targeted one – aiming very specifically at those whom it considered to be a threat to the regime. For the majority of ordinary Germans beyond those groups, the sense of threat from the Gestapo remained, at worst, theoretical. Indeed, a post-war oral history study concluded that some 80 per cent of respondents felt 'no fear' of arrest.[3] So much for a generalised terror.

Nonetheless, the Gestapo was still intimately involved in the persecution and extermination of the Nazi regime's perceived opponents, and beyond Germany in the occupied lands the mask of civility was usually abandoned altogether. Gestapo prisons, such as the infamous Pawiak in Warsaw, or Montelupich in Kraków, were among the very worst addresses in wartime Europe.

Gestapo headquarters at 8 Prinz-Albrecht-Strasse in Berlin.

In addition, Gestapo officers were often brought in to supervise the *Einsatzgruppen* killing squads responsible for the mass murder of Jews and others in Eastern Europe. One example of many is that of Walter Blume, who had been a senior Gestapo officer in Berlin until he was called upon to establish Einsatzkommando 7a during the invasion of the Soviet Union in 1941. At his trial in 1947, Blume was found guilty of direct involvement in the murder of 996 people.[4] He was responsible for sending some 40,000 more to their deaths at Auschwitz.

At the Nuremberg Trials the Gestapo was branded a criminal organisation and its leading members condemned as war criminals. 'Gestapo Müller', however, was not amongst them. He disappeared in Berlin in the last days of the war, and was widely thought to have escaped using a new identity. Though the suggestion has been disputed – not least in 2013, when it was claimed that his body had been found and reburied in 1945[5] – the idea of his escape chimes perfectly with the popular perception that the Gestapo itself sought to present, that of a mysterious, diabolically capable organisation.

1   R. Gellately, *The Gestapo and German Society: Enforcing Racial Policy, 1933–1945* (Oxford, 1992), p. 44.

2   Moorhouse, *Berlin at War*, p. 224.

3   E. Johnson & K.-H. Reuband, *What We Knew: Terror, Mass Murder and Everyday Life in Nazi Germany* (London, 2005), p. 355.

4   Einsatzgruppen Trial, Case 9, Ohlendorf Indictment, November 1947 – see www.legal-tools.org/en/doc/ce5c31.

5   See www.spiegel.de/international/germany/nazi-war-criminal-heinrich-mueller-buried-in-jewish-cemetery-in-berlin-a-930995.html.

# 40 Hitler's Germania Sketch

*Alongside his hideous political career,* Hitler has long been characterised as a frustrated artist who found solace in architectural plans. First through Paul Ludwig Troost, and then through Albert Speer, amongst others, he found an outlet for his artistic yearnings in doodling capitals and rooflines, footprints and façades, on projects such as the planned rebuilding of Linz or a new Berlin Opera House.

> *'It is the classic example of Hitler's "architectural fantasies",*
> *monumental in scale and grandiose in conception.'*

The sketch overleaf, however, was part of an altogether more substantial undertaking – the wholesale redesign and reconstruction of the German capital itself, and its transformation into 'Germania'. Given the green light in 1937, with Speer appointed at its head, the Germania plan did not want for ambition. It foresaw a thoroughgoing reorganisation of Berlin, centred on two grand intersecting boulevards, but also encompassing rail infrastructure, new suburbs, airports, parkland, and even allowing for the elimination of the city's non-native flora. When he saw the plans, Speer's own father commented: 'You've all gone completely crazy.'[1]

The two boulevards – the east–west axis and the north–south axis – would be home to Germania's most iconic buildings, which were intended, in Hitler's words, to inspire a 'sense of heroism' in the German people and symbolise German greatness for future generations. They included the monumental 'Great Hall', which would stand over 300 metres high and accommodate 180,000 of the Nazi faithful, and the 'Circus', a 200-metre-wide fountain, replete with bronze statuary and a central sculpture of Apollo.

The heart of the plan, however, was the Triumphal Arch, seen here in Hitler's original sketch. It was, Speer recalled, the classic example of Hitler's 'architectural fantasies', monumental in scale and grandiose in conception. And, though he tried to revise and tone down his leader's plans, he had to concede defeat. The arch was Hitler's design – and Speer noted as much on the resulting plans, cryptically giving the architect's name as 'XXX', though, he said, 'Everyone would know who the anonymous architect was.'[2]

Intended to serve as a memorial to the German fallen of World War I – whose 1.8 million names were to be inscribed upon its walls on seventy-five huge marble panels – the Triumphal Arch was so vast, at 117 metres high, that its Parisian counterpart could have comfortably fitted beneath its 80-metre central span. The scale can be gleaned when one realises that the tiny squiggles that Hitler added, bottom right on the sketch, are people.

Such were the arch's gigantic proportions, indeed, that the very limits of physics were seemingly reached. In the southern suburbs of the capital, not far from where the arch was to be built, a 12,600-ton solid concrete block was created – the *Schwerbelastungskörper*, or 'heavy load-bearing body' – complete with measuring equipment to assess the capacity of Berlin's soil to carry huge weight.

It is not clear whether the results of those tests might have prevented construction of the arch, or reined in Hitler's soaring ambition, but the war served to kill the project off and 'Germania' was formally abandoned in 1943, with little of substance having been completed. Ironically, the *Schwerbelastungskörper* test-bed survived; too large to destroy and now rain-stained and weather-worn, it stands as a peculiar monument to Nazi megalomania.

Hitler's sketch of the grand Triumphal Arch.

1  Quoted in Moorhouse, *Berlin at War*, p. 110.

2  Speer, *Inside the Third Reich*, p. 199.

# 41 Gas Mask and Canister

*This fluted metal canister* was one of the most characteristic items of German military equipment in World War II. Often seen hanging at a soldier's back, it was designed to hold a gas mask and accessories, and was required to be worn at all times. It was an instruction that was indicative of the widespread fear – among civilian populations and soldiers alike – that poison gas would be used during World War II.

The Germans had been the first to use poison gas in warfare in 1915, and in a major chemical assault at Ypres in April of that year they released clouds of chlorine against Canadian and French Colonial troops. The British responded in kind with a chlorine attack in September 1915, but the wind blew it back on their own troops, underlining the unreliability of gas as a weapon and the necessity of gas masks for both sides. Phosgene and mustard gas attacks followed.

A German Army gas mask with its metal canister, plus gas cape bag
with decontamination fluid bottle and a torch.

## 'All sides feared gas attack when war broke out again in 1939.'

At first, simple damp cloths and chemically infused mouth pads were used to try to counter the horrific effects of such weapons, but then both sides developed more effective masks. By the end of 1915, the Germans were producing a rubberised cloth face piece with two circular windows for eyes and a cylindrical filter attached by a screw thread to the part covering the mouth and nose. This was the basic design that would be used by German soldiers for the next three decades. By the start of World War II, then, German forces had two gas mask models – the M30 and M38 – both very similar except that the body of the M30 consisted of rubberised canvas, whereas the M38 – as in this example – was all rubber.

Mindful of the experience of World War I, all sides feared gas attack when war broke out again in 1939. Though chemical warfare had been banned in the Geneva Protocol of 1925, its use had persisted, in isolated incidents such as in 1935, when Fascist Italy deployed mustard gas during its invasion of Abyssinia. Consequently, all sides continued their research into both new chemical and nerve agents as well as possible countermeasures; while the Germans stockpiled 'Tabun' and 'Sarin', the British had a number of agents, including 'Lewisite', 'Paris Green' and chlorine.

German troops wearing gas masks in training.

However – though there is anecdotal evidence of the isolated use of chemical weapons by the Germans on the Eastern Front – their military deployment was never officially sanctioned by any combatant nation during World War II in Europe. Hitler's experience of being gassed in 1918 is often cited as a reason for him staying his hand, as is the contention that the Germans feared reprisals and that they would not risk a chemical weapon release, because they lacked an effective equine gas mask.[1] Which explanation is true, if any, is not clear.

For the ordinary German soldier then, chemical and gas warfare became a threat that remained unrealised. Little wonder, perhaps, that as the war dragged on those canisters were increasingly unlikely to contain a gas mask, and more likely to contain extra rations.

1   S. P. Lovell, *Of Spies & Stratagems* (New Jersey, 1963), p. 78

# 42 Volkswagen Beetle

*This front cover of the Motor Schau* ('Motor Show') magazine, published in Berlin in July 1938, features the launch of the Kraft durch Freude-Wagen ('Strength through Joy Car') – abbreviated to KdF-Wagen on the number plate of the vehicle in the illustration. Modern readers will know the car as the Volkswagen Beetle (Volkswagen is literally 'People's Car'). It is a motoring icon, and it owes its genesis to the personal patronage of Adolf Hitler.

---

*'The car shall bear the name of the Strength through Joy movement, which made all this possible.'*

---

On 26 May 1938, just two months before the publication of this magazine, Hitler had laid the foundation stone of the new Volkswagen factory near Fallersleben in Lower Saxony. At the ceremony he gave a speech outlining the purpose of the car that was to be built there: 'As the National Socialist Movement came to power in 1933,' he said, 'it seemed to me that this area was particularly well-suited to open the campaign against unemployment – the problem of motorisation!'[1] He insisted that Germany needed to catch up in car manufacturing with the rest of the world – especially the USA – and that workers could be employed making cheaper cars for the average family. A car should not be a luxury – like a Mercedes – but the major mode of transport for everyone. Therefore, it could only have one title he declared: 'The car shall bear the name of the Strength through Joy movement, which made all this possible.'[2]

A model settlement for workers – the city that would become Wolfsburg – was established nearby. Hitler explained that it was to serve 'as a prototype for the future of social housing projects and city design . . . We wish to demonstrate how National Socialism sees, approaches, and resolves such problems.'[3] Clearly, much was invested in the launch of the People's Car.

The concept of a small, affordable, car had been around since the 1920s, but Hitler had recognised its political and propaganda potential, and at the Berlin Motor Show in 1933 had announced his intention to motorise the German nation. He gave designer Ferdinand Porsche the task of developing a car that could transport two adults and three children at 100 kmh, with fuel economy of no less than 32 miles per gallon, and all for the price of 990 Reichsmarks – a fraction of the cost of other models. For the first time, it seemed, motoring was within the reach of the ordinary man and woman.

Front cover of the *Motor Schau* magazine, published in Berlin in 1938 and featuring the launch of the Kraft durch Freude-Wagen, 'People's Car'.

Porsche's response was an air-cooled, rear-engine car with the characteristic, aero-dynamically efficient 'beetle' shape, which bore some similarities to an existing Tatra model, the T97. Huge sums of money were pumped into the project and, as a result, the first batch of prototypes – the Type 60 – were produced in the autumn of 1935.

Understandably, perhaps, German consumers were enthused – seeing in the 'KdF-Wagen' a glimpse of the shining new world that Nazi propaganda promised them. They dutifully signed up for their new cars, purchasing 'stamps', at a value of 5 Reichsmarks each, which would be stuck into a savings book and would count towards the cost of the car. A third of a million Germans subscribed. Money was thrown at the project and, as a result, the vehicle

Hitler dedicates the cornerstone of the Wolfsburg Volkswagen plant on 26 May 1938.

was submitted to the same quality of tests reserved for aircraft, making it a superbly robust and efficient design. Prototype cars were driven by the SS in all conditions, with each vehicle covering 100,000 km.[1]

Buyers were to be disappointed, however. Though the final KdF-Wagen prototypes were completed in 1938, they were presented to Nazi dignitaries rather than ordinary customers; Adolf Hitler himself received one on his fiftieth birthday in April 1939. Then, with the outbreak of war later that year, production at Wolfsburg was switched to making military vehicles such as VW's military variant, the Kübelwagen, and the amphibious Schwimmwagen. No KdF-Wagens were ever presented to ordinary subscribers by the Nazi regime, despite the fact that 278 million Reichsmarks had been paid into the scheme.

In 1945, the Wolfsburg factory was taken over by the British occupation authorities, who began to seek a buyer. However, when Allied motor manufacturers turned down the opportunity to acquire it, considering its product to be 'unattractive', it was decided to restart production, to provide work as well as a few hundred vehicles for use by the occupying forces. Production swiftly grew, and by March 1946, the factory was producing 1,000 cars per month. Rebadged as the iconic 'Volkswagen Type 1', the KdF-Wagen successfully shed its Nazi past and became a symbol of Germany's post-war economic rebirth.

1   B. Taylor, *Volkswagen Military Vehicles of the Third Reich* (Cambridge, 2004), p. 17.

2   S. Parkinson, *Volkswagen Beetle* (Dorchester, 1996), p. 15.

3   Taylor, *Volkswagen Military Vehicles*, p. 18.

4   B. Gilmour, 'The KdF Brochure', *VW Trends*, 4/85, p. 47.

# 43 *Mutterkreuz*

*In the Third Reich, everything was militarised.* Adolescent boys undertook paramilitary training under the auspices of the Hitler Youth, and the workers of the Reich Labour Service paraded with spades instead of rifles. Even motherhood was harnessed for the struggle.

Rewards for multiple motherhood were nothing new: the French Republic had founded a 'Medal of Honour of the French Family' in 1920. But the German equivalent – the Ehrenkreuz der Deutschen Mutter, 'Honour Cross of the German Mother' – was a much more politically motivated award. Introduced in 1938, the *Mutterkreuz*, as it was popularly known, was an elongated Iron Cross design, enamelled in blue, with a slim white border, which was intended to be worn around the neck. At its centre, surrounded by a golden radiant spread, was a roundel containing a black enamelled swastika, ringed with the words '*Der Deutschen Mutter*'. 'To the German Mother'. On the reverse was engraved the date of the award's foundation – 16 December 1938 – along with a facsimile of Hitler's signature.

> '*Some sneeringly referred to the medal as the Kaninchenorden,*
> *"The Order of the Rabbit".*'

At first glance, the award criteria of the *Mutterkreuz* were straight-forwardly maternal: it was conferred in three classes – bronze, silver and gold – for those with four, six and eight or more children respectively. Yet, the conditions for conferral reflected the Nazis' racist and social prejudices; Jews and Gypsies were ineligible, and recipients (and their spouses) both had to be of German (Aryan) origin, and free from hereditary diseases. In addition, both parents had to be 'worthy' of the award, that is faithful, law-abiding, not workshy and of sound moral standing. Consequently, research into a recipient's eligibility could be extensive and about 5 per cent of applicants were rejected.[1]

The first recipient – on 21 May 1939 – was 61-year-old Louise Weidenfeller from Munich, who had successfully raised eight children and so was awarded the *Mutterkreuz* in gold. In the years that followed, it is estimated that over 4 million German women received the medal in ceremonies overseen by the local Nazi Party leaders and usually scheduled for Mothers' Day.[2] Recipients could generally expect preferential treatment, not only in their interactions with the Nazi state, but also from their fellows; Hitler Youth boys were instructed to salute them, and an official order proclaimed that they were to receive the same privileges as the war wounded.[3] Perhaps for this reason, some sneeringly referred to the medal as the *Kaninchenorden*, 'The Order of the Rabbit'.

Amid the brutal, murderous realities of Nazi rule, a subject such as the *Mutterkreuz* might seem rather trivial, an inconsequential footnote to a much more urgent story. But it is nonetheless very instructive. It not only demonstrates the effective militarisation of German society under Nazism – the awarding of medals to exhausted mothers could scarcely show anything else – it also shows that Nazi Germany saw itself in a 'demographic war', just as much as it would soon be engaged in a real one. Alongside the fashion for eugenics and the use of sterilisation for those considered racially 'undesirable', it was indicative of the extraordinary importance that the Nazis attached to the biological wellbeing of the nation. It signified, in effect, the politicisation of the German womb.

The Mother's Cross: militarised motherhood.

1   Nicole Kramer, 'Anmerkung zur Einführung des Mutterkreuzes im Mai 1939', at www.zeitgeschichte-online.de/print/kommentar/anmerkungen-zur-einfuehrung-des-mutterkreuzes-im-mai-1939.

2   Wolfgang Benz, *Die 101 wichtigsten Fragen – Das Dritte Reich* (Munich, 2006), p. 24.

3   *Völkischer Beobachter*, No. 25, 1938.

# 44 'Ein Volk, Ein Reich, Ein Führer' Card

*This postcard commemorates* Nazi Germany's annexation of Austria – the *Anschluss* – in March 1938. Proclaimed with the slogan '*Ein Volk, Ein Reich, Ein Führer*' – 'One People, One Empire, One Leader' – the take-over of the land of Hitler's birth marked another step in his determination to fulfil the pan-German nationalist goal of bringing together all German-speaking people in a 'Greater Germany'. The card shows Hitler's head, and the *Reichsadler* or 'Imperial Eagle' superimposed on a simple map of the new Germany, incorporating Austria and showing all the great German cities, as well as the province of East Prussia that had been separated from Germany by the creation of the Polish Corridor after World War I. The slogan *Ein Volk, Ein Reich, Ein Führer* had been coined by the Austrian Nazi Hubert Klausner, and had become a constant refrain in Nazi propaganda, reinforcing the idea of the German nation being united under the leadership of one man – Adolf Hitler.

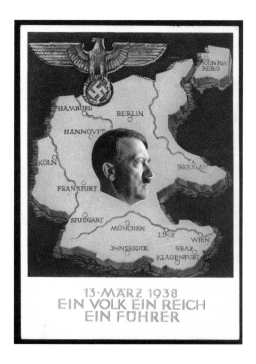

Greater Germany is born – the *Anschluss* of March 1938.

Austria had never been part of Germany's Wilhelmine Empire, but instead had headed a multi-national empire of its own. Like Germany, however, it had collapsed after defeat in World War I, and had been divided into the new nation states of Czechoslovakia, Hungary and Yugoslavia, with the German-speaking rump of Austria becoming an independent republic. Yet, when the Versailles Treaty specifically banned the union of Austria with Germany, another complaint was added to Germany's litany of inter-war grievances. For the moment, the dream of the German right, and of Hitler – of establishing a 'Greater Germany' incorporating all German-speaking peoples in one state – would have to wait.

When Hitler came to power in 1933, he began to put pressure on Austria, and its diminutive Chancellor, Engelbert Dollfuss. But Dollfuss refused to let the Austrian parliament be bullied into accepting German overtures, and instituted an authoritarian clerical dictatorship of his own, known as the Fatherland Front. Frustrated and enraged, Hitler instructed the SS to destabilise the country. The Sicherheitsdienst (SD), the intelligence agency of the SS, had links with the Austrian Nazi Party and encouraged ruthless methods to undermine Dollfuss, launching a terror campaign, blowing up government offices and railways, and attacking the Fatherland Front's supporters.

---

*'Hitler's triumph culminated in a packed rally in Vienna's Heldenplatz attended by a quarter of a million delirious Austrians.'*

---

On 25 July 1934 the pressure came to a climax when a detachment of over 150 Austrian Nazis dressed as soldiers seized the Chancellery building in Vienna, while others took over the capital's radio station. Though Dollfuss's ministers escaped, the Chancellor was shot in the neck, and callously left to bleed to death. Nonetheless, the coup was defeated when Austria's Justice Minister, Kurt von Schuschnigg, rallied government forces. Dollfuss's killers were hanged, and Schuschnigg took over as chancellor.

Such was the international alarm at the attempted coup in Vienna that Italian dictator Benito Mussolini, not yet closely allied with Hitler, sent four army divisions to the Brenner Pass on the Italian–Austrian border. Hitler backed off from his immediate intention of annexation but Austrian Nazis renewed their terrorist campaign. An economic boycott of Austria by Germany, crippling its tourist trade, put further pressure on Schuschnigg. Though an Austro-German treaty was signed in 1936, it did little to ease the tension; Hitler agreed to respect Austrian independence and not meddle in its internal affairs, but the deal was designed to appease Mussolini more than anything else.

Matters came to a head in March 1938, when Schuschnigg was summoned to Hitler's mountain home, the Berghof, and presented with an ultimatum demanding that he unban the Austrian Nazi party and accept its leaders into his government. Returning to Vienna, Schuschnigg attempted to spike Hitler's guns by calling a referendum on whether Austria should remain an independent state. Realising it was mainly young people who were the most fanatical supporters of Hitler, he set the minimum voting age at twenty-four. Hitler was furious, and demanded that he cancel the poll and hand over power or face invasion. Schuschnigg appealed to Britain and France for support, but when no help was forthcoming he resigned on 11 March. The next day, German troops crossed the border and a leading Austrian Nazi, Arthur Seyss-Inquart, became the country's new chancellor and signed the *Anschluss* into law.

When Hitler entered Austria he was surprised by the enthusiasm of the Austrian crowds that lined the streets to welcome him. The years of Nazi terrorism might have caused the general population to be suspicious of outright annexation, but now they cheered him rapturously as he enjoyed a tour of the country, visiting his parents' grave and his former Austrian homes. His journey culminated in a packed rally in Vienna's Heldenplatz attended by a quarter of a million delirious Austrians. For Hitler, it was a triumphal return to the land of his birth, as he reminded the audience in his speech.

> If Providence once called me from this city to assume the leadership of the Reich, it must have charged me with a mission, and that mission can only have been to restore my dear homeland to the German Reich. I have believed in this mission, have lived and fought for it, and I believe I have now fulfilled it.[1]

A plethora of Nazi propaganda posters and postcards celebrated his achievement. 'Greater Germany' was born, but it was one more step on the road to war.

Hitler crosses the border into Austria in March 1938.

---

1   J. Fest, *Hitler* (London, 2002), p. 548.

# 45 *Wilhelm Gustloff* Bracelet

*For most people living in the Third Reich*, a cruise aboard the liner *Wilhelm Gustloff* was the stuff of dreams, a once in a lifetime experience. Commemorative postcards would be sent home and daily menu cards pinched and secreted in luggage. Other souvenirs available onboard included enamel badges, or china teapots, or ashtrays, all emblazoned with an image of the ship. For those passengers who wanted a more personal reminder of their voyage, a souvenir bracelet such as this was just the thing. It spelled out W.I.L.H.G.U.S.T.L.O.F.F. in nautical signal flags and ended the sequence with a swastika.

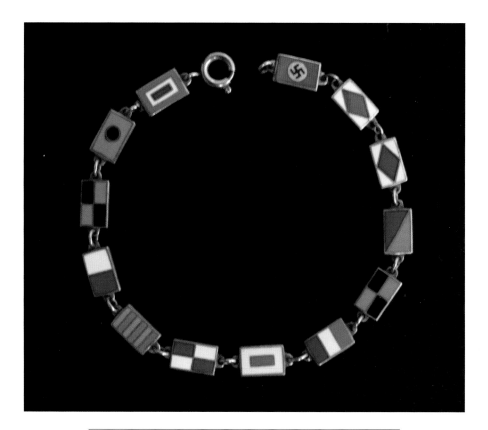

A souvenir bracelet from the *Wilhelm Gustloff, c.* 1938.

Launched in 1937, and entering service the following year, the MV *Wilhelm Gustloff* was the first cruise liner to be purpose-built for the Nazi leisure-time organisation Kraft durch Freude, KdF or 'Strength through Joy'. At more than 25,000 tons and measuring over 200 metres from stem to stern, it was considerably larger than Hitler's so-called 'pocket battleships'.

The ship was named after the leader of the Swiss branch of the Nazi Party, who – but for being assassinated by a Jewish gunman in 1936 – would doubtless have remained in total obscurity. It is said that Hitler briefly toyed with the idea of naming the vessel after himself, but was dissuaded because of the possible propaganda effects if the ship were ever to sink. So, when the MV *Wilhelm Gustloff* was launched, it was Gustloff's widow Hedwig who smashed the champagne across the vessel's bow.

> *'For those who had scarcely even had a holiday before,*
> *a cruise was an almost unbelievable prospect.'*

The *Gustloff*'s 616 cabins, spread across four decks, were able to accommodate over 1,400 passengers, each with a sea-view, in line with its 'classless' ethos. Toilet and washing facilities were shared. In addition, its seven bars, two restaurants, two dance halls, concert hall, library, hair-dressing salon and swimming pool were all accessible to all passengers. As the Nazi minister Robert Ley boasted at its launch: 'We Germans do not use any old crate for our working men and women. Only the best is good enough.'[1]

Alongside the *Wilhelm Gustloff*, there were another ten ships in the KdF fleet by 1939. Cruises, heavily subsidised of course, could be paid for in instalments, with 59 Reichsmarks charged for a five-day tour of the Norwegian fjords and 63RM for a week in the Mediterranean, rising to 150RM for a twelve-day tour around Italy, and 155RM for a two-week voyage to Lisbon and Madeira. With average weekly wages at around 30RM per week, it is easy to see the enormous popular appeal that such trips had. For those who had scarcely even had a holiday before, it was an almost unbelievable prospect.

The logic behind such elaborate KdF enterprises was quite simple. It was a seduction, first and foremost, a crude bid for the German workers' allegiance and an attempt to undermine their traditional loyalty to socialism. It was also an exercise in forging the *Volksgemeinschaft*, the German 'national community', that was meant to transcend all class or regional divides.

In addition, there was a vital economic rationale behind the KdF programme, that of maximising production by fostering a contented and, above all, motivated workforce. And, as Hitler darkly hinted to one of his ministers, there was an important political logic too, that of ensuring that German workers were tempered, militarised and ready for any eventuality – even war.

Of course, once war broke out in September 1939, all KdF cruises – and most of the organisation's myriad other activities – were suspended, with the exception of entertaining German troops. By that time, some 750,000 passengers had already sailed with the KdF fleet, around 75,000 of them aboard the *Wilhelm Gustloff*.

By the end of the war, such frivolities were a distant memory, and the *Wilhelm Gustloff* lay, mothballed, in the harbour at Gdynia in occupied Poland. Pressed into service one last time to ferry desperate German refugees westward, away from the approaching Red Army, it was torpedoed by a Soviet submarine in the Baltic Sea on the night of 30 January 1945. Hideously overcrowded, the liner sank beneath the freezing waters in less than an hour, with the loss of some 10,000 lives – thus making its sinking the worst maritime disaster in history.

Long the subject of exploratory and recreational dives and exposed to looting, the wreck of the *Wilhelm Gustloff*, which lies in forty metres of water off the Polish coast, is now protected as a war grave. The only items remaining to tell its story, therefore – and of the morale exercise of which it was part – are the trinkets that were once purchased on board.

The *Wilhelm Gustloff* in the Elbe estuary, Hamburg, 1938.

1   See Roger Moorhouse, *Ship of Fate: The Story of the MV Wilhelm Gustloff* (London, 2016).

# 46 Jerrycans

*The pressed-steel rectangular Wehrmachtskanister,* with its inbuilt handle, was originally developed in Germany in 1937 by Vinzenz Grünvogel, chief engineer at the Müller company in Schwelm, near Wuppertal. It was the product of a design competition, initiated by Hitler in 1936, to find the perfect fuel-carrying can for the Wehrmacht. The result was a design classic which is still used around the world today.

The 20-litre container marked a significant improvement on earlier designs, not least as it was self-contained, requiring no additional tools or funnels for operation. Its distinctive crossed indentations gave it strength and allowed the contents to expand or contract according to temperature, while a ingenious cam-lever cap and short spout provided for easy opening and smooth pouring. It was also designed to float in water when full, due to an internal air pocket. The *Wehrmachtskanister* made its military debut during the annexation of Austria in 1938.

Pressed-steel *Wehrmachtskanister* for carrying fuel, also known as jerrycans.

That design brilliance was soon being appreciated internationally, despite being jealously guarded. With the outbreak of war, the British encountered the cans for the first time and swiftly ordered an exact copy to be made – aided by an example smuggled out of Germany the previous year by an American engineer, Paul Pleiss. Until then, British fuel came in 4-gallon cans which, though cheap and easy to produce, were less than robust and were consequently known as 'flimsies'. The 'jerrycan' in contrast – with the British slang term for 'German' acknowledging its provenance – was strong and easy to use. It quickly found favour over the 'flimsy', and captured stores were highly prized. In time, both the British and Americans would mass-produce jerrycans, which would transport

US-style jerrycans at Savannah Quartermaster Depot, Savannah, Georgia, 1943.

fuel to every corner of the globe, easing the Allied advance. In 1944, US President Franklin Roosevelt was unequivocal in praising their significance: 'without these cans', he said, 'it would have been impossible for our armies to cut their way across France'.[1]

Hitler's use of *Blitzkrieg* warfare in Europe certainly speeded the emergence of motorised technology thirsty for fuel – aircraft, tanks and transport trucks – and the jerrycan played an important role in that process, providing a strong, reliable fuel container that was easy to transport and easy to use.

---

*'The result was a design classic which is still used around the world today.'*

---

But the can's significance to Germany's war should not perhaps be overstated. The German Army in World War II was not as motorised as its propagandists would have had the world believe. For all the newsreel images of rumbling tanks and armoured vehicles, only a fifth of German forces belonged to motorised or Panzer divisions, and horses were still widely used to shift supplies. With three million horses and mules requisitioned during the war and thousands of German servicemen employed to look after them, one might conclude that bales of animal fodder were just as necessary as jerrycans in keeping the Wehrmacht on the move.

1   Cited in 'The Amazing Jerry-Can' at www.thinkdefence.co.uk/2012/08/the-amazing-jerry-can.

# 47 Waffen-SS Camouflage

*This tree-pattern camouflage smock* produced for the Waffen-SS – the military arm of Hitler's elite SS – was one of the first examples of camouflage textiles worn by soldiers in combat. German innovation in the field of military camouflage came as a result of preparations for war in the 1930s. The Wehrmacht had learned many lessons from the Great War and had begun to devise a new form of mobile warfare – later dubbed *Blitzkrieg* – based in part on the experience of its fast-moving stormtrooper units in 1917–18. Their combat clothing had included helmets decorated with disruptive pattern camouflage, contrasting shapes and colours that break up the outline of a soldier's uniform. During World War I, disruptive patterning had been developed

A camouflage smock produced for the Waffen-SS, one of the first examples of camouflage combat clothing worn by soldiers.

for use on static positions, aircraft and battleships but, with very few exceptions, was rarely used for uniforms. In June 1930, however, the German Army ordered a camouflaged triangular tent sheet/poncho called a *Zeltbahn*, which was issued in the following year, replacing the standard grey tent sheet. The pattern chosen was known as *Splitter* or 'splinter' and consisted of angular shapes in green and brown against a tan background overlaid by broken green lines. It was Germany's first step in what was to become the most comprehensive use of printed camouflage textiles by any armed force in the world up to 1945.

By the mid-1930s, the Waffen-SS wanted to devise a camouflage pattern that would differentiate it from the Wehrmacht's *Splitter* pattern. Sturmbannführer (SS Major) Wim Brandt, commander of reconnaissance for the SS-Standarte *Deutschland*, chose a series of patterns inspired by nature, which mimicked the dappled effect of sunlight through trees.[1] This experimentation resulted in three main designs that suited the needs of the Waffen-SS perfectly. The early *Platanenmuster*, or plane tree pattern, was quickly supplanted by the *Eichenlaubmuster* or oak-leaf pattern, which was produced in both green and brown versions and in a ringed variant, the *Beringt Eichenlaubmuster*, with the addition of a dark edge around the leaf clusters.

---

*'German thinking on camouflage was well ahead of the curve.'*

---

This prototype camouflage was tested in field exercises by the SS-Standarte *Deutschland* in December 1937 and was estimated to reduce casualties by 15 per cent. The following summer, the Reich Patent Office registered the patterns for use on a camouflage helmet cover, pullover smock, and a sniper face-mask. The textiles were reversible, which meant they could be worn in either their 'spring green' or 'autumn brown' colouring. They thereby became the characteristic camouflage of the Waffen-SS.

Once placed into production, these camouflage patterns encountered some teething problems. Hand screen-printing processes proved too time-consuming, so with the urgency of war, roller printing was introduced, using dyes developed by IG Farben, which resulted in 33,000 camouflaged smocks – most of them made by concentration camp prisoners – being delivered to the Waffen-SS in the summer of 1940. As the war progressed, however, material shortages ensured that such clothing remained the preserve of elite assault soldiers. By 1943, further restrictions meant that the cloth was no longer reversible and an all-seasons green and brown colouration was adopted.

Despite such difficulties, in 1944 yet another pattern was developed, this time made to be worn as an all-season uniform, rather than merely a smock to be pulled over the regular field-grey. *Erbsenmuster*, or 'Pea Pattern', used a base brown over which a lighter brown and three shades of green were arranged in an erratic dot pattern. Issued to Waffen-SS units, it would become the most common camouflage type encountered by Allied soldiers. By the later stages of the war, camouflage was so closely associated with the Waffen-SS that the US Army declined to equip its own troops with camouflage uniforms in case they were mistaken for Germans. In part this decision was motivated by the political stigma that clung to anything associated too closely with the SS, but military analysts in Washington were also unimpressed with the practical value of camouflage in combat, as a 1945 report into the subject made clear, casting doubt on its effectiveness with a moving object and questioning whether the meagre results justified the effort.[2]

Despite this negative assessment, German thinking on the use of camouflage for combat uniforms was well ahead of the curve. As time would show, every modern army in the twentieth century would soon follow suit in adopting disruptive patterning. That which was once considered experimental would quickly become the norm.

Waffen-SS cavalrymen, part of a brigade formed in August 1941,
on patrol in Russia wearing camouflage smocks.

1   T. Newark, *Camouflage* (London, 2007), p. 136.

2   Ibid., p. 133.

# 48 Badenweiler March

*Though now largely forgotten*, the Badenweiler March would have made audiences very excited during the Third Reich – it was a signal that Hitler was about to appear.

The march was composed at the start of World War I by the Bavarian composer Georg Fürst, to commemorate the German victory over the French at Badonviller in Lorraine in August 1914. As such, it was little different from any of the other military marches composed around that time, except for two aspects: the first was its jaunty, brass fanfare introduction, which made quite an impression; the second was the fact that Hitler was said to have liked it.

---

*'For a generation of Germans, the Badenweiler March became completely synonymous with their Führer.'*

---

Consequently, a piece that had been merely one of many in the German military repertoire – it was number 256 in the Prussian Army March Collection – was selected under the Third Reich for a very particular role, that of Hitler's personal *'Führer March'*. It was to be used, for the benefit both of audiences at speeches and also for the masses listening on the radio, as a fanfare for Hitler, to build excitement and anticipation by announcing his imminent arrival on stage – in the same way that 'Hail to the Chief' is employed as a fanfare for American presidents.

To this end, in 1939, it was forbidden to perform the Badenweiler March in public in Germany except in Hitler's presence, with transgressors being liable to a 150RM fine, or six weeks in prison.[1] Of course, for those who wanted to listen to the march at home without Hitler present, a record was required, and this was duly made available – in this example performed by the music corps of Hitler's own SS-*Leibstandarte*.

So, for a generation of Germans, the Badenweiler March became completely synonymous with their *Führer*, a musical cue to Nazi ceremonial and an integral part of the cult of personality that was created around Hitler. It is perhaps ironic, then, that the focus of that cult appears not to have been quite as keen on the march as his acolytes had once imagined. In her memoir, Hitler's secretary Traudl Junge recalled that he once complained to her that he could never say that he liked a piece of music without finding it eternally played for him and proclaimed as his favourite. 'The same thing happened', he said 'with the Badenweiler March.'[2]

Hail to the Chief. A wartime record of the Badenweiler March,
performed by the music corps of the SS-*Leibstandarte*.

---

1  Polizeiverordnung gegen den Mißbrauch des Badenweiler Marsches, 17 May 1939, Reichsgesetzblatt I, p. 921.

2  Junge, *Until the Final Hour*, p. 81.

# 49 Georg Elser's *Stolperstein*

*Until comparatively recently, Georg Elser* was almost completely unknown. Remarkably, until the 1990s, the man who – after Claus von Stauffenberg – came closest to assassinating Adolf Hitler was scarcely commemorated in Germany, with barely a small memorial and a provincial street to his name.

Unlike Stauffenberg, who became the poster-boy of the German resistance – and Germany's post-war conscience – Georg Elser was quietly forgotten. Yet his feat had been no less impressive. In November 1939, he had installed a home-made bomb in a beer hall in Munich, where Hitler was due to give his customary speech to the 'Old Fighters' of the Nazi movement, to mark the anniversary of the attempted *Putsch* of 1923. His intention, he later confessed to his interrogators, was that he wanted to kill Hitler so as 'to prevent greater bloodshed'.[1]

Elser's bomb detonated as he had planned – at 9.20 p. m. – and killed eight of those present in the room. Hitler, however, was not among the casualties. Due to bad weather preventing him travelling by air, he had left the hall early that evening, thirteen minutes before the explosion, in order to take the train back to Berlin. Had he not left, there is little doubt that he would have been killed.[2]

Elser, who was apprehended that same night trying to cross the Swiss frontier, always maintained that he had worked entirely alone. Yet, the heightened tensions of that first autumn of the war, as well as the complexity of his bomb, meant that he was scarcely believed. The Gestapo, after attempting to beat him into confessing that he was a British agent, then ordered him to build an exact replica of his detonator – which he duly did – but still refused to believe him. Then, as Elser was sent to solitary confinement for the remainder of the war, the bizarre rumour spread on the

Georg Elser: forgotten no longer.

German left that he had been a patsy, a cat's paw employed by the Nazis to stage the bombing so as to generate popular sympathy and support for Hitler.[3] When Elser was finally executed by his SS jailers in April 1945, few Germans would even have remembered his name.

So it was that Georg Elser became the forgotten man of the German Resistance, a man whose story – where it was mentioned at all – was hedged with caveats and dark insinuations of complicity with the regime. It was only in the 1970s that such rumours began to be contradicted, and a new narrative emerged: Elser had been the creature of neither British intelligence, nor the Gestapo; he had conceived, planned and carried out his remarkable assassination attempt completely alone.

It was only then, therefore, that he began to be commemorated, and memorials followed in Berlin, Munich, Freiburg, Konstanz and elsewhere. One of the most notable among them was a *Stolperstein* installed in 2009 at the site of the house where Elser was born, in Hermaringen in Swabia. *Stolpersteine*, or 'Stumbling stones', are an initiative begun in 1992 by an artist called Gunter Demnig, which is intended to commemorate individual victims of the Nazis. They consist of a 10 cm x 10 cm brass plate, set in concrete, which is placed in the pavement, most usually at the individual's last place of residence. They contain only sparse information – the name, life dates and fate of the victim – but are intended to give an identity to the otherwise imponderable millions. In Elser's case, the inscription reads:

Elser's *Stolperstein*, in Hermaringen, Germany.

Here lived
GEORG ELSER
Born 1903
Assassination attempt on Hitler
8.11.1939
Arrested while escaping
8.11.1939
Sachsenhausen
Shot 9.4.1945
Dachau

*Stolpersteine* have been a remarkably successful memorial, both in Germany and beyond. Their small size and subtlety mean that they can be easily missed, or can be stumbled across by passers-by, giving a brief, poignant reminder of past injustices and horrors. Since the first one was laid – in Cologne in 1992 – they have spread rapidly. By the end of 2015, some 56,000 stones had been laid in over 1,200 towns and cities across Europe, from Spain to Russia, Greece to Norway, with over 7,000 installed in Berlin alone. Strangely, one of the few places to reject the *Stolperstein* initiative is the city where Elser carried out his assassination attempt, Munich, where the authorities have stated that they prefer to commemorate victims of the Nazis in their own way.[4]

> '*When Elser was finally executed by his SS jailers in April 1945,*
> *few Germans would even have remembered his name.*'

Given that the vast majority of *Stolpersteine* are laid in memory of victims of the Holocaust, it is remarkable that one was set aside to honour Georg Elser, and it marks another stage in the would-be assassin's long-overdue rehabilitation. Gunter Demnig told the press that one unintended consequence of the small text on Elser's stone was that 'those that want to read the inscription have to bow down, before the victim and his story'.[5] It is no less than Georg Elser deserves.

1   Gestapo Interrogation Report (November 1939), Bundesarchiv Koblenz, signatur R 22/3100.

2   See Chapter 3 of Roger Moorhouse, *Killing Hitler* (London, 2006).

3   Ibid., p. 57.

4   http://www.faz.net/aktuell/politik/inland/keine-stolpersteine-in-muenchen-zum-gedenken-an-ns-opfer-13725160.html.

5   'Vor Georg Elser verneigen', in *Heidenheimer Neue Presse*, 6 Oct. 2009, available at www.georg-elser-arbeitskreis.de/texts/hnp20091005.htm.

# 50 Ration Cards

*Nazi Germany introduced rationing* a few days before the outbreak of war, on the morning of Sunday 27 August 1939. From that point on, the supply of most foods, as well as of clothing, footwear and coal, was strictly controlled.

The rationing system was infernally complex. Firstly, all German citizens and permanent residents were categorised: adults were divided into three classes, based on the physical intensity of their work: an office worker, for instance, would be classed as a 'normal consumer', while a train driver might be classed as a 'heavy worker' and a coal miner would fall into the category of a 'very heavy worker'. Additional categories were established for infants, children and youths.

The category decided the ration allocation: a 'normal consumer' would receive 2,400 calories per day, while supplements would provide a 'heavy worker' with an additional 1,200 calories daily, and a 'very heavy worker' would receive a daily total of 4,200 calories.[1] Ration cards would be reissued every month, thereby giving the authorities the chance to revise allocations according to supply. Soldiers home on leave were given a special ration card, as a 'gift from the *Führer*'.

A ration card for a soldier home on leave.

| 125 g Butter **1** 20. 11.—26. 11. 39 | 125 g Butter **3** 4. 12.—10. 12. 39 | **Gültig vom 20. 11. bis 17. 12. 1939** **Reichsfettkarte** | 80 g Margarine oder Kunstspeisefett oder Speiseöl **a 2** 20. 11.—17. 12. 39 | 80 g Margarine oder Kunstspeisefett oder Speiseöl **a 1** 20. 11.—17. 12. 39 |
|---|---|---|---|---|
| 200 g Butter **2** 27. 11.—3. 12. 39 | 125 g Butter **4** 11. 12.—17. 12. 39 | | 62,5 g (¹/₈ ₢) Margarine oder Kunstspeisefett oder Speiseöl **b 2** 11. 12.—17. 12. 39 | 90 g Margarine oder Kunstspeisefett oder Speiseöl **b 1** 20. 11.—17. 12. 39 |
| 62,5 g (¹/₈ ₢) Schweineschmalz oder Speck oder Talg **2** 27. 11.—10. 12. 39 | 125 g Butter **4** 12.—17. 12. 39 | EA: _____ Name: _Anna Jokubec_ Wohnort: _Wn._ Straße: _Feldkellergasse 64_ | 62,5 g (¹/₈ ₢) Käse oder 125 g Quark **2** 11. 12.—17. 12. 39 | 62,5 g (¹/₈ ₢) Käse oder 125 g Quark **2** 27. 11.—3. 12. 39 |
| 62,5 g (¹/₈ ₢) Schweineschmalz oder Speck oder Talg **1** 20. 11.—3. 12. 39 | 62,5 g (¹/₈ ₢) Schweineschmalz oder Speck oder Talg **3** 4. 12.—17. 12. 39 | Ohne Nameneintragung ungültig! Nicht übertragbar! Sorgfältig aufbewahren! Falls die Abschnitte a 1 u. a 2 nicht für die Rantine oder Werküche benutzt werden, empfiehlt es sich, zur Erleichterung des Abwiegens auf diese Abschnitte und b 1 250 g Margarine usw. in einer Menge zu beziehen. | 62,5 g (¹/₈ ₢) Käse oder 125 g Quark **1** 4. 12.—10. 12. 39 | 62,5 g (¹/₈ ₢) Käse oder 125 g Quark **1** 20. 11.—26. 11. 39 |

A Reich 'fats card', from 1939.

The ration cards were colour-coded: blue cards for meat, yellow for fat and cheese, white for sugar and jam, pink for flour, rice, tea and oatmeal, orange for bread, green for eggs, and purple for sweets and nuts. They were printed on stiff paper, which was perforated into small, tear-out coupons – known as *Marken* – each of which carried the name of the product and the quantity allowed. These were stamped or exchanged – accompanied by the necessary payment – for the allocated ration

> 'As one wit noted, the system was so convoluted that "those who survive the war will end up in a lunatic asylum".'

In addition to food, the ration system also covered soap, footwear and clothing. Allocation of these was arranged by a points system. Each consumer was allocated a fixed number of points – 100 for an adult, 60 for teenagers and 70 for a small child – which were available to them for purchases over a period of around 18 months. The items rationed all had a points value, 80 points, for instance, for a suit, 18 for a skirt, 14 for a child's pullover and 10 for a pair of underpants. Shoes, too, were strictly controlled, with only two pairs generally permitted to each consumer, and with a permit for a new pair only being issued upon submission of a declaration that one of the older pairs had worn out. Whatever one purchased, however, the total points value could not be exceeded. On this basis, it was envisaged that a 'normal' wardrobe would consist of barely a full set of clothes and a change of underwear.[2] Additional, and even more restrictive, rules were applied to Germany's Jewish population.

The rationing system served its purpose; food supply (of sorts) was maintained right up to the final collapse of 1945. Yet, needless to say, it was grossly unpopular, not least for its complexity. As one wit noted in 1939, the system was so convoluted that 'those who survive the war will end up in a lunatic asylum'.[3] In addition, the ration allocations, though initially generous as a sop to public opinion, were soon reduced as the realities of wartime bit. Increasingly, too, even those reduced allocations became largely theoretical, with only empty shelves greeting shoppers, whether they had the right ration cards or not.

Moreover, the rationing system forced a generation of Germans to seek alternative sources of food. *Ersatz* ('substitute') products became commonplace, most notably 'coffee' made from acorns or chicory, but also *ersatz* honey, *ersatz* egg powder and *ersatz* sugar. Bread, too, was redefined, with flour increasingly adulterated with bone meal or sawdust, and sometimes taking on an unsavoury greenish hue. The definition of 'meat' became similarly elastic, with brain, lungs and udders all supplied by butchers under that name. Unsurprisingly, perhaps, those who could began growing their own vegetables, or keeping rabbits or chickens; others, such as city dwellers for whom such options were rarely suitable, were forced to rely on the black market, or on the newly vibrant barter economy, or on petty theft – known colloquially as 'organising'.

Of course, those with money, or connections, could always find a way around the rules. When Berlin delicatessen owner August Nöthling was arrested in 1943, it was discovered that he had been supplying his well-heeled customers – many of whom were senior Nazis and military men – with chocolates and other delicacies, without requesting ration cards. Known as 'Mr Shopping Bags', Nöthling would commit suicide in his prison cell. None of his customers were prosecuted.[4]

1   Jeremy Noakes (ed.), *Nazism 1919–1945*, Vol. 4: *The German Home Front in World War II* (Exeter, 1998), p. 512.

2   Ibid., p. 525.

3   Quoted in Terry Charman, *The German Home Front 1939–1945* (London, 1989), p. 47.

4   Moorhouse, *Berlin at War*, pp. 98–9.

# 51 Enigma Code Machine

*The Enigma machine was the main encoding device* of the German armed forces in the Third Reich. Intended to produce encryption so complex that even the world's finest brains could not crack it, it was devised by a Dutchman in 1919, but it was a German, Dr Arthur Scherbius, who bought the patent and made the machine. In 1923, it was marketed by Scherbius's company as the 'Enigma', a device for sending confidential business information over public telegraph systems. It remained in commercial production until 1929, by which time the German military had begun to take an interest.

Not enigmatic enough: a late-war four-rotor version of the Enigma cipher machine.

The Enigma looked something like a portable typewriter, albeit with some additions. It functioned via a complex electro-mechanical encryption process, by which messages could be securely encoded and then decoded only by another machine working on the same settings as the original.

An operator would type a letter on the keyboard, sending an electrical signal through a changeable plugboard, followed by three rotors, each of which would transpose the letter into another letter. The signal would then pass through a 'reflector', before coming back through the rotors and the plugboard, and lighting an output letter porthole on the accompanying lamp-board. Each original letter, therefore, was transposed at least six and perhaps eight times, producing a message, now apparently gibberish, which could be sent via Morse code.

---

*'Berlin's enemies faced a seemingly impossible task in their efforts to read German signals.'*

---

A receiving Enigma operator would reverse the process. Using the correct plugboard, ring settings and rotor settings, which were usually changed daily, the baffling, randomised stream of letters would be typed into the keyboard and would produce the original message – letter by latter – via the lamp-board.

Enigma became the standard cipher machine for the German Army from 1926 onwards, and would also be used by the Luftwaffe, Navy, SS, and even German railways. Further modifications increased security: rotors with a selection of different internal wiring arrangements could be placed in the machine in different orders, and versions employing four rotors were introduced for use by the U-boat arm and by the Abwehr military intelligence service. In this way, many billions of combinations were possible and Berlin's enemies faced a seemingly impossible task in their efforts to read German signals.

Undeterred, from 1932 a group of mathematicians employed by the Polish cipher bureau, Marian Rejewski, Jerzy Różycki, and Henryk Zygalski, were already studying Enigma messages. Within just four and a half months they worked out the machine's basic design and the wiring pattern of its then limited set of rotors. It was an inspired breakthrough.

Later that year, the Poles received a huge boost from Captain Gustave Bertrand, the head of decryption in French intelligence, who provided photographs of hundreds of secret documents supplied by a German spy working in the Berlin cipher department, Hans-Thilo Schmidt, including operating instructions for Enigma. This information, together with their own deductions, enabled the Polish team to build their own Enigma machine, and just weeks after Hitler came to power in January 1933, they were already regularly reading German Enigma messages.

This state of affairs continued until 1938, when the Germans changed their system, making their messages much harder to read. Needing more resources, the Poles met with their French and British counterparts in Paris and in Warsaw, and all sides shared their information. The British were enormously impressed by the work of the Poles and pledged their co-operation. In August 1939, just two weeks before the outbreak of World War II, Captain Bertrand was met at Victoria Station in London to deliver a Polish copy of the Enigma machine.

It was just in the nick of time. At dawn on 1 September 1939, Nazi Germany invaded Poland and rapidly overcame Polish resistance to capture Warsaw. Though many of the Polish code-breakers, among them Rejewski, Różycki and Zygalski, escaped via Romania to France, other members of their team were less fortunate and were captured and executed by the Germans. With the Polish cryptographers scattered, it was up to the British to turn their discoveries into a reliable war-winning code-breaking system.

The centre of British code-breaking was a rambling country house at Bletchley Park, some 80 km north-west of London. It was officially called the Government Code and Cypher School (GC&CS) and was headed by Commander Alastair Denniston, with an eccentric civilian, Alfred Dillwyn 'Dilly' Knox – a veteran of Britain's successful naval code-breaking in World War I – leading the code-breaking department. Knox headed a brilliant team of mathematicians, decoders and translators, many of them academics from Oxford and Cambridge Universities, including the genius Alan Turing, a pioneer of computing. Those code-breakers were given a toe-hold by the Enigma's flaws – no letter could stand for itself and numbers had to be spelled out – but, for all their brilliance, they might have made little progress but for the opportunities given them by the repeated errors made by German Enigma operators.

Bletchley Park, where German Enigma messages were broken.

At the height of its activity, some 10,000 people worked in the house and huts at Bletchley Park. The intelligence that they produced – codenamed Ultra – was of huge significance to the outcome of the war, giving an immeasurable advantage to Allied forces in every theatre. Most significantly, Berlin never suspected that its Enigma traffic had been broken. For all its technological brilliance, the Enigma machine was emblematic of Nazi Germany's hubristic faith in its own superiority.

Decoding a signal with an Enigma machine in typically cramped confines aboard a U-boat.

# 52 Wolfgang Willrich Postcard

*Just as Nazi Germany had been quick to embrace* the new medium of radio, so it was also keen to exploit the older media in its propaganda. Cheap to produce, postcards were an essential part of that strategy, and the work of artist Wolfgang Willrich featured strongly.

Born in Göttingen in 1897, Willrich was already an established artist by the 1930s and thanks to his growing reputation as a portraitist, particularly of ethnic German subjects, he began to receive commissions from Nazi organisations to produce collections of sketches of the Nazi leadership, ethnic Germans abroad (*Volksdeutsche*) and German peasants.

Wolfgang Willrich's 1939 postcard of U-boat captain Günther Prien, the 'Hero of Scapa Flow'.

His portraits typically consisted of a head and shoulders, often viewed in profile, showing the contours of the face and the bone structure of the subject to best advantage. Representative subjects were entitled: 'Pomeranian Fisherman', 'Peasant from Hanover', or 'Farmer's Daughter from Oldenburg'. Executed in pencil and charcoal, but sometimes wholly or partly overpainted in watercolour, his portraits betrayed the same bluff heroism – all cheekbones and rippling muscles – that was common to much Nazi art.[1]

With the outbreak of war, Willrich found new opportunities. He petitioned Erwin Rommel, then commanding a Panzer division, to be permitted to accompany the troops as a war artist, and in that capacity took part in both the Polish and the French campaigns, sketching ordinary soldiers as he went. He also produced sketches of the military heroes of the day, including Admiral Karl Dönitz, Luftwaffe ace Werner Mölders and Rommel himself. Another subject – as in this example – was the U-boat captain Günther Prien, commander of *U-47*, who scored an early German success by sinking the British battleship HMS *Royal Oak*, at anchor in Scapa Flow, in October 1939.

---

*'His portraits showed the same bluff heroism – all cheekbones and rippling muscles – that was common to much Nazi art.'*

---

Prien was swiftly propelled to celebrity status. Fêted in the German capital, he was awarded the Knight's Cross of the Iron Cross – the first sailor of the U-boat arm to receive the award – presented personally by Hitler. The following year, as well as sinking a further 160,000 tons of enemy shipping, he received the Oak Leaves to the Knight's Cross, and found time to write a best-selling biography. Prien quickly became ubiquitous, his face adorning postcards, picture books, news magazines, even children's games. He was one of the first military figures to be actively marketed by the Nazi regime but only briefly, as he was killed on operations in 1941.

In an age before television, celebrity culture was seen as a vital way to extend the propaganda message beyond the traditional circles of those who read the newspapers or listened to the radio, and especially to target the young. Postcards had long been a part of the Nazi propaganda effort, from those commemorating the Nuremberg rallies or the movement's martyrs to the stern-faced image of Hitler. But with the advent of war, and especially the victories of 1940, the medium really came into its own.

Willrich found a vast market; his chisel-jawed, pale-eyed heroes and sturdy peasant girls proved enormously popular, particularly amongst children. His postcards would be eagerly collected, or traded in the schools and playgrounds. Their artistic worth may have been dubious, but their propaganda value was incalculable.

---

1   See, for instance, Wolfgang Willrich, *Des Edlen ewiges Reich* (Berlin, 1939) or *Die Männer unserer Luftwaffe* (Berlin, 1940).

# 53 Nazi Eagle

*The Reichsadler – 'Imperial Eagle' –* had long been a symbol of German nationhood. Stretching back to the Holy Roman Empire, when it underlined that state's supposed continuity from Imperial Rome, its use was re-established by the German Empire in 1871, taking its traditional form of black plumage and red beak and talons. Such was its symbolism that the Weimar Republic adopted a rather plainer version in 1919, leaving Hitler to revise the design after 1933.

In line with the union of the German state with the Nazi Party toward which Hitler strived, his version of the Imperial Eagle combined the bird with an oak-wreathed swastika held in its talons. This new *Reichsadler* took a number of forms. The most familiar, perhaps, was the stylised design showing the bird's wings fully spread – the so-called *Hoheitsabzeichen* or insignia – which was used on official letterheads, passports and on the uniform of every German soldier.

The designer of the *Hoheitsabzeichen* was sculptor Kurt Schmid-Ehmen. Born in 1901 in Torgau, Schmid-Ehmen studied in Leipzig and Munich before making his name

A symbol of defeat: a battered Nazi eagle recovered from the ruins of the Reichstag after Berlin's fall.

with a series of portrait busts of luminaries, including scientists and composers. In 1930, after joining the Nazi Party, his friendship with the architect Paul Ludwig Troost brought him close to Hitler, and a number of official commissions followed. In 1933, for example, he created the memorial – off Munich's Odeonsplatz – on the site where members of the Nazi Party had been killed during the Beer Hall *Putsch* of 1923.[1]

---

*'It was used on official letterheads, passports and on the uniform of every German soldier.'*

---

Following that, Schmid-Ehmen produced a series of monumental eagles for Nazi buildings, including two six-metre examples which oversaw Nazi Party rallies at the Luitpold Arena in Nuremberg. It is one of these eagles that is the opening image in Leni Riefenstahl's 1935 propaganda film *Triumph of the Will*. The tallest of Schmid-Ehmen's creations, however, was a nine-metre bronze eagle surmounting the German Pavilion at the 1937 World Exhibition in Paris, for which he received the Grand Prix of the République Française.

Perhaps the most famous of Schmid-Ehmen's eagles, however, is the one on the previous page – one of two *Reichsadler* that were incorporated into the New Reich Chancellery, opened in Berlin in 1939. Made from copper alloy and weighing a quarter of a ton, it stands over 1.5 metres tall and has a wingspan of nearly 3 metres; its base bears the inscription: 'Schmid-Ehmen. Munich. Year of Destiny 1938'. Now displayed at the Imperial War Museum in London, and bearing the prominent scars of the Battle for Berlin, it is the only surviving example of Schmid-Ehmen's monumental eagles – eagles that once symbolised Hitler's Reich.

---

1  J. W. Baird, *To Die for Germany* (Bloomington, 1992), p. 49.

# 54 Stick Grenade

*Like the Stahlhelm steel helmet*, the stick grenade or *Stielhandgranate* – 'stalk hand grenade' – is one of the most widely recognisable German icons of World War II, which nonetheless had its origins in the First.

When it first appeared in 1915, the stick grenade – dubbed the 'potato-masher' by the British – consisted of a hollow wooden handle, with a 170g charge of TNT contained in its cylindrical steel head. To use it, a soldier would pull on a small porcelain ball, attached to a cord which ran inside the handle, thereby activating a five-second friction fuse. The beauty of the design was that the wooden handle enabled the grenade to be thrown as much as twice the distance of the contemporary British example – the egg-shaped 'Mills bomb'.

In the years after World War I, the stick design was revived in Germany as the M24 grenade. Essentially the same as the original, it had a smaller explosive head and a longer handle, thereby making it easier to use and throw. Also, as with the 1917 version, its detonator cord was safely stowed behind a metal screw cap in the base of the handle, so that it could not be set off accidentally.

> *'The wooden handle enabled the grenade to be thrown as much as twice the distance of the contemporary British example.'*

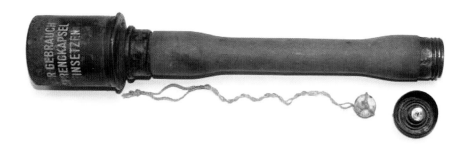

German stick grenade or *Stielhandgranate.*

Further versions would later be developed, such as the M39 'egg grenade', and the simplified M43, which dispensed with the hollow wooden shaft and so was better suited to mass-production. But it was the M24 stick grenade that would become a staple weapon of German soldiers after 1939. Over 75 million examples were manufactured – some containing a smoke charge and others with an additional fragmentation sleeve for maximum effect. In the field, a number of M24 grenades could be connected together to make an improvised 'bundle charge', for use against larger targets such as tanks or buildings. Used in every theatre, the M24 stick grenade was ubiquitous, even iconic. It can often be seen in contemporary photographs, tucked into German soldiers' belts or into the tops of their boots, ready for action.

A young SS soldier prepares for action with a stick grenade and a belt of machine-gun ammunition.

# 55 Type VII U-Boat

*The Type VII U-boat once struck fear* into the hearts of Allied merchant seamen. The workhorse of the German submarine arm in World War II, it was produced from 1935, over eight variants, and made up over 70 per cent of the U-boat fleet, remaining in service to the very end of the war. If you were a German submariner during World War II, chances are you would have served aboard a Type VII.

Technically, the Type VII – like its contemporaries – was a submersible rather than a true submarine; it spent much of its time on the surface, powered by its twin diesel engines, and ordinarily submerged only to attack or to evade its enemies. It was also rather small, being barely 6 metres in beam and 50 metres in length, and displacing less than 800 tons. As U-boat ace Reinhard 'Teddy' Suhren described, the narrow passageway that ran down the spine of the ship, 'from the bow-room for'ard to the electric motor room aft' was 'flanked by bunks, cables, valves and hand-wheels, tubes and instruments, radio apparatus and electric galley . . . everything was crammed together in the smallest possible space'.[1]

*U-995* at Laboe, the last surviving Type VII U-boat.

Squeezed into that cramped interior would be the forty-five-strong crew, working in eight-hour shifts and sleeping in hammocks and drop-cots slung beneath, between and alongside their complement of fourteen torpedoes. Space was always at a premium, but was especially tight at the beginning of a patrol, when all manner of supplies: bread, sausages, sacks of potatoes and assorted food cans, would be stowed into every available nook and cranny. The men had to endure tours of up to three months at sea; beards grew and personal hygiene became a rare luxury. Submariners often joked that they could smell their comrades before they saw them.

## 'The Type VII sank more Allied shipping than any other U-boat type.'

Their primary objective, of course, was to sink Allied merchant vessels in the North Atlantic and so undermine Britain's ability to wage war. In this respect, the Type VIIs were rather well suited; with a top speed on the surface of 17 knots and a range of 15,000 km, they were highly effective in patrolling the Atlantic and terrorising merchant convoys right up to America's eastern seaboard. Until early 1943, when Allied countermeasures turned the tide, U-boat crews cut a deadly swathe through Allied convoys, sinking fully three-quarters of their wartime total.[2]

Though the larger, ocean-going Type IX U-boats enjoyed greater success on a ship-for-ship basis, due to its sheer numbers the Type VII sank more Allied shipping than any other U-boat type. Type VIIs were responsible for the sinking, amongst many others, of HMS *Courageous*, HMS *Barham*, HMS *Ark Royal* and the civilian liner SS *City of Benares*. In addition, a number of Type VII commanders achieved fame (or infamy). Günther Prien, for instance, commanding *U-47*, scored an early success by sinking HMS *Royal Oak* in Scapa Flow in October 1939. Two darlings of the German Navy – Otto Kretschmer and Joachim Schepke – wrought havoc in the mid-Atlantic in their Type VIIs, *U-99* and *U-100* respectively, sinking over 400,000 tons between them, until their raiding was halted by the former's capture and the latter's death in March 1941. *U-48* meanwhile – a Type VII launched in 1939 – became the most successful U-boat of the war, sinking fifty-five vessels for a total of 321,000 tons.

Perhaps the most famous Type VII, however, was *U-96*, which sank twenty-seven ships in its two-year career on active service, before being retired to a training capacity. Its fame would be primarily post-war, however. *U-96* was immortalised after taking a young war correspondent named Lothar-Günther Buchheim on one of its patrols. Buchheim later used his experiences aboard to write the novel *Das Boot*, upon which the hit film and TV series of the same name were based. As a result, the popular image of a U-boat for a generation was of the cramped, claustrophobic interior of a Type VII.

Despite their former ubiquity, almost all Type VII U-boats were either sunk by enemy action, scuttled by their own crews, or destroyed in 'Operation Deadlight', the Royal Navy's post-war mass scuttling of 116 surrendered vessels off Northern Ireland. Consequently, only a dozen survived beyond 1946, and only one survives intact to this day – the example pictured above – *U-995*.

A Type VII in a heavy sea *c.* 1941.

Launched in 1943, *U-995* enjoyed a comparatively unspectacular wartime career, taking part in nine patrols, mainly in the Barents Sea, and sinking six ships for a total of just under 10,000 tons. At the end of the war, it was surrendered to the British at Trondheim in northern Norway, before being transferred to Norwegian command in 1946 and renamed the *Kaura*.

When it was stricken from the Norwegian Navy in 1965, *U-995* was then sold to the German government for the symbolic price of 1 Deutschmark. Restored to its 1945 specifications, it was put on display as a museum ship in 1971, perched on the shore of the Bay of Kiel close to the Laboe Naval Memorial – the last of a maritime icon.

1  Teddy Suhren, *Ace of Aces: Memoirs of a U-boat Rebel* (London, 2011), p. 67.

2  For details, see http://uboat.net/allies/merchants/losses_year.html.

# 56 Junkers Ju 87 Stuka

*The Junkers* Ju 87 'Stuka' took its name from the acronym for the German *Sturzkampf-flugzeug*, meaning 'dive-bomber'. It first gained its fearsome reputation in the Spanish Civil War, before becoming synonymous with Hitler's early *Blitzkrieg* victories, when it served in a vital ground-attack role. It would be World War II's first 'terror weapon'.

With its distinctive cranked wings and fixed undercarriage, the Ju 87 was made by Junkers in Dessau, which, despite starting out making boilers and radiators in 1895, had become a prominent aircraft producer by the inter-war years. Spurred by the patronage of Ernst Udet, a World War I fighter ace who, as head of Luftwaffe development was a keen advocate of dive-bombing tactics, the first Stuka prototype flew in 1935, before going through a number of versions – one even with a Rolls Royce Kestrel power plant – as engineers wrestled with the high speeds and G-forces experienced in a dive.

A Stuka in flight over the North African coast in 1941.

In its first mass-production model – the Ju 87 B-1 – the Stuka already had its established features; the Junkers Jumo 211 inverted V-12 engine, the greenhouse canopy, and the propeller-driven sirens – dubbed 'Jericho trumpets' – which were fixed ahead of the landing gear; their screaming sound intended to intimidate the enemy. The new version could withstand a dive speed of 600 kmh, and had automatic diving brakes that helped control the aircraft as the pilot struggled with extreme G-forces. It had a crew of two, with the pilot accompanied by a rear gunner, and was armed with two forward-firing machine guns and one to the rear.

---

*'The Stuka was synonymous with Hitler's early Blitzkrieg victories.'*

---

The Stuka was first deployed during the Spanish Civil War and was judged to be a success, taking part in a bombing raid on the port of Barcelona in 1939. It then carried out the very first air raid of World War II, targeting Polish units holding the vital rail bridge at Tczew on the Vistula in the early hours of 1 September 1939.

In the early *Blitzkrieg* campaigns that followed, Stukas were well-suited to hitting enemy targets and softening up ground forces. But when they were used in the Battle of Britain later in 1940, their vulnerability to attack from faster fighters quickly became evident, and they were soon withdrawn from the theatre.

The Stuka posed in its characteristic dive.

With this failure, the Stuka's fearsome reputation was certainly dented, but it was partially restored after 1941, on the Eastern Front, where the aircraft successfully served once again as a dive-bomber, and increasingly as a tank-destroyer. Indeed, Germany's most highly decorated serviceman of World War II, Hans Ulrich Rudel, scored most of his successes – including over 500 tanks, one battleship, one destroyer, four armoured trains and over 800 assorted military vehicles – flying Stukas in a ground-attack role.[1] So it was that this iconic aircraft remained in Luftwaffe service until 1945.

1   Gordon Williamson, *Aces of the Reich* (London, 1989), p. 141.

# 57 Mercedes-Benz 770 Limousine

*Hitler was a keen fan of cars, particularly those of Mercedes-Benz.* It was a long-standing relationship. While in prison in Landsberg in 1924, Hitler placed an order with a dealer in Munich for a supercharged Mercedes – probably a 24/100 – which he purchased upon his release for the huge sum of 26,000 Reichsmarks.[1]

A number of vehicles followed through the 1920s. Hitler was an avid reader of car specifications and kept up to date with the latest developments.[2] He even said he had sent sketches to Mercedes-Benz, and thereby claimed 'fatherhood' for some of the marque's later designs.[3] In 1931, he took delivery of the latest model, the 8-cylinder, 7.7-litre, 770 limousine, at the time the most expensive passenger car made by the firm. It was delivered to him, in person, by the racing driver Rudolf Caracciola.[4] Clearly Mercedes-Benz were keen to cultivate their up-and-coming customer.

The Führer's Benz of choice.

Though Hitler was able to drive, he didn't – citing the potential political consequences of him having an accident – and so employed a succession of drivers, who doubled as bodyguards. In the years before the seizure of power, he criss-crossed the country, seated in the passenger seat, map in hand, logging hundreds of thousands of kilometres, relishing the thrill of speed. 'I love automobiles', he said in 1942, 'I have to say that I owe the best moments of my life to the automobile.'[5]

After coming to power in 1933, Hitler was well placed to add to his growing fleet. In 1935, four vehicles were allocated to his bodyguard detail; the following year it was eight.[6] In total, Hitler's Chancellery would order over sixty cars from Mercedes-Benz.

*'When he saw the 770, Hitler said: "In future I will use only this car."'*

Within the fleet, there were a number of curiosities. There was, for example, the cross-country Mercedes G4, with its triple axle and off-road tyres, or the armoured 540K saloons that were used extensively for official Reich business. The most remarkable, however, was the 770KW150, the first of which was delivered to Hitler in April 1939.

The standard Mercedes-Benz W150 was a modified version of the older flagship 770 limousine, with hydraulic brakes and uprated suspension. However, Hitler's cars – such as the example shown here, from the Car & Technology Museum at Sinsheim – boasted a number of additional features, including 40 mm bulletproof glass all round, 18 mm steel doors, run-flat tyres and a 10 mm steel reinforced floor; all of these were designed to make the car impervious to attack with handguns and with up to half a kilogram of explosives. All that extra steel and glass made the car hugely heavy, of course, pushing its kerb weight up to 5 tons and giving horrific fuel economy figures of barely 6 miles per gallon.[7]

Hitler was undeterred, however, and when he saw the first example of the model, he said: 'In future I will use only this car.'[8] He was so impressed that he also commissioned cars – only ten of them were made – which were to be gifted to his allies, among them Finland's Field Marshal Gustav Mannerheim, Romania's Ion Antonescu, Norway's Vidkun Quisling, Spain's General Francisco Franco and Bulgaria's King Boris.

For all his enthusiasm, Hitler did not insist on using 'only' the W150, and often used the smaller 540K vehicles from the Reich Chancellery motor pool, which were also armoured. Whichever car he was in, his security men employed state-of-the-art techniques to keep him safe. On public appearances, Hitler's car would usually be part of a convoy of at least four vehicles, including a pilot car and two for Hitler's bodyguards. Anyone interrupting its progress would get short shrift. As the British military attaché noted in 1938, Hitler's convoy was 'bristling with tommy-guns and other lethal weapons'. 'There was something terribly sinister', he wrote, 'about that string of shining black Mercedes, rolling along inexorably towards Vienna'.[9]

However, for all the ingenuity of Hitler's security regime, it is doubtful how far such cars might have protected him in the event of a serious attack. After all, Hitler's own

Mercedes were almost all cabriolet vehicles, and his habit was to stand in the passenger footwell – in plain view – to receive the adulation of the crowd. In such circumstances, a determined assassin armed with a pistol or a hand-grenade would have been untroubled by the car's bullet-proof windscreen and armoured doors. Hitler evidently considered being safe was of secondary importance to being seen.

Bulletproofed, but vulnerable.

1   Trevor-Roper (ed.), *Hitler's Table Talk*, p. 284.

2   Ullrich, Hitler: *Ascent 1889–1939*, p. 404.

3   *Hitler's Table Talk*, p. 284.

4   Ullrich, *Hitler: Ascent 1889–1939*, p. 405.

5   Quoted in ibid., p. 404.

6   Hoffmann, *Hitler's Personal Security*, p. 65.

7   Ibid.

8   Kempka, *I was Hitler's Chauffeur*, p. 24.

9   Moorhouse, *Killing Hitler*, p. 23.

# 58 Luger Pistol

*The Luger – or more properly* the Pistole Parabellum 1908 – was the classic semi-automatic pistol used by German armed forces during the Third Reich era. Its distinctive shape – with its slim barrel and sharply raked handgrip – made it instantly recognisable.

Designed by Austrian Georg Luger, the Pistole Parabellum was patented in 1898 and manufactured by the Berlin Deutsche Waffen und Munitionsfabriken (DWM) company from 1900. A semi-automatic pistol, with an eight-round magazine in the grip, it was easy to use and reliable, and took its name from the Latin phrase '*Si vis pacem, para bellum*' – 'If you want peace, prepare for war.'

Luger's design had drawn on the work of Hugo Borchardt, who had developed the earlier C-93 model, which had been the world's first self-loading pistol. Luger improved that design, making it smaller and more efficient, and incorporated it into his own. It was this 'Borchardt-Luger System' that gave the Luger its distinctive shape, with a hinged toggle-lock mechanism above the grip, which used the recoil to expel the spent cartridge and load the next round.

The Luger semi-automatic pistol, used by German armed forces throughout the Third Reich.

*'The Luger's distinctive shape – with its slim barrel and sharply raked handgrip – made it instantly recognisable.'*

For all its later fame, the Luger was rather slow to catch on. The Swiss Army first adopted it in 1900 and then the German Imperial Navy made a large order for it in 1904. Four years later, the German Army adopted it as its main front-line sidearm and it became known as the Pistole 08. Thereafter, its predominance among German forces was unchallenged until the emergence of the Walther PP and P-38 models in the late 1930s. And, though the Luger was officially dropped as a standard-issue Wehrmacht sidearm in 1938 – in favour of the P-38, it was still manufactured and remained in widespread service until 1945. In total, it is thought that some 3 million Lugers were made.

As something of a German icon, the Luger was greatly prized as a souvenir by Allied soldiers during World War II. In some instances this enthusiasm was exploited by German forces, and a discarded Luger would be used as bait, rigged to a booby-trap or land mine to explode when disturbed.[1] Though this made Allied soldiers rather more wary when seeking their prize, perversely it did little to diminish the Luger's fame.

A German soldier holds a Luger pistol during the invasion of Russia in 1941.

---

1   G. Rottman, *World War II Axis Booby Traps and Sabotage Tactics* (Oxford, 2011), p. 49.

# 59 Gleiwitz Radio Tower

*Modern guidebooks will tell you* blandly that the radio tower at Gliwice in south-western Poland is – at 118 metres – the tallest wooden structure in Europe. However, its historic significance is much greater. Arguably it was there that World War II started.

The radio tower was constructed in 1935, when Gliwice was in Germany, close to the border with Poland, and went under the German name of Gleiwitz. Built using a lattice of impregnated larch beams linked by 16,000 brass bolts, it was intended as a broadcasting relay station for the Reichssender radio signals from the nearby regional capital of Breslau (now Wrocław).

Nonetheless, when the Nazis needed a *casus belli* against Poland, and wanted to justify their actions in the eyes of the world, Gleiwitz became the focus of their plotting. On the evening of 31 August 1939, shortly after the 8.00 news bulletin, a team of seven members of the SS Sicherheitsdienst, led by Alfred Naujocks, burst into the radio station. Their mission was to broadcast an incendiary message in Polish, which would show the world that irregular Polish forces had captured the station in an act of unprovoked aggression.

> '*When Hitler spoke to the assembled Reichstag later that day, he posed as the victim, stating that German forces were now "returning fire".*'

After taking the German staff hostage and locking them in the cellar, the SS raiders encountered a problem: the Gleiwitz station did not have a broadcast studio, the town's other station – 3 km away – had the studio. Making the best of their error, they decided to broadcast over the so-called 'storm microphone', which was used to warn local listeners of impending bad weather. Opening the channel, they read the message 'Here is Gleiwitz. The radio station is in Polish hands . . .', before the connection was lost. As the SS squad departed in frustration, they shot and killed a 43-year-old captive – Polish farm labourer Franciszek Honiok – whose body was left behind to add authenticity to the scene, and to 'prove' that the Poles had been behind the attack.[1]

It is not known how many listeners actually heard the SS broadcast – few, one suspects – but two hours later its message was reported in full across the German radio network. Germany would awake the following morning to the astonishing news that it had been attacked by Polish irregulars, and when Hitler spoke to the assembled Reichstag later that day, he posed as the victim, stating that German forces were now 'returning fire'.[2]

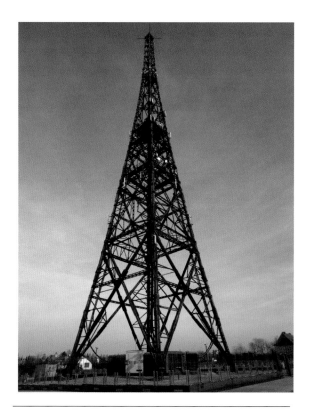

The Gleiwitz radio tower and transmitter station: where World War II began.

Gleiwitz was one of a pattern of 'provocations' that autumn, all aiming at destabilising and discrediting Poland. There was also a raid on a German customs post at Hochlinden, a bomb attack at Tarnów rail station and an assault on a forester's refuge in Pitschen.

So-called 'false flag' operations such as these were very fashionable among the totalitarian powers, for whom might was right, and international law was an irritant to be circumvented. The Japanese, for instance, mounted a false flag action at Mukden in 1931, as a pretext for their declaration of war on China. A month after Gleiwitz, the Red Army would shell its own border post at Mainila on the Finnish frontier, thereby delivering the spurious grounds for its invasion of Finland. Of all such operations, however, Gleiwitz is the most famous, the most symbolic of the sneering brutality of totalitarian *Realpolitik*. Remarkably the tower beneath which it all happened still stands – 118 metres tall – in the suburbs of Gliwice.

1    Alfred Spieß, *Heiner Lichtenstein, Das Unternehmen Tannenberg* (Wiesbaden, 1979), p. 141.

2    Terry Charman, *Outbreak 1939* (London, 2009), p. 81.

# 60 Germany–Soviet Treaty Border Map

*On 23 August 1939, the world was shocked to learn* that Adolf Hitler and Joseph Stalin – Nazi Germany and the USSR – had agreed a non-aggression pact. The world order, as many contemporaries had understood it, seemed to have been turned on its head; the two states whose ideological conflict had defined the age were now cosying up together; where once they had traded insults, they now praised one another's virtues. As one commentator recalled, it was a relationship that was so sinister that it appeared to foreshadow the destruction of civilization itself.[1]

A short time later, and much of what the doomsayers had feared had already come to pass. A week after the signature of the Nazi–Soviet Pact, Hitler had invaded Poland and his refusal to withdraw had brought an Anglo-French declaration of war. Two weeks after that, the Red Army then invaded Poland as well, to ensure that Stalin got the share of the spoils promised to him by his new partner. Poland was being systematically destroyed by the two invaders, its armies decimated, its people persecuted and expropriated, its towns and cities reduced to rubble.

By the last days of September 1939, the German and Soviet military campaigns in Poland were drawing to a close, and already the two dictatorships were looking to the next stage of their collaboration. German foreign minister Joachim von Ribbentrop was in Moscow for talks once again, and a second agreement was being prepared, this one grandly entitled 'The German–Soviet Boundary and Friendship Treaty'.

Apart from both sides agreeing not to resurrect a Polish state and establishing a framework for ongoing collaboration, much of the discussion was taken up with drawing the new German–Soviet frontier, which would run through the very heart of occupied Poland. Naturally, given that many among both the German and Soviet negotiating teams were less than entirely clear on the minutiae of Polish geography, this large-scale physical map of Poland was supplied by the German Embassy in Moscow to aid their deliberations.

The map was laid out on a table-top in the Kremlin and the new frontier was drawn across it as agreement was reached. In the original Nazi–Soviet Pact, the prospective line of division between the two had been agreed to run almost directly through the centre of Poland, along the middle reaches of the River Vistula – Warsaw would have found itself on the border – but this was now to be revised. In return for the cession of Lithuania to the Soviet 'sphere of influence', Stalin was prepared to scale back his demands on Polish territory and accept the line of the River Bug as his new frontier.

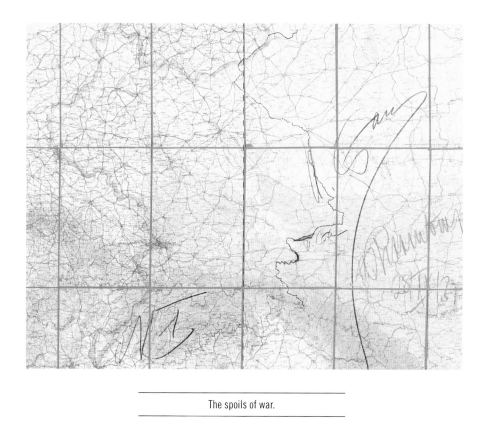

The spoils of war.

The black line was duly drawn down the map, following the line of the River Bug, past Brest, where Soviet and German forces had met a week earlier, and on southwards to Czerwonogród, where it followed the River Sołokija westwards before winding its way down, along the upper course of the San, to the border with Hungary at the village of Sianki in the Beskid Mountains. At only two locations was there disagreement or confusion – east of Przemyśl and north of Lubaczow – where the frontier line was evidently adjusted or corrected.

When they were finished, Poland had been neatly divided into two almost equal halves: Germany taking 201,000 square kilometres of territory and 20 million inhabitants, and the USSR taking 188,500 square kilometres with 12 million souls.[2] The two sides then signed the map to signify their agreement – Ribbentrop appended his signature in a flourish of red pencil, with the date of '28 IX 39', while Stalin signed with a swirl of blue, adding an initial next to the two adjustments. He then asked his guest cheekily: 'Is my signature clear enough for you?'[3]

The German–Soviet Boundary and Friendship Treaty is much less well-known than its predecessor, the Nazi–Soviet Pact, but it is nonetheless significant in that it perfectly reflected the new constellation of power in central Europe after the first month of World War II. Poland was prostrate, facing imminent defeat, and to its aggressors had already ceased to exist, its lands ripe for division and partition. The only powers that held any importance were Hitler's Germany and Stalin's Soviet Union, and – with astonishing arrogance – those two drew a black line down a map and divided the territory between them. For the second time in 150 years, Poland had disappeared, consumed by its neighbours.

*'Stalin asked his guest cheekily: "Is my signature clear enough for you?"'*

Those – at the time and since – who have sought to defend the Nazi–Soviet Pact often say that it was merely a non-aggression pact, just like the various other similar treaties that were briefly fashionable in the 1930s. Yet, this follow-up agreement – the German–Soviet Boundary and Friendship Treaty – which was signed just over a month later in Moscow, demonstrates that the Nazi–Soviet Pact was something rather different. It was the opening of a twenty-two-month relationship between the Germans and the Soviets, a relationship that would spawn a further four economic treaties and a whole host of diplomatic and political contacts. Moreover, as the map shows, it was a relationship that was founded, not on non-aggression, but on its very opposite.

New friends: Ribbentrop and Stalin at the signing of the
Nazi–Soviet Pact in August 1939.

1  'Chips' Channon, quoted in Roger Moorhouse, *The Devils' Alliance: Hitler's Pact with Stalin, 1939–1941* (London, 2014), p. 142.

2  Moorhouse, *Devils' Alliance*, p. 51.

3  Andor Hencke, quoted in Laurence Rees, *World War II Behind Closed Doors* (London, 2009), p. 33.

# 61 *Verdunkelung* Poster

*In Nazi Germany, the blackout was ordered* on the very first day of the war in 1939. In order to minimise the threat of aerial attack, it was stipulated that all light sources were to be extinguished, filtered or shaded during the hours of darkness. Shutters and curtains could be employed, as well as thick blackout card, which could be taped to the inside of windows. Car headlights were to be shrouded, and restaurants and bars had to take particular precautions to prevent light escaping when their customers entered and left the premises. The order stated that no light should be visible from a height of 500 metres. If an enemy couldn't see a city, the logic ran, he wouldn't be able to bomb it.

The blackout order was not just advisory, or voluntary, it was rigidly enforced. Information booklets were circulated containing useful tips for homeowners, and the local Nazi Party representative, the block warden, would also help ensure compliance. In addition, posters such as this one were printed to encourage the population. One of the most common German posters of the war, it shows a ghoulish skeletal figure atop an enemy bomber, hurling his bombs down on a careless resident below who is briefly illuminated by an open doorway. The text reads: 'The enemy sees your light: Blackout!'

Those who were unmoved by such orders and failed to comply would initially receive a formal warning; a notice would be fixed to the door of the offending property proclaiming 'This house is badly blacked out' and warning of the consequences of continued non-compliance. Those consequences could be severe: beginning with an interview with the Gestapo, and ending, in some cases, with a spell in the local concentration camp. Unsurprisingly, those who were able to compare judged that Germany's blackout in the early stages of the war was much more thorough and complete than that of its neighbours. Blacked-out Paris was like the 'city of lights', in comparison to Berlin, one commentator noted.[1]

> *'If an enemy couldn't see a city, the logic ran,*
> *he wouldn't be able to bomb it.'*

The blackout also had some notable social and technological consequences. Accidental deaths skyrocketed, as did petty crime and road accidents. Sales of phosphorescent paint soared; kerbs were whitewashed, and blue-filtered light bulbs were employed, because their shorter wavelength did not carry as far as an enemy aircraft. Ironically, the blackout also spurred the development of radar measures. Soon after this poster was produced, in 1942, the RAF began installing the primitive H2S radar set in its bomber aircraft, which aided target identification without the need for visual verification.

It has been argued that the blackout had as much a political function – fostering compliance and militarising community spirit – as a practical one.[2] Either way, it soon became an established air-defence measure across all combatant nations, and had a huge impact on life on the home front.

'The Enemy sees your Light!' – an exercise in propaganda, or civil defence?

1   Moorhouse, *Berlin at War*, p. 35.

2   M. R. D. Foot, in *The Oxford Companion to the Second World War* (Oxford, 1995), p. 134.

# 62 *Erkennungsmarken*

*By the start of World War II, most European armies* had instituted a formal system of identification for their soldiers, motivated at least in part by the chaos of World War I, in which millions of dead were left unidentified.

The German system of the *Erkennungsmarke* – or 'identification disc' – was a variation of that which had been in use from 1917, and consisted of a single, oval, tin disc, which each soldier was required to wear around his neck. Perforated along its centre, the disc had the soldier's unit, roll number and blood group stamped on both sides of the perforation. So, this example signifies a soldier of the 5th SS Panzer Division *Wiking*, with the roll number 588 and blood group B. Its wearer used the hessian pouch to keep the metal disc from his skin.

Identifying the dead: German *Erkennungsmarke* from a soldier of the SS *Wiking* Division.

In the event of a soldier's death, the lower half of the *Erkennungsmarke* would be snapped off by a comrade and handed to a commanding officer to begin the process of notifying the family, leaving the other half *in situ* to identify the body. In due course, notice of the death would be passed to the central administrative office, the Wehrmachtauskunftstelle (WASt or 'Wehrmacht Information Centre'), which would send out a pro-forma letter to the registered next of kin. In some cases, the commanding officer might also send his personal condolences, particularly if the deceased soldier was well known to him.

---

*'Most usually, German dead would simply lie where they fell.'*

---

The soldier's body, meanwhile, might initially be afforded only a rudimentary burial. In time – and if the military situation allowed – it would be disinterred for reburial in a formal war cemetery, with a simple wooden cross, bearing the soldier's name and date of death. Only the most senior officers would expect their remains to be repatriated after death in the field.

While German forces were on the advance, and rear areas could be secured and bodies identified and buried, then the system worked well. However, once the advance stalled, or – worse still – German forces found themselves in retreat, then it collapsed entirely. As a result, the numbers of German soldiers listed simply as *vermisst*, or 'missing', increased exponentially through the war, easily outnumbering the named and registered dead. The situation was most acute on the Eastern Front, where the heightened passions of ideological warfare meant that no quarter was given, even to the deceased. In some cases, German dead would be gathered together by the Soviets and – like their own dead – interred, unmarked in mass graves. More usually, however, they would simply lie where they fell. Only after 1991 could any systematic attempt be made to recover such remains, and to date only 800,000, of the 3.4 million German soldiers who are thought to have died in the war against the USSR, have a grave, and only about half of those are actually named.[1]

Such difficulties have been grievously exacerbated in recent years by the growing trend for amateur battlefield archaeology and 'trophy hunting'. *Erkennungsmarken* are easily found on auction websites, and many of those that are genuine and intact will have been taken from human remains – remains which now lie unidentified.

---

1  See 'Germany Still Burying Eastern Front Dead', in *Spiegel International*, at http://www.spiegel.de/international/europe/germany-to-open-last-wwii-war-cemetery-in-russia-a-914093.html.

# 63 *Der Ewige Jude* Film Poster

*When the notorious film Der Ewige Jude* – 'The Eternal Jew' – premiered in Berlin in November 1940, it marked a new low in Nazi propaganda.

The film claimed to be 'a documentary about world Jewry' – as the subtitle on this contemporary poster proclaimed – and was even narrated by Harry Giese, the voice of Germany's newsreels. In truth, however, it was Nazi propaganda of the most egregious sort. Its stark message, delivered in brutal terms, was that Jews were little more than vermin, 'the parasitical destroyers' of European civilisation.

The origins of the film lay in Nazi attempts actively to propagate anti-Semitic attitudes amongst the German population. Passive anti-Semitism was already quite widespread in Germany, but the Nazi leadership wanted more. Stung by the mixed popular reaction to the *Kristallnacht* pogrom in 1938, Goebbels had begun an intensification of anti-Semitic propaganda, to prepare the German public for the harsher measures against the Jews that were to come.[1] To this end, cinema was considered the ideal medium. Goebbels saw it as a vital tool in moulding public opinion and had taken a personal hand in expanding the German film industry, nationalising it in 1937 and consistently pushing both higher standards and increased political content thereafter. He even hoped that German films would one day rival those of Hollywood.[2]

So the German film industry was harnessed to the Nazi project and propaganda films – such as Leni Riefenstahl's iconic *Triumph of the Will* from 1935 – soon began to appear on the nation's cinema screens, alongside the usual love stories and dramas. By 1940, when *The Eternal Jew* appeared, in the same year as *Jud Süss* and *Die Rothschilds*, it was part of a cinematic, anti-Semitic offensive. But the film nonetheless marked something of a departure. While the other offerings, as fictional or historical features, adopted the more usual and rather subtler approach to their propaganda message, *The Eternal Jew* – with its images of swarming rats and graphic depictions of ritual animal slaughter – knew nothing of subtlety.

The film drew on an earlier exhibition of the same name, which had been shown across Germany between 1937 and 1939, and had defamed and de-humanised Jews by perpetuating numerous anti-Semitic myths. Now Goebbels's propagandists had the opportunity to adapt those odious messages for the new medium of cinema. *The Eternal Jew* included the same prejudicial pseudo-history, the same crude anti-Semitic tropes and the same racial mythology, but crucially it reached a far wider audience than the exhibition ever did.

158

For the release of what he called 'the Jew film', Goebbels gave specific instructions. In Berlin alone, *The Eternal Jew* opened in sixty-six cinemas, the occasion hyped by the publication of this poster, with its faux-Hebrew text and the malevolent, bile-yellow face staring out over a stereotyped hooked nose. Some versions were even overlaid with a tantalising disclaimer about the film's gory content, advising that women and children should attend a censored showing.

Soon, Nazi journalists were dutifully frothing over the film's 'horrifying scenes' and expressing their 'deep gratitude' to those working on the task of 'solving the Jewish problem'.[3] SS 'mood reports' concurred, claiming that the 'high expectations' regarding the film had been borne out, that it had been deemed 'especially impressive' and that in Munich audiences had even applauded.[4]

*Der Ewige Jude* film poster from 1940 – propaganda, but not for the faint-hearted.

But the German people were less than uniformly enthused, it seems. Those same SS reports noted that though audiences may have applauded in Munich, some in Breslau walked out, claiming to have 'had enough of Jewish filth'. Others fainted. Certainly viewing figures – estimated at barely 1 million – were a fraction of those reported for *Jud Süss*, making the film a commercial failure. The SS explained the drop by suggesting that only the 'politically active sector' of the population had seen the film. But the Jewish diarist Victor Klemperer wrote that, despite the 'ballyhoo' surrounding it, *The Eternal Jew* had swiftly disappeared due to the 'weariness and disgust' of the public.[5] Both may have been right.

The cover of the brochure for the
'Der Ewige Jude' exhibition, Berlin 1938.

Thanks to its deserved notoriety, *The Eternal Jew* might be assumed to be an archetype of a Nazi propaganda film: crude, blunt and shocking. But, in truth, it was an exception. Goebbels was too intelligent not to appreciate that propaganda had to be a rapier, not a blunderbuss; it had to seduce rather than confront, persuade rather than hector. To his frustration, perhaps, he understood that audiences were not automata, passively waiting to be programmed by their leaders. And, for this reason, his usual approach was much more subtle than *The Eternal Jew* would have suggested, consisting more often of subliminal propaganda, wrapped in an apparently apolitical context. Indeed, it is worth remembering that the most successful film of the Nazi period was hardly even propaganda at all, it was *Die Grosse Liebe* – 'The Great Love' – the story of a romance between a singer and a fighter pilot.

1   David Welch, *The Third Reich: Politics and Propaganda* (London, 1993), p. 82.

2   See Peter Longerich, *Goebbels* (London, 2015), pp. 285–8.

3   Saul Friedländer, *The Years of Extermination: Nazi Germany and the Jews, 1939–1945* (London, 2007), pp. 101–2.

4   Heinz Boberach (ed.), *Meldungen aus dem Reich*, Vol. VI (Herrsching, 1984), p. 1918.

5   Victor Klemperer, *I Shall Bear Witness* (London, 1998), p. 348.

# 64 Pervitin

*In mid-November 1939, a young Wehrmacht soldier* wrote home from occupied Poland to Cologne, sending his greetings to his parents and siblings and asking that they send him 'some Pervitin'.[1]

Pervitin was an early, low-dose version of what would now be called crystal meth, or methamphetamine hydrochloride: 'speed'. Inspired by the American use of Benzedrine during the Berlin Olympics of 1936, Pervitin was developed by the pharmaceutical company Temmler and first introduced onto the German market in 1938, in tablet form. Marketed as a stimulant, an 'alertness aid' to ease symptoms of everything from depression to lack of libido, it quickly proved popular with the civilian population.[2]

Inevitably, the popularity of Pervitin soon brought the drug to the attention of the German military, and by the summer of 1939 Dr Otto Ranke of the Berlin Academy for Military Medicine was already carrying out experiments to assess its effectiveness on military subjects. After tests using Wehrmacht drivers during the Polish campaign of September 1939, he noted that the drug's effects were similar to those of adrenaline: a heightened state of alertness, increased self-confidence, reduced inhibitions and a greater willingness to take risks. It was easy to conclude that Pervitin would help Germany win the war.

So, in the spring and summer of 1940, more than 35 million Pervitin tablets – known colloquially as 'Stuka-tablets' – were distributed to the German military. Users were advised to take one or two 3-milligram tablets, as required, to 'maintain sleeplessness'.

Pervitin, one of the unlikely drivers of *Blitzkrieg*.

The possible military effects of so much methamphetamine have provoked much speculation. It seems obvious, perhaps, that soldiers who were alert, self-confident, willing to take risks and able to stay awake for three days on end would prove to be highly effective fighters. Indeed, contemporary accounts suggest that Pervitin was indeed vitally important. The supply officer of the 1st Panzer Division during the Battle for France, for instance, was obliged to carry some 20,000 tablets of the drug – speeding his soldiers in their headlong drive westward.[3] Modern commentators have gone further, some suggesting that *Blitzkrieg* itself was powered as much by amphetamines as by machinery.[4]

---

### 'It must have seemed that Pervitin would help Germany win the war.'

---

Pervitin's spell didn't last, however. Though its initial benefits to men in combat were self-evident, Wehrmacht doctors became increasingly concerned about the drug's side-effects, the growing resistance evident amongst users, and of course the high incidence of addiction. In fact, moves were already afoot in 1940 to have it added to a list of restricted substances.

It is perhaps telling in this respect that the soldier above, who wrote home to request fresh supplies of Pervitin, was doing so in November 1939, more than a month after combat operations in the Polish campaign had been concluded. The battle was long over by that point, but he clearly still needed his fix.

1   Heinrich Böll, quoted in Andreas Ulrich, 'Hitler's Drugged Soldiers', *Der Spiegel*, May 2005.

2   Norman Ohler, *Blitzed: Drugs in Nazi Germany* (London, 2016), p. 41.

3   Karl-Heinz Frieser, *The Blitzkrieg Legend* (Annapolis, 2013), p. 119.

4   Nicolas Rasmussen, *On Speed: The Many Lives of Amphetamine* (New York, 2009), p. 54.

# 65 MP 40 Submachine Gun

*The first submachine gun was developed* by Hugo Schmeisser at Bergmann Waffenfabrik in Suhl in 1918. Known as the Bergmann MP 18, it was fed by a drum magazine and was issued to German stormtroopers in the final months of World War I. Well suited to the confined spaces of the trenches, it was considered a success and so had a number of post-war imitators, including the improved MP 28 and the Steyr MP 34. Its most notable successor, however, was the MP 40, the iconic German submachine gun of World War II.

Developed as a simplified version of the earlier MP 38, the MP 40 was the first gun of its type to be made purely from metal and plastic, with no wooden elements. With its signature folding skeleton stock and 32-round stick magazine, its primary components were stamped rather than machined, thereby easing mass production. In action, the MP 40 was easy to use, and with a theoretical rate of fire of 500 rounds per minute and an effective range of 100–200 metres, it could deliver overwhelming firepower, even if the soldier was not a skilled marksman. Nonetheless, the weapon had a few flaws, being prone to jamming in dirty or dusty conditions, or when its characteristic magazine was used as a grip, thereby causing it to move out of line with its feed.

The Allies erroneously called the MP 40 a 'Schmeisser' – and though Hugo Schmeisser had had nothing directly to do with developing either the MP 38 or MP 40, he had designed the earlier MP 36 prototype and held the patent for the gun's distinctive

An MP 40 submachine gun.

163

magazine. The rather more prosaic German designation, meanwhile, used the year of first manufacture with the prefix MP, meaning 'machine pistol', as the weapon used 9 mm calibre pistol ammunition.

At the beginning of the war, the Kar. 98k rifle was the standard German infantry weapon and barely 8,000 MP 38s were distributed, usually to platoon or squad commanders. However, as the war progressed and urban street fighting became an increasingly important form of combat, the MP 40 was issued in greater quantities, with over a million being manufactured by the time production was halted late in 1944.

The iconic status of the MP 40 owed something to Hollywood's post-war depictions, which suggested that its use was more widespread than it was, but it was also due to the weapon's advanced features and rugged usability, which made it a favourite 'souvenir' for soldiers of all sides.

A German Army soldier on the lookout with his MP40.

# 66 Waffen-SS Recruiting Poster

*This poster from 1940 was aimed* at recruiting Flemish men in German-occupied Belgium to the ranks of the Waffen-SS, the military arm of the SS. It sought to evoke the medieval past of Flanders, with its characteristic buildings and an image of an armoured warrior superimposed upon the emblem of the region – the lion rampant. Beneath, it shows a stylised SS-man, with a camouflaged helmet. The text reads: 'Report to the Waffen-SS and the Volunteer Legion Flanders'.

A Waffen-SS poster aimed at recruiting Flemish men in occupied Belgium.

The result of this recruitment drive was the first 1,000 of the estimated 40,000 Belgians to join the Waffen-SS.[1] First designated in 1941 as the SS Volunteer Legion *Flandern* within the SS-Panzer Division *Wiking*, the Flemish SS served exclusively on the Eastern Front, initially seeing combat around Leningrad before being wiped out in January 1943. Reformed as the 6th SS Volunteer Brigade *Langemarck* and sent to the Ukraine, it was again effectively annihilated in August 1944, with its surviving remnant being refitted and renamed as the 27th SS Volunteer Division *Langemarck*. It finished the war defending eastern Germany against the Red Army and surrendered at Mecklenburg in May 1945. Of those who survived to return home, some thirty former volunteers were sentenced to death and executed.[2]

---

*'The Germans found many nationalities keen to fight against the brutal regime of Stalin.'*

---

The grim experience of the Flemish SS units was by no means extraordinary. Yet, curiously perhaps, there was rarely a shortage of foreign volunteers for the Waffen-SS. As a result, the organisation expanded rapidly, particularly after its successful performance during the invasion of the Soviet Union in 1941. Its commander, Reichsführer-SS Heinrich Himmler, saw foreign recruits not only as a vital source of manpower, but as the vanguard of Nazi warriors, crusaders against Bolshevism, perfectly suited to the new ideological war.

In truth, however, motivations for joining up ranged widely. Some, certainly, enlisted out of ideological conviction, sharing the Nazis' racist ideology, or seduced by their narrative of an 'anti-Bolshevik' crusade. For most, however, the motivation was more mundane: a desire for military adventure, the need to escape the privations of occupation in their homelands, a way of demonstrating a tactical loyalty to the Nazi regime, or – particularly for Soviet national minorities – an opportunity of getting back at their pre-war oppressors.

Applying strict racial criteria, Himmler first sought out those with what he regarded as Nordic blood, with Waffen-SS foreign recruits coming from Scandinavia and the Low Countries, most of whom were collected in the 5th SS Panzer Division *Wiking* – its very name drawing on that common Nordic heritage. Following the rapid German conquests of 1941, Himmler then loosened the criteria for membership of the Waffen-SS, allowing ethnic Germans located in Croatia, Serbia, Hungary and Romania to join the 7th SS Volunteer Mountain Division *Prinz Eugen*, for deployment in anti-partisan operations. Again, the division name had a historical resonance, as Austria's Prince Eugene of Savoy had been a Habsburg commander in the wars against the Turks in the eighteenth century – another crusade against a supposedly barbaric foe.

However, the needs of the German war machine – fighting campaigns on numerous fronts and chronically short of manpower – forced Himmler to water down his racial criteria even further and, in 1943, he permitted the creation of the first 'non-Germanic' Waffen-SS division. The 13th SS Mountain Division *Handschar* (1st Croatian) included

Bosnian Muslims, the descendants of the very Ottoman Turks once battled by Prince Eugene, and even took its name from an Ottoman sword. They were later joined by the 21st SS Mountain Division *Skanderbeg* (1st Albanian), mainly composed of Albanian Muslims, although it took its name from a medieval warlord who had battled the Ottoman Empire.

In the Soviet Union, the Germans found many nationalities keen to fight against the brutal regime of Stalin. Some among the Baltic nations, especially Latvians and Estonians, volunteered to join the 15th, 19th and 20th Waffen-SS Divisions, primarily to avenge themselves on the Soviets following Stalin's vicious occupation of their countries in 1940–1. In addition, the 14th Waffen-Grenadier Division *Galizien* of the SS, established in 1943, was made up primarily of Ukrainians from the former Polish district of Galicia. They saw their service in German colours as an important step towards the attainment of Ukrainian independence.

This Waffen-SS poster invites Norwegians to join *Den Norske Legion* in the battle against Bolshevism; a symbolic Viking longboat is in the background, *c.* 1941.

Although not forming separate Waffen-SS divisions, many other minorities also fought alongside the Nazis on the Eastern Front in SS units, including Tatars, Cossacks, Azeris, Chechens and Turkic tribesmen from central Asia. All these collaborators would pay a heavy price when Stalin won back control of the Soviet Union, facing execution or a grim fate in the camps of the *Gulag*.

In total, nearly a million soldiers served Nazi Germany as foreign 'volunteers', some 600,000 of them within the thirty-eight divisions of the Waffen-SS, where they quickly outnumbered native Germans.[3] Many of those units, certainly, were of dubious quality; some never achieved full combat strength; a few scarcely saw action; many gained an unenviable reputation for cruelty and war crimes. But, taken together, the Waffen-SS was possibly the largest multinational army ever to fight under a single flag.

1   G. H. Stein, *The Waffen SS: Hitler's Elite Guard at War* (London, 1966), p. 139.

2   Rolf-Dieter Müller, *The Unknown Eastern Front: The Wehrmacht and Hitler's Foreign Soldiers* (London, 2012), pp. 129–30.

3   Stein, p. 287.

# 67 Psychiatric Asylum Iron Bed

*A leading principle of Adolf Hitler's Third Reich* was the purification of the Aryan race from what he considered foreign and unfit elements. While the Holocaust was intended to deal with the former, the latter were to be exterminated through the so-called 'Aktion T4', the Nazi euthanasia programme.

Eugenics – the idea of improving the genetic quality of a people by encouraging the breeding of supposedly superior elements at the expense of those with less desirable traits – was nothing new. This controversial 'science' was very popular in the early twentieth century, with many developed countries experimenting with various methods. But it struck a particular chord with Hitler and the Nazis, who promulgated the idea of 'racial hygiene'. To their mind, eugenics not only gave pseudo-scientific justification to their anti-Semitism, it also legitimised the concept of euthanasia: the 'mercy killings' of the disabled.

As early as 14 July 1933, Hitler passed the Law for the Protection of Hereditary Health, which allowed the enforced sterilisation of anyone deemed likely to pass on inherited

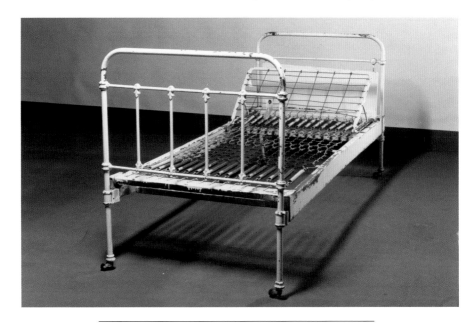

Iron bed from the Sachsenburg psychiatric asylum.

## 'Next of kin would receive a spurious notification that their loved one had died of pneumonia or a heart condition.'

defects, including blindness and deafness. With the outbreak of war in 1939, he was prepared to go one step further and enact a widespread euthanasia programme. That autumn, he signed a decree allowing for the 'mercy killing' of 'incurably ill patients', and authorising a programme of assessment, which was to be administered from a building at Tiergartenstrasse 4 in Berlin – hence the code-name 'T4'.

Over the following two years, over 70,000 patients from psychiatric hospitals were murdered across Germany, Austria and occupied Poland. Most were killed by poison gas, at six centres in Germany – Grafeneck, Sonnenstein, Hartheim, Hadamar, Bernburg and Brandenburg – where SS doctors in white coats escorted their victims into the gas chambers. After cremation, next of kin would receive a spurious notification that their loved one had died of pneumonia or a heart condition.

Though the T4 programme was formally suspended in 1941, it did not end completely; it was merely devolved to the authority of local institutions. One of those was the psychiatric asylum at Sachsenburg in Schwerin, from where this iron-framed ward bed comes. In all, it is thought that around 1,000 mentally or physically handicapped people – including many children – were killed at Sachsenburg; condemned to death by their doctors, they were given lethal doses of barbiturates or

Disabled children at Schönbrunn Psychiatric Hospital in 1934, photographed by the SS.

morphine, and then cremated.[1] They were, in Nazi parlance, 'lives unworthy of life'.[2]

Around 100,000 disabled people are thought to have been killed by the Nazis in the T4 programme and beyond. Of course, it is a number that is dwarfed by the dead of the Holocaust, and the wider death toll from Hitler's wars, yet the victims of T4 are nonetheless hugely significant. Not only was the T4 programme a rehearsal for the Holocaust – with much of the practical expertise gained in killing the disabled directly transferred to the genocide against the Jews – it also revealed the dark heart of Hitler's racial state with brutal clarity.

1   K. Haack, E. Kumbier, 'Verbrechen an psychisch Kranken und Behinderten in der Zeit des Nationalsozialismus. Eine Bestandsaufnahme unter besonderer Berücksichtigung von Mecklenburg und spezifisch Rostock', in G. Boeck & H.-U. Lammel (eds), *Die Universität Rostock in den Jahren 1933–1945. Referate der interdisziplinären Ringvorlesung des Arbeitskreises 'Rostocker Universitäts- und Wissenschaftsgeschichte'* (Rostock, 2012), pp. 227–42.

2   M. Burleigh, *Death and Deliverance: Euthanasia in Germany, c. 1900–1945* (Cambridge, 1994), p. 189.

# 68 *Afrika Korps* Field Cap

*The Deutsches Afrika Korps (DAK)* – German Africa Corps – was formed in January 1941 to assist Hitler's Italian ally, Benito Mussolini, in his faltering efforts to conquer North Africa as part of a new Fascist Roman Empire. Commanded by Erwin Rommel – the 'Desert Fox' – it was initially subordinated to the Italian chain of command, but quickly grew in size and strength, with Rommel's brilliant use of mobile warfare scoring some notable victories, such as the taking of Tobruk in June 1942.

The soldiers of the *Afrika Korps* encountered extreme conditions in North Africa: vast open expanses, blinding blue skies, and daytime temperatures regularly over 35°C. But, unlike German forces fighting on the Eastern Front, they were already well-equipped. The previous autumn, when an intervention in the theatre had appeared necessary, the Tropical Institute of the University of Hamburg had been tasked with developing a range of suitable uniforms.

A sun-bleached *Afrikamütze*.

> *'Many soldiers deliberately bleached their caps, as a faded cap*
> *was the hallmark of a seasoned desert veteran.'*

The results drew heavily on the British Army's tropical dress, providing pith helmets, high, laced boots and breeches, some of which proved to be less than entirely suitable for the desert. However, the most famous item supplied to the *Afrika Korps* was the humble peaked field cap. It would become synonymous with the campaign and with the soldiers who wore it.

Modelled on the *Bergmütze* worn by German mountain troops, the *Afrikamütze* cap was made from light olive canvas material, with a long peak to give protection to the eyes and two metal grommets each side of the crown to provide ventilation. As with this example, insignia for all ranks consisted of a woven silk eagle and swastika on a tan background, and a silk cockade in the national colours of black, white and red. Earlier versions also featured an inverted chevron of coloured braid, above the cockade, which denoted the wearer's branch of service.

Though the field caps were originally olive green in colour – like the uniform – they swiftly faded in the strong desert sun, down to a sandy beige, or even to cream. Many soldiers deliberately bleached their caps, as a faded cap was the hallmark of a seasoned desert veteran, while the original olive green was very much the preserve of the new arrival.

Wearing their field caps, *Afrika Korps* soldiers ride their machine-gun-armed motorcycle and sidecar combination in typical sandy conditions.

Despite its successes, after defeat at the Second Battle of El Alamein in November 1942, and the Anglo-American landings in Morocco and Algeria that same month, the DAK was forced into retreat, overwhelmed by the materiel and logistical superiority of its enemies. It finally surrendered in Tunisia on 12 May 1943, its commander General Hans Cremer signalling: 'Ammunition shot off. Arms and equipment destroyed. In accordance with order received, *Afrika Korps* has fought itself to the condition where it can fight no more.'[1]

The significance of the defeat of the Afrika Korps was substantial, marking as it did the first major British and American success against German land forces. As was his wont, Churchill summed it up pithily, if not entirely accurately: 'Before Alamein, we never had a victory, after Alamein we never had a defeat.'[2]

---

1   Quoted in David Rolf, *The Bloody Road to Tunis: The Destruction of Axis Forces in North Africa* (London, 2001), p. 277.

2   Winston Churchill, *The Second World War* (London, 1959), p. 630.

# 69 Flak Tower

*The Allied bombing of Germany*, which began in the early summer of 1940, was designed initially to target solely military installations; only leaflets were to be dropped over civilian areas. Soon, inevitably, the cities themselves were targeted, with Berlin being raided in late August 1940 in reply to an (apparently accidental) German raid on the London suburb of Harrow. Hitler's response was immediate and dramatic: as well as promising that the Luftwaffe would 'wipe out' enemy cities, he ordered a huge programme of bunker-building to reassure worried civilians. In Berlin alone over 3,000 bunkers and shelters were planned, ranging from converted cellars to large-scale, purpose-built structures.

When one considers the Nazis' bloodthirsty reputation, this might seem peculiar. But the motivation behind the programme was clear. Aside from the obvious propaganda benefits, Hitler was terrified of 'losing' the Home Front – as Germany's leadership had done during World War I – and so went to great lengths to reassure the civilian people that everything possible was being done to ensure their safety. In addition, as a totalitarian state, Nazi Germany could ill afford any expression of popular discontent, for fear that it might develop into opposition and resistance. So, for the Nazis, a state-of-the-art system of civilian protection was a political necessity.

The centrepieces of this huge building programme were the flak towers, eight of which were constructed in Berlin, Hamburg and Vienna. They were built to three different designs, but they all served the dual purpose of providing air-raid defence as well as civilian protection. The most impressive were the first generation, of which three were built in Berlin and one in Hamburg. Nearly 40 metres tall and 70 metres across, they consisted of seven floors, with walls 2.5 metres thick and a bombproof 3.5-metre-thick reinforced roof. On top of that roof was an array of anti-aircraft weaponry, from 27 ton, twin 128 mm giants to the smaller quadruple 20 mm guns, which could fire an astonishing 1,800 rounds a minute.[1]

---

*'For the Nazis, a state-of-the-art system of civilian protection was a political necessity.'*

---

As one eye-witness noted, the towers looked: 'like fantastic monstrosities from another world'.[2] Yet they offered a precious refuge for civilians. As well as storage, a hospital floor and living quarters for the gun crews, four floors in each tower were set aside for air-raid protection, designed to hold some 15,000 people. Conditions were spartan, all bare concrete and little natural light, but with the benefit of an independent supply of both power and water.

The flak tower at Berlin Zoo, a 'monstrosity from another world'.

As the war neared its end, overcrowding in the flak towers became rife, with perhaps three times the design capacity – as many as 45,000 people – desperately seeking safety in each one. The towers would be the very last places in Berlin to fall to the Soviets, with that at Humboldthain being last to surrender, at 2 p. m. on 2 May 1945.

After the war, two of Berlin's towers were demolished, with only one – Humboldthain – defying French dynamite to be transformed into a 'rubble mountain'. Those in Hamburg and Vienna were left standing as vast, mute witnesses to the remarkable durability of reinforced concrete – and to the Nazis' incongruous 'duty of care' to the German people.

1   Michael Foedrowitz, *The Flak Towers* (Berlin, 2007).

2   Howard Smith, quoted in Moorhouse, *Berlin at War*, p. 310.

# 70 *Prinz Eugen* Propeller

*When work began* on the heavy cruiser *Prinz Eugen*, in Kiel in August 1936, it was an event of profound significance. Ordered in the wake of the Anglo-German Naval Agreement of 1935, which permitted Germany a naval strength of 35 per cent of that of the Royal Navy, the ship was seen as symbolic – like its later sister ships the *Blücher* and the *Admiral Hipper* – of Germany's restored military honour.

Hitler had set great store by expanding his navy, broadly matching British naval spending in the 1930s in an effort to build a surface fleet that he hoped would one day challenge the Royal Navy.[1] Launched in 1938, the *Prinz Eugen* was an integral part of that expansion programme. It was certainly an impressive vessel. Named after Prince Eugene of Savoy, an Austrian general of the eighteenth century, it displaced over 16,000 tons and was over 200 metres from stem to stern, with a crew of nearly

One of the *Prinz Eugen*'s three propellers, now on display at Laboe.

1,600 officers and men. Its armament was provided by a potent battery of eight 20 cm main guns, mounted in pairs of twin turrets, fore and aft. With a top speed of 32 knots and a cruising speed of 20 knots, it was powered by three steam turbines driving triple bronze propellers such as this, each one over 4 metres in diameter and weighing over 11 tons.

---

*'Prinz Eugen was known to its crews as the lucky ship.'*

---

Yet, for all its impressive scale and specifications, fortune did not entirely smile on the *Prinz Eugen*. While fitting out in Kiel in July 1940, it was damaged in an RAF air raid; then, the following April, it hit a mine in the Baltic and was forced to head to port for repairs. Returning to action in May 1941, it then joined the *Bismarck* in the Battle of Denmark Strait, scoring vital hits on both HMS *Hood* and HMS *Prince of Wales*.

Ordered to break off the engagement, the *Prinz Eugen* retired to Brest for repairs, while the *Bismarck* was chased down by the Royal Navy and sunk.

The following year, after successfully returning to the Baltic via the English Channel – the so-called 'Channel Dash' – the *Prinz Eugen* was torpedoed by the British off the Norwegian coast, before being repaired and then withdrawn to the safety of the Baltic to serve as a training ship. Returning to combat duty in 1943, as a gunnery support vessel for the Eastern Front, it collided with the cruiser *Leipzig* in heavy fog off the Pomeranian coast in October 1944, during which incident the two unfortunate vessels were locked together for some fourteen hours. After another round of repairs, the *Prinz Eugen* remained in the Baltic, largely in

The Prinz Eugen's forward gun turrets ready for action.

support of the German retreat in East Prussia, before steaming to Copenhagen, where it was surrendered to the British on 8 May 1945.

The *Prinz Eugen* was known to its crews as 'the lucky ship'. This was presumably because it was the only one of Hitler's ten largest ships to survive the war, rather than any reference to its record – despite all its efforts, it did not sink a single Allied vessel. Ironically, though it was supposed to be symbolic of the restoration of the German Navy as a fighting force, the *Prinz Eugen*'s war record was rather more indicative of the wider shortcomings of the Kriegsmarine's surface ships. Despite the bravery of its crews and the technological brilliance of its vessels, Hitler's navy was simply outnumbered and outgunned by its adversaries. As Admiral Erich Raeder noted glumly in the very first days of the war: Germany's surface forces were 'so inferior in number and strength . . . that they can do no more than show that they know how to die gallantly'.[2]

Ultimately, the *Prinz Eugen* would join its fellows on the seabed. Allocated to the Americans as war booty, it sailed for Boston in January 1946, before being re-named USS *Prinz Eugen* and being towed through the Panama Canal into the Pacific, bound for Bikini atoll. That summer, it was used as a target ship in two atomic tests – an air-burst and a submerged detonation – being moored some 1,100 metres from the epicentre of both. Lightly damaged but heavily irradiated, it was then towed to Kwajalein Atoll, 350 km away, where it began to list. On 22 December 1946, the *Prinz Eugen* capsized and sank.

One can view precious little of Hitler's navy today without getting wet – a few ships' bells and other artefacts survive in museums, and the stern eagle from the *Graf Spee* languishes in a Uruguayan Navy warehouse in Montevideo. This bronze propeller, therefore – salvaged from the wreck of the *Prinz Eugen* in 1979, and now on display at the German Naval Memorial at Laboe on the Baltic – provides a rare glimpse both of Nazi Germany's maritime ambition, and its failure.

The USS *Prinz Eugen* being prepared for the atomic tests at Bikini, 1946.

1   A. Tooze, *The Wages of Destruction* (London, 2006), p. 251.

2   Quoted in Shirer, *Rise and Fall of the Third Reich*, p. 750.

# 71 Hampel Postcard

*Otto and Elise Hampel were supposed* to be the sort of people who formed the very backbone of the Nazi national community – the *Volksgemeinschaft*. They were solid, ordinary, working-class Germans: he worked for Siemens in the Berlin suburb of Reinickendorf; she was a member of the National Socialist Women's League.

However, something happened to change their reflexive loyalty to the Third Reich. In the summer of 1940, Elise's younger brother Kurt was killed in the invasion of France. His death hit the childless couple hard, shaking them out of their complacency. That autumn, they began actively to resist Nazi rule.

With little money and no political connections, the Hampels did not have the means to make much of an impact, but they found a simple solution: they would write postcards with anti-Nazi slogans, which they would then distribute in public areas – such as stairwells – around their home suburb of Wedding in north Berlin. Their cards were crudely written, sometimes with disjointed, misspelled text. They often called for civil disobedience, or demanded that their fellow Germans 'wake up', or denounced the Nazi Winter Aid scheme as fraudulent.

This example – dating from 1941 – is typical. It begins with the heading 'Free Press' – presumably proclaiming itself a counterpoint to Nazi propaganda – and goes on to demand a popular struggle against the 'Hitler regime' (which is spelled wrongly). The Nazis are described as 'exploiters', 'riff-raff' and 'murderers' who are dragging the German people 'into the abyss'. 'Down with the despicable Nazi regime!' it demands on the reverse, 'Down with the Hitlerite war!'

---

*'What is most astonishing about the case is the petty nature of the crime versus the severity of its punishment.'*

---

For almost two years, the Hampels continued their counter-propaganda campaign, writing over 200 postcards in the process. They left their last one on 20 October 1942, in Nöllendorfplatz, where they were spotted by a passer-by, who called the police. Under interrogation by the Berlin Gestapo both proclaimed that they were 'happy' with the idea of protesting against the Nazi regime. They were less happy with what followed. On 22 January 1943, they were sentenced to death by the People's Court for undermining military morale and preparing high treason. They were executed, by guillotine, on 8 April 1943.[1]

The Hampels would have languished in total obscurity were it not for the fact that their story was picked up after the war by the novelist Hans Fallada, and – at the request of the incoming communist administration in Berlin – was woven into what was intended to be the definitive novel of wartime resistance. The Hampels became the Quangels, the brother became a son – but otherwise Fallada remained reasonably true to the original. The book – published in English as *Alone in Berlin* – would be Fallada's last, but would become a posthumous bestseller.

Aside from its remarkable publishing history, what is most astonishing about the case is the petty nature of the Hampels' crime versus the severity of its punishment. It reminds us that totalitarian systems could tolerate no contradiction; there was no capacity for the airing of discontent, however justified – everyone had to march in lock-step. It also reminds us that, under such regimes, 'resistance' could have an extremely broad definition – even extending to brave, futile acts of littering.

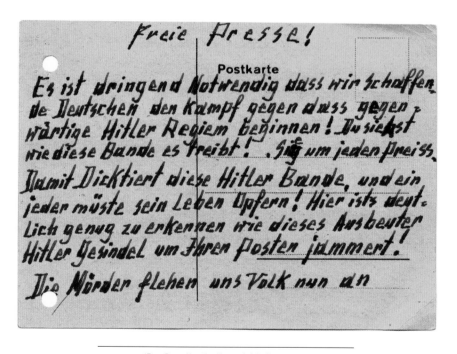

'Free Press!' – the Hampels' futile protest.

1   Johannes Groschupf, 'Das Ehepaar Hampel allein in Berlin', in *Die Zeit*, 16 April 2011. Available at www.zeit.de/kultur/literatur/2011-04/hans-fallada-widerstand/komplettansicht.

# 72 Rudolf Hess's Underpants

*When Rudolf Hess took off* from the Augsburg-Haunstetten airfield, on the evening of 10 May 1941, he was travelling light. Flying solo, he had crammed everything that he would need into the pockets of his Luftwaffe flying suit: charts of his route, a wallet with family photos and an assortment of homeopathic remedies. Hitler's deputy, and one of the most senior figures in the Third Reich, he was flying to Britain with a peace offer, on what he would later call 'a mission of humanity'.[1]

Unfortunately for him, Hess would not receive a warm welcome when he parachuted to earth over lowland Scotland later that evening. Initially captured by a ploughman, he identified himself as 'Hauptmann Alfred Horn', before being handed over to the Home Guard and taken to the local scout hut at Giffnock, where he was first searched and most of his possessions confiscated. Confessing his true identity, Hess asked to see the Duke of Hamilton, near whose estate he had come down, for whom he said he had an urgent message.

> *'Hess sank into a deep depression and began to show symptoms of mental instability and illness.'*

Yet Hess's revelation of his identity and his mission changed little. Viewed as a curiosity rather than an emissary, he was interviewed and interrogated – not least by the Duke of Hamilton – but scarcely taken seriously. While Hitler was provoked into an impotent rage by his flight, Churchill refused to change his plan to see the latest Marx brothers' film.[2]

In time, Hess was dispatched, first to the Tower of London, then to a Surrey country house, Mytchett Place near Farnborough. It was soon after his arrival in Surrey that Hess was subjected to a further indignity – the confiscation of his woollen long johns. Oddly, the Ministry of Economic Warfare petitioned the British Intelligence Service to ask permission to examine Hess's underwear, in the hope that 'something of propaganda value' – presumably that he wore something luxurious or embarrassing – might be gleaned. Permission was granted, and the long johns were duly procured, but disappointingly they turned out to be extremely plain and unremarkable, as the head of SIS sniffily noted 'of the cheapest variety'.[3] Their manufacturer, Benger-Ribana from Stuttgart – far from being purveyors of frilly lingerie to the German elite – was mainly responsible for Wehrmacht-issue battledress. With that, the propaganda scheme was quietly dropped, and Hess's long johns disappeared into the archive.

Thereafter, Hess sank into a deep depression and began to show symptoms of mental instability and illness. He grew paranoid, complaining of stomach cramps and persistently accusing his guards of trying to poison him. In mid-June he even attempted suicide by throwing himself over the banisters, succeeding only in breaking his left leg on landing.

Already by that point, only a month after his arrival, Hess would have realised – despite his delusions – that he had failed in his mission. Rather than being lauded as a peacemaker, he was a prisoner and a helpless tool of British propaganda. Bereft of his underwear, he was already being derided as a lunatic.

Rudolf Hess's woollen underwear, 'of the cheapest variety'.

1    Quoted in Peter Padfield, *Hess: The Führer's Disciple* (London, 1991), p. 212.

2    Quoted in ibid., p. 217.

3    Keith Jeffery, *MI6: The History of the Secret Intelligence Service, 1909–1949* (London, 2011), pp. 758–9.

# 73 Knight's Cross, Oak Leaves and Swords

*This military decoration* – one of the highest awarded by the Third Reich – was introduced by Adolf Hitler on 15 July 1941, shortly after his invasion of the Soviet Union. Intended only for the bravest and most distinguished members of the German armed forces, it became the foremost symbol of Nazi Germany's cult of heroism during World War II.

The Iron Cross – *Eisernes Kreuz* – had long been the iconic German military honour. It had originated in the Kingdom of Prussia and was first awarded in 1813, during the 'War of Liberation' against Napoleon, taking its characteristic shape from the

Knight's Cross with Oak Leaves and Swords, one of the highest military decorations in the Third Reich.

black 'Maltese' cross worn by the Teutonic Order of medieval crusading knights. Re-instituted for each major conflict, it was awarded in both the Franco-Prussian War of 1870–1 and World War I; but appeared to meet its end with the German Empire's demise in 1918. However, Hitler re-established the Iron Cross on 1 September 1939, as his forces invaded Poland.

In its 1939 iteration, the Iron Cross initially had four classes; though the highest – the Grand Cross of the Iron Cross – was awarded only once during World War II, to Hermann Göring. Of the remaining three classes, the lowest – Second Class – was awarded for courage or exemplary conduct in combat, and was presented on a red, white and black ribbon, and was worn tucked into the top tunic buttonhole. It was awarded to around two and a half million individuals, including the test pilot Melitta von Stauffenberg, sister-in-law of Claus von Stauffenberg.[1] The Iron Cross First Class, in contrast, took the form of a pin badge, which was worn on the left breast pocket. It was awarded for outstanding bravery and around 300,000 were presented during the war.[2]

---

*'Army slang quipped that those eager for the award – which was worn at the neck – were suffering from "a sore throat".'*

---

Above the Iron Cross First and Second Class came the Knight's Cross of the Iron Cross, which was slightly larger and was worn on a long ribbon at the neck. Replacing the *Pour le Mérite* or 'Blue Max', which had been awarded by the Kaiser, the Knight's Cross could only be conferred by Hitler, and was available to any recipient showing exemplary leadership, regardless of his rank. Among those who received the award were Erwin Rommel for his *Blitzkrieg* victories in France in 1940, and tank ace Michael Wittmann, who was decorated in January 1944, after destroying sixty-six Soviet tanks on the Eastern Front.

As the war progressed, Hitler devised additional grades to reward the further triumphs of his soldiers. In June 1940, a silver oak-leaf cluster was added to the ribbon hanger of the Knight's Cross to create 'The Knight's Cross with Oak Leaves'. Over 800 examples of this grade were awarded from June 1940, and it was colloquially known to soldiers as 'the cauliflower'. Its first recipient was Major-General Eduard Dietl, who commanded the German 3rd Mountain Division in the conquest of Narvik during the Norway campaign.

As Hitler planned his assault on the Soviet Union in 1941, a higher grade of decoration was instituted in anticipation of the heroic efforts required to overcome his great enemy. Crossed swords were added beneath the oak leaf cluster to create 'The Knight's Cross with Oak Leaves and Swords'. Only 159 of these decorations were awarded during the war, one being a posthumous presentation to Admiral Isoroku Yamamoto for his role in commanding the Japanese attack on Pearl Harbor.

The very first example of this award was presented to Luftwaffe air ace Oberstleutnant (Lt.-Col.) Adolf Galland on 21 July 1941. Galland was the perfect choice; a flamboyant

German war hero, he was a veteran of the Condor Legion in the Spanish Civil War, where he had developed his ground-attack skills flying the Heinkel He 51 biplane. He then switched to the more advanced Messerschmitt Bf 109 to fly in a combat role in the French campaign and the Battle of Britain in 1940. Having shot down sixty-nine Allied aircraft by the eve of Operation Barbarossa, his total tally of kills by war's end would be 104. When the commander of the German Fighter Force, Werner Mölders, was killed in an air accident in November 1941, Galland succeeded him as General der Jagdflieger – 'General of Fighter Aircraft'.

When Galland oversaw the use of air power to protect the return of German battleships from western France through the English Channel to their home bases in 1942, he received the next award up the scale: 'The Knight's Cross with Oak Leaves, Swords and Diamonds', which had been devised by Hitler in July 1941. This medal – encrusted with fifty-five diamonds on the oak-leaf spray – was awarded only twenty-seven times during the war; twelve to representatives of the Luftwaffe, eleven to those from the Army, and two each to the Navy and the Waffen-SS.

Field Marshal Rommel wearing his Knight's Cross with Oak Leaves, Swords and Diamonds. Just visible underneath is the *Pour le Mérite* he had won in WWI.

The highest variant, introduced by Hitler in December 1944, was the Golden Oak Leaves, Swords and Diamonds to the Knight's Cross. It was only awarded once, to Oberst (Colonel) Hans-Ulrich Rudel, a Stuka pilot, who was credited with destroying over 500 tanks, mainly on the Eastern Front, and had been shot down no fewer than thirty times.

In all its grades, the Knights Cross was the primary outward symbol of a 'heroic career' in Hitler's armed forces. As such, it was highly prized, but ordinary soldiers were rather more equivocal, mindful that such awards for the ambitious – or the reckless – often came at the expense of their own lives. For this reason, army slang quipped that those eager for the award – which was worn at the neck – were suffering from 'a sore throat'.[3]

1   See C. Mulley, *The Women Who Flew for Hitler* (London, 2017), p. 164.

2   G. Schulze-Wegener, *Das Eiserne Kreuz in der deutschen Geschichte* (Graz, 2012), p. 148.

3   Schulze-Wegener, p. 150.

# 74 *Judenstern*

*Jews have long been subjected to public stigmatisation.* From the Middle Ages to the seventeenth century, from Baghdad to Britain, bells, badges, hats and pendants were variously ordered to be worn by Jews to identify themselves publicly. The Nazi *Judenstern* – or 'Jewish Star', therefore, was heir to a long and hateful tradition.

In the form of a crudely drawn Star of David, the *Judenstern* had featured strongly in Nazi propaganda, most memorably perhaps during the Jewish Boycott of April 1933, when it was daubed on many Jewish-owned shop windows in order to dissuade customers from entering.

> *'The intention was simple, that of further isolating Jews from German society, and spurring popular prejudice.'*

Most notoriously, however, the *Judenstern* was used to identify individual Jews. A yellow cloth badge, with the word '*Jude*' (Jew) written in Hebrew-style lettering in the centre, on a yellow background, the star was ordered to be fixed to the left side of the outermost item of clothing, and was to be worn by all Jews from the age of six, when out in public. Those affected were obliged to purchase the star, at a cost of 10 pfennigs, and sign a declaration that they understood the new regulations. Failure to comply, or covering the star, would incur a fine. Repeat offenders risked a spell in a concentration camp.

The intention was simple, that of further isolating Jews from German society, and spurring popular prejudice. At a stroke, any anonymity that German Jews had previously enjoyed was removed, and their public humiliation was complete.

Though *Judenstern* legislation was already mooted by the Nazis in 1938, following *Kristallnacht*, the introduction of the star was held off, largely for fear of provoking a political response from America. By the time it was introduced in the German Reich, therefore, in the autumn of 1941, such legislation was already in force in the German-occupied areas of Poland and the Soviet Union, as well as in the territories controlled by some of Germany's allies, such as Slovakia. It would subsequently be extended to occupied France, Belgium and Holland, but due to widespread opposition from local authorities and populations, was only incompletely enforced.

The introduction of the *Judenstern* marked something of a watershed in Germany. Though it appears to belong to the earlier period of piecemeal discrimination and persecution – a period in which Jews were successively banned from employing non-Jews, owning radios, keeping pets, sitting on park benches, and a thousand other restrictions – it came at a time when Nazi policy towards the Jews was shifting into a decidedly more murderous phase. Only a month later, in October 1941, the Nazi regime began deporting Reich Jews to the ghettos of Łódź and elsewhere, preparatory to their wholesale extermination. The *Judenstern*, therefore, signified the beginning of the end for German Jewry.

A petty humiliation and a sign of new horrors to come.

# 75 Bells of Lübeck Marienkirche

*They hardly look like bells any more.* The mass of twisted, shattered metal beneath the south spire of St Mary's Church – the Marienkirche – in Lübeck is what is left of the church's oldest bell – the 2-ton 'Sunday Bell' from 1508 – and its largest – the 7-ton 'Pulse Bell' from 1669. The crumpled remains now stand as a memorial to the city's firebombing in 1942.

The bells had sounded together for centuries. Eighteen bells had been installed in a belfry in the south tower and in a flèche above the nave: eleven to give the church its great peal and seven to sound the time. However, on the night before Palm Sunday, 28 March 1942, they all came crashing to the ground. Lübeck was targeted by the RAF; 234 Wellingtons and Stirlings approached from the Baltic Sea and dropped over 400 tons of bombs on the city's old town. According to the German police, over 300 people were killed and 15,000 rendered homeless. The city's ancient heart was burnt out.

The authorities had taken some precautions to protect the elaborate interior of the *Marienkirche*; altarpieces had been removed, artworks and other immovable objects had been packed with sandbags and enclosed in wooden shuttering. But such measures were little help against 25,000 incendiaries. Once the roof had been damaged and the incendiaries penetrated the eaves, the church's wooden structures were swiftly consumed; the high Gothic vaulting collapsed and the twin spires were burnt out.

> *'Some Lübeckers proclaimed that the attack was God's judgement; if so, many did indeed pay for their sins with their lives.'*

It is said that the massive updraught of the fire caused the bells in the tower to ring in a final atonal swansong before they crashed down, shattering the tiled floor beneath. On the ground, the heat of the fires surrounding them softened and deformed their remains. Bell bronze typically begins to melt above 650°C.

The bombing of Lübeck was the first of the RAF's large-scale operations against German civilian targets. On the ground, some Lübeckers proclaimed that the attack was God's judgement; if so, many did indeed pay for the Nazis' sins with their lives. In London, 'Bomber' Harris would not have disagreed; he considered the raid a success, coldly describing the city as 'more like a firelighter than a human habitation'.[1]

Other targets would soon follow for the RAF: Hamburg, Cologne, Kassel, Essen, Darmstadt, Berlin, Schweinfurt, Pforzheim, Dresden, and a thousand other places. In total, Allied air forces would drop some 1.6 million tons of bombs on Germany during the war, fully twenty times the amount dropped on the UK by the Luftwaffe over the same period.[2] The German civilian death toll from aerial bombing was estimated at 600,000. For most Germans on the home front, it would become the defining experience of the war – the war that they had unleashed.

Lübeck was not the first German city to be bombed by the RAF, nor was it the most grievously affected, but it was one of its first large-scale raids. The old port city – and the bells of its Marienkirche – received an early taste of the whirlwind to come.

The shattered, melted bells of the Lübeck Marienkirche.

1 Quoted in Horst Boog, *The Global War: Germany and the Second World War* (Oxford, 2001), p. 565.

2 For statistics see John Ellis, *The World War II Data Book* (London, 2003), pp. 233–5.

# 76 'Goliath' Miniature Tank

*Nazi Germany had a deserved reputation for innovation* in military technology. In this respect, the V-2 rocket or the StG-44 assault rifle are well known, but the 'Goliath' tracked mine is a rather more exotic example.

Properly designated the Sd. Kfz. (or 'special vehicle') 302/303 – and known to the Western Allies as the 'Beetle Tank' – the Goliath was developed in 1940 from an earlier, remote-controlled mine clearance vehicle. Standing only 56 cm tall and 90 cm in length, the 370 kg Goliath was initially powered by twin electric motors, before an uprated 2-cylinder, 2-stroke petrol engine was fitted in 1943. This example, preserved in the technical museum at Sinsheim in Germany, is the earlier, electrically-powered 302 model. On top is the control unit, which was worn by the 'driver' and connected by a 600 m cable, via which the 'tank' could be steered and detonated. Designed to be expendable, the Goliath could deliver a 60 kg explosive charge to its target. Over 7,000 of both models were built.

A surviving 'Goliath' – the future of warfare?

> *'Too fragile and unreliable to be genuinely effective, it was more memorable to Allied soldiers as a captured plaything.'*

Despite substantial teething difficulties, not least the vulnerability of the 'tank' and its control wire to damage from enemy fire, Goliaths were deployed with some moderate success at Sebastopol and against the Allied landings at Anzio. At the Battle of Kursk, for instance, in July 1943, they were used effectively in their original mine-clearing capacity, in support of heavy tanks. Alternatively, during the German suppression of the Warsaw Rising in the summer of 1944, they were employed to some effect in urban siege warfare against enemy barricades.[1] The following spring, they were used once again, this time in resisting a Soviet siege during the battle for Breslau, where they were described by one civilian eye-witness – who had presumably never seen one before – as a 'land torpedo'.[2]

Ultimately, the Goliath is considered to have been a failure. Too fragile and unreliable to be genuinely effective, it was perhaps more memorable to Allied soldiers as a captured plaything than as a real threat. Nonetheless, it did not represent a technological dead-end. After all, as a remote-controlled weapon system, it foreshadowed the development of the modern drone.

American ordnance men examine three captured Goliaths, Normandy, 1944.

---

1   See Robin Cross, *The Battle of Kursk* (London, 1993), p. 163, and Hanns von Krannhals, *Der Warschauer Aufstand 1944* (Frankfurt am Main, 1964), p. 141.

2   Quoted in Horst Gleiss, *Breslauer Apokalypse 1945* (Wedel, 1986), Vol. III, p. 909.

# 77 Sophie Scholl's Matriculation Card

*Sophie Scholl is one of the most famous* active opponents of the Third Reich. Born in 1921, one of six children, she was raised in a Lutheran household in Württemberg in south-western Germany. After initial enthusiasm for National Socialism, she began to reject it by her late teens, spurred by her father's free-thinking criticism of the Nazi regime and the arrest of her brothers in 1937 for membership of a banned scouting group. After finishing school, Scholl became a kindergarten teacher and might have settled – like countless others did – into an 'inward migration', a passive rejection of Nazism. But everything changed when, in the spring of 1942, she was admitted to Munich University.

'Not a joiner': Sophie Scholl's matriculation card.

This document is Sophie Scholl's university registration, or matriculation certificate. Dated from the summer semester of 1942, it gives Scholl's details: her name, date and place of birth – Forchtenberg, 9 May 1921 – as well as her home address – Münsterplatz 33, Ulm – and her term-time address – Dittlerstrasse 10, in the Munich suburb of Solln. Tellingly, the section where a student's Nazi Party membership details would be entered was left blank, as was the section for membership of the National Socialist Students League (NSDStB); she was clearly not a 'joiner'. At bottom right, the dates of Scholl's Reich Labour Service – a precondition for those wishing to study at University – are given as 6 April 1941 to 28 March 1942.

---

*'Everything changed when, in the spring of 1942,
she was admitted to Munich University.'*

---

Scholl intended to study biology and philosophy; however, she soon found herself a member of an active oppositional cell, which would become known as 'The White Rose'. That summer, she found a flyer penned by the White Rose, which – using high-flown prose and religious imagery – called for passive resistance against the Nazi regime. And, when she discovered that one of the authors had been her elder brother, Hans, who was also a student in Munich, she joined the group.

Motivated primarily by religious and philosophical considerations, the White Rose was a small grouping of students – and a professor – at Munich University who began writing and distributing oppositional leaflets in the summer of 1942. In total, they authored six flyers, which variously denounced the Nazi regime for the Holocaust against the Jews, declared that the war was lost, and called for resistance against 'the contemptible tyrant', Hitler.

Emboldened by the fact that they had not been discovered, and enraged by the costly German defeat at Stalingrad, the White Rose stepped up its activities in February 1943, distributing its flyers across Germany and even daubing slogans on Munich walls. Their final flyer, issued that month, upped the rhetoric, describing Hitler as a 'dilettante', demanding the smashing of National Socialist terror, and declaring that 'the day of reckoning has come'.

On the morning of 18 February 1943, Sophie and Hans Scholl came to the university with a briefcase full of leaflets, which they left in stairwells and empty hallways for the students to discover. Before leaving, Sophie decided to get rid the last of the batch and so hurriedly climbed to the second floor and threw the flyers over the balustrade into the atrium. In doing so, she was spotted by the university janitor and reported to the Gestapo. That same afternoon, she was arrested.

Four days later, Sophie and two other members of the White Rose, her brother Hans and Christoph Probst, were arraigned before the notorious 'People's Court' in Munich – the first of three related trials – on charges of high treason and undermining the war effort. Harangued by the Third Reich's infamous 'hanging judge', Roland Freisler, they were, inevitably, found guilty and, unusually, were ordered to be executed by guillotine that very afternoon.

Sophie went to her death in a philosophical frame of mind: 'Such a fine, sunny day, and I have to go,' she said, 'but what does my death matter, if through us, thousands of people are awakened and stirred to action?' The executioner would later recall that he had never seen someone die with such bravery as Sophie Scholl.[1] She was twenty-one years old.

That last hope – that the people might be 'stirred to action' – would ultimately prove misplaced; it would be military defeat, rather than a popular uprising, that would bring about the demise of Nazism. But Sophie Scholl's principled resistance to tyranny would echo far beyond Munich. Those same leaflets that she threw into the university atrium would be smuggled out of the country, reprinted in their thousands and, that summer, dropped over Germany by the RAF.[2]

Sophie Scholl

1  'Hinrichtungen im Dreiminutentakt' (article about executioner Johann Reichart), *Augsburger Allgemeine,* 14 November 1996.

2  W. Benz & W. Pehle (eds), *Encyclopedia of German Resistance to the Nazi Movement* (New York, 1997), p. 253.

# 78 Tiger I Tank

*The Tiger I tank illustrated overleaf – now known as 'Tiger 131' –* was captured intact by British forces in April 1943, in Tunisia, when a round from a Churchill tank wedged beneath the barrel and jammed the turret traverse, rendering the monster defenceless. Sent to the UK for inspection, it was restored after the war and is now kept as a star attraction at the Bovington Tank Museum in Dorset. It is the last remaining functioning example of the iconic German heavy tank of World War II.

Tanks were central to Germany's military tactics – popularly known as *Blitzkrieg*. The invasions of Poland, the Low Countries and France in 1939–40 had been led by columns of armoured vehicles that had pierced Allied front lines and rapidly overcome resistance. But German tanks of the period were not the armoured behemoths of later in the war: the mainstay of tank forces used in the French campaign, for instance, was the decidedly modest Mark II, which weighed in at barely 9 tons.[1]

Yet, when Hitler's forces turned east and invaded the Soviet Union in 1941, hoping to repeat their *Blitzkrieg* successes, they got a nasty surprise. There they faced Soviet tanks – the heavy KV-1 and medum T-34 – which seemed worryingly immune to their anti-tank fire, were more manoeuvrable, and could inflict significant damage with their powerful 76.2 mm guns. Despite its overall success in 1941, German armour suddenly seemed less invincible than it had earlier appeared. The answer, according to German tank designers, was to build bigger.

> 'Tiger tanks were always outnumbered by their opponents
> and eventually that weight of numbers proved telling.'

Though the Panther Tank (Panzer Mk V) would be the direct product of those early encounters with Soviet tanks – incorporating heavy, sloping armour, a powerful Maybach V-12 engine and a potent 75 mm gun – the existing plans for another German heavy tank, the Tiger I (Pz. Kpfw. VI), were also amended in response. Produced by Henschel & Co., of Kassel, the Tiger boasted an uprated 88 mm gun, able to penetrate a T-34's turret from around 1,800 metres, as well as 100 mm frontal armour which was impervious to all but close range artillery. Those amendments came at the cost of added weight, however, and at a massive 57 tons, the Tiger I was the heaviest tank in service when it made its combat debut on the Eastern Front in 1942.

The world's last surviving Tiger I tank in running order can be seen at Bovington Tank Museum in Dorset, UK.

With these new 'breakthrough tanks', Hitler had reason to be confident that his forces would no longer be halted. But when the Tiger had its baptism of fire, near Leningrad on 29 August 1942, its shortcomings were made swiftly apparent, with two of the four Tigers engaged becoming bogged down in marshy ground.[2] Rushed into service, the Tigers also suffered significant teething problems, particularly as their tremendous weight put huge strain on the suspension and gear-train, and made battlefield recovery difficult. In addition, their piecemeal deployment across all theatres and fronts made for a debilitating shortage of spare parts and mechanical support. Though they proved their worth in combat, with their 88 mm gun being particularly effective, the over-engineered Tigers were difficult to keep in the field. Indeed, they only reached the same levels of maintenance and repair as their stable-mates, such as the Panzer Mk IV, by the middle of 1944, nearly two years after their debut.[3]

The Tiger's first major test would come in the monumental battle at Kursk in July 1943, where some 7,000 tanks were deployed either side of a vast salient. While the Germans had delayed their attack, wanting to maximise the numbers of Tigers and other new tanks available to them, the Soviets had taken the opportunity to prepare their defences well, using trenches and minefields to slow the expected German advance. Heavily outnumbered, the German assault faltered, and when the Red Army counter-attacked with its T-34s, carnage ensued, with hundreds of tanks destroyed.

Despite the defeat, the Tigers performed rather well at Kursk: of the 120 that were sent into battle, few were destroyed, though breakdowns meant that only a handful were still operational at the end of the battle. They certainly proved a formidable foe, as one T-34 commander recalled:

His first shot blew a hole in the side of my tank, his second hit my axle. At a range of half a kilometre I fired at him with a special calibre shell, but it bounced off him . . . It didn't penetrate his armour. At literally 300 metres I fired my second shell – same result. Then he started looking for me, turning his turret to see where I was. I told my driver to reverse fast and we hid in some trees.[4]

Despite such prowess in combat, the primary problem that the Tiger tanks had was their sheer lack of numbers. Tigers were expensive both in material and labour, and consequently costs were prohibitive: at 300,000 RM per unit, Tigers were around five times more expensive to produce than American M4 Shermans or T-34s.[5] As a result, production numbers could never match those of their Soviet or American rivals: in total 1,350 Tiger Is were built, compared to around 50,000 for the M4 Sherman and nearly 60,000 for the T-34. The Soviets produced as many T-34s in a month as the Germans produced Tigers in three years.[6]

Allied vehicles pass a Tiger I abandoned in a Tunisian ditch early in 1943.

One engagement exemplified the problem. In the summer of 1944, following the Allied landings in northern France, German tank aces, such as Michael Wittmann, who had gained tremendous experience on the Eastern Front, began to take a heavy toll of Allied armour. At Villers-Bocage in Normandy, for example, Wittmann commanded a company of six Tiger tanks and knocked out some fourteen Shermans and Cromwells of the British 7th Armoured Division with ease, in the process raising his own overall tally of kills to 138. Two months later, however, Wittmann was ambushed by eight British Shermans. He destroyed three, but the other five combined their fire and blew his Tiger apart.

As Wittmann's fate showed, the lesson of tank warfare in World War II was that quantity could overwhelm quality. For all their firepower and technological ingenuity, Tiger tanks were always outnumbered by their opponents and eventually that weight of numbers proved telling.

1   Heinz Guderian, *Panzer Leader* (London, 1952), p. 472.

2   T. Jentz & H. Doyle, *Tiger I Heavy Tank: 1942–45* (Oxford, 1993), p. 21.

3   T. Jentz, *Panzertruppen 2: The Complete Guide to the Creation & Combat Employment of Germany's Tank Force 1943–1945* (Atglen, PA, 1998), p. 202.

4   Quoted in L. Clark, *Kursk* (London, 2011), pp. 239–40.

5   W. Spielberger, *Der Panzerkampfwagen Tiger und seine Abarten* (Stuttgart, 1997), p. 106.

6   Ellis, *World War II Databook*, pp. 303–4.

# 79 Wannsee Villa

*Had it not been for the events of 20 January 1942,* the elegant lakeside villa at 56 Am Grossen Wannsee would have remained in obscurity and would now likely be home to a wealthy businessman or banker. But history wanted it otherwise, and the villa – for all its beauty – has become one of the most infamous buildings in the world.

Built in 1914 for a Berlin industrialist, Ernst Marlier, it was designed in the Italian style by the renowned architect Paul Baumgarten. Three stories, with a garden terrace down to the lake, it occupied a prime site, 20 km south-west of the centre of Berlin and surrounded by woodland and the waterways of the Havel. Marlier did not enjoy it for long, however. Exposed as a fraudster, he found himself in financial difficulties after World War I, and was forced to sell the house in 1921 to another industrialist, Friedrich Minoux, for the sum of 2.3 million Marks – then about $30,000 or £7,500.

> 'The Wannsee villa has become one of the most infamous buildings in the world.'

The villa's new owner was scarcely more upstanding than the last. Minoux made a great deal of money buying up failing businesses during the hyperinflation of 1923 and became a notable figure in interwar German politics, dabbling as a deal-maker between the political right and their anti-republican allies. He even met Hitler in Munich in 1923, but was alarmed by the latter's anti-Semitic and revolutionary intentions. Eventually, Minoux's sharp practices caught up with him and in 1940 he was arrested on fraud charges. Sentenced the following year to five years' imprisonment, and seeking to offset a looming fine, he sold the Wannsee villa – to the SS – for 1.95 million Reichsmarks.

Though the villa's new owner was formally the SS subsidiary Nordhav Foundation, its real master was Reinhard Heydrich, Himmler's deputy and the head of the SS security service, the Sicherheitsdienst. Heydrich swiftly converted the villa into a guest house for the SS, to be used by visiting dignitaries or senior personnel with business in the capital. It is often suggested that he also planned to use it as his own Berlin residence – and given that the first purchase of the Nordhav Foundation had been an estate on the Baltic island of Fehmarn, which he used as a holiday home, it is quite possible that he intended a similarly neat solution for the Wannsee villa.

But notoriety was beckoning. Late in 1941, Heydrich invited thirteen senior civil servants – representing the Party, the Gestapo, the Foreign, Justice and Interior

The Wannsee Villa: a beautiful place for an odious act.

Ministries, as well as SS and SD personnel – to a top secret meeting at the villa, where the 'Final Solution of the Jewish Question' would be discussed.[1] After a number of postponements, the group finally convened – in the dining room – at midday on 20 January 1942. Heydrich spoke for about an hour, then thirty minutes of questions and discussion followed before the meeting was brought to a close with a buffet lunch.

Though it is often lazily described as a 'planning meeting' for the Holocaust, the 'Wannsee Conference' was in fact something a little more complex. Given that the Holocaust was already effectively under way, the conference might more accurately be described as an exercise in administrative infighting.[2] Before an audience of potential rivals, Heydrich was setting out his bona fides as the prime mover in Nazi policy towards the Jews, and challenging those present to acquiesce. The subtext was that they would all be working together, but he was in charge, and nobody would be able to claim later that they had understood things differently.

Ironically, the dark chapter of the Wannsee Conference might never have been preserved were it not for the naked ambition of one of its participants. Heydrich sent out the fifteen-page minutes of the meeting – via his factotum Adolf Eichmann – to those who had been present. But while most of the copies of those minutes were subsequently destroyed, one set – that of an under-secretary in the Foreign Ministry, Martin Luther – survived, to be discovered in the archive in 1947. The reason for the document's survival was that Luther had been caught scheming against his superior, Foreign Minister Joachim von Ribbentrop, and had been sent to a concentration camp in 1944, and so had been unable to 'weed' his filing cabinet of sensitive material at war's end.

After the war, the Wannsee villa was used by the Red Army, then as a socialist training college, and then as a school. The suggestion that it should be made into an exhibition and education site for the Holocaust was first aired in 1966 by Auschwitz survivor and historian Joseph Wulf; however, the idea initially gained little traction. Finally, in 1992, the Wannsee villa opened as a memorial and museum, documenting the conference that took place within its walls and the wider history of the Holocaust.

| L a n d | Zahl |
|---|---|
| **A.** Altreich | 131.800 |
| Ostmark | 43.700 |
| Ostgebiete | 420.000 |
| Generalgouvernement | 2.284.000 |
| Bialystok | 400.000 |
| Protektorat Böhmen und Mähren | 74.200 |
| Estland      – judenfrei – | |
| Lettland | 3.500 |
| Litauen | 34.000 |
| Belgien | 43.000 |
| Dänemark | 5.600 |
| Frankreich / Besetztes Gebiet | 165.000 |
| Unbesetztes Gebiet | 700.000 |
| Griechenland | 69.600 |
| Niederlande | 160.800 |
| Norwegen | 1.300 |
| | |
| **B.** Bulgarien | 48.000 |
| England | 330.000 |
| Finnland | 2.300 |
| Irland | 4.000 |
| Italien einschl. Sardinien | 58.000 |
| Albanien | 200 |
| Kroatien | 40.000 |
| Portugal | 3.000 |
| Rumänien einschl. Bessarabien | 342.000 |
| Schweden | 8.000 |
| Schweiz | 18.000 |
| Serbien | 10.000 |
| Slowakei | 88.000 |
| Spanien | 6.000 |
| Türkei (europ. Teil) | 55.500 |
| Ungarn | 742.800 |
| UdSSR | 5.000.000 |
|    Ukraine     2.994.684 | |
|    Weißrußland aus- | |
|    schl. Bialystok     446.484 | |
| Zusammen:    über | 11.000.000 |

A page from the Wannsee Protocol – listing Jewish populations across Europe.

1 Text of Heydrich letter to Martin Luther, 29 November 1941, in Christa Schikora et al., *Die Wannsee-Konferenz und der Völkermord an den europäischen Juden* (Berlin, 2006), p. 114.

2 See Mark Roseman, *The Lake, The Villa, The Meeting: Wannsee and the Final Solution* (London, 2002).

# 80 Zyklon-B Canister

*Hydrogen cyanide was originally developed* in the late nineteenth century for use as a pesticide. By the early 1920s, it was produced in a white pellet form – with the addition of a warning eye-irritant – under the trade-name Zyklon-B, or 'Cyclone-B', and was awarded a German patent in 1926.

Prior to 1942, Zyklon-B was still used as a pesticide and fumigation agent. In Germany, it was produced under licence by two plants, as a by-product from the processing of sugar beet. With the chemical tell-tale added, Zyklon-B was distributed across 'Greater Germany' for delousing clothes and for the disinfection of agricultural and industrial buildings. Distribution was divided, with the Frankfurt firm of Heerdt-Lingler responsible for the western half of the country, and Tesch & Stabenow of Hamburg responsible for the eastern half.

Given that the Nazis viewed their racial enemies as little more than vermin, it is brutally logical that Zyklon-B would, in time, also be used for the killing of human beings. The first experimental instance of killing using Zyklon-B, it appears, was in early September 1941, in the main camp at Auschwitz, when a group of Soviet POWs, along with some Polish prisoners, were gassed in the cellar of Block 11 – the

A used Zyklon-B canister, from the memorial site at Auschwitz.

199

punishment block. That first experiment was not an overwhelming success. As a Polish prisoner, August Kowalczyk, recalled, the gassing was not entirely effective – either because insufficient Zyklon-B had been used, or the resulting gas had escaped – and some of the prisoners were still alive the following morning.[1] Nonetheless, soon after, a second experimental killing took place, with the camp commandant Rudolf Höss in attendance.[2]

Despite such blunders, the process of killing with Zyklon-B was soon refined until it was simple and relatively swift. Victims would be ordered to strip before entering a gas chamber, often disguised as a shower block, with a gas-proof door sealed behind them. Then, Zyklon-B pellets would be dropped from a canister through a hatch in the roof or the wall. With exposure to heat and moisture, the pellets would quickly degrade and give off hydrogen cyanide gas. For those victims closest to the pellets, death would occur within minutes; those further away took longer to succumb.[3] For all of them, massive cell death caused loss of consciousness followed by cardiac arrest. Eye-witness testimony suggests that all of the victims were dead within around fifteen minutes, their bodies often exhibiting a tell-tale pink colouration, sometimes with blue blotches on the skin caused by cyanosis.

---

*'For those victims closest to the pellets, death would occur within minutes; those further away took longer to succumb.'*

---

Within months of those first experiments, gassing with Zyklon-B became the preferred method of mass killing at the larger, nearby facility of Auschwitz II-Birkenau. The extermination camp at Majdanek followed suit and other smaller-scale killings using the product took place at the concentration camps at Mauthausen, Ravensbrück, Dachau and Buchenwald. In all, around 1 million people were murdered by the Germans using it, mostly at Auschwitz II-Birkenau. That camp alone would consume over 24 tons of Zyklon-B between 1942 and 1945.[4]

Ironically, the inventor of Zyklon-B, Walter Heerdt, was an opponent of the Nazis, who was removed from all positions of influence in 1942. His rival, the chemical's distributor Bruno Tesch, was less circumspect. Tried as a war criminal in 1946, Tesch would claim that he had been unaware of the murderous purpose to which his deliveries had been put – but his defence was fatally undermined when it was shown that he had visited Auschwitz to brief SS guards on Zyklon-B's use.[5] Tesch was hanged in Hamelin Prison in May 1946.

1  Laurence Rees, *The Holocaust* (London, 2017), p. 227.

2  Christopher Browning, *The Origins of the Final Solution: The Evolution of Nazi Jewish Policy, 1939–1942* (London, 2004), pp. 356–7.

3  Peter Hayes, *From Cooperation to Complicity: Degussa in the Third Reich* (Cambridge, 2004), p. 273.

4  Ibid., pp. 295–6.

5  Angelika Ebbinghaus, 'Der Prozeß gegen Tesch & Stabenow', in *Zeitschrift für Sozialgeschichte*, Vol. 13 (1998), p. 22.

# 81 Death Card

*Death is the constant companion of warfare,* and never more so than in the wanton slaughter of World War II. The total German death toll from the conflict is not known, but estimates range between 7 and 8 million, with the vast majority being military deaths.[1]

In such circumstances 'death cards' became very common during the Third Reich. The *Totenzettel*, or 'death card', was a long-established part of Catholic funeral culture in Germany and would be presented to mourners at the church service for the fallen, and sent out to those who could not attend, to act as a *memento mori*.

Death cards did not have a standard format, but ordinarily consisted of a photograph of the deceased (usually in uniform), along with their life dates and place of death. In addition, a short biography might be added, perhaps giving their peacetime occupation, and the military unit in which they served. Some were extremely simple and modest; others were double-sided, with facsimiles of Christ on the Cross, a short prayer, and the names of the bereaved. This example commemorated the death of a 21-year-old Wehrmacht private, who was killed west of Moscow on New Year's Day 1942.

A reminder of one of the many.

Beyond the private importance of the death card, they were also politically significant. With a death toll approaching 10 per cent of the population, few German families were untouched by the war and that posed a profound political challenge to the Nazi regime regarding how to 'manage' the growing undercurrent of grief and mourning. To this end, a narrative of heroism was propagated, so that every military death might be celebrated as a hero's fall, fighting in defence of Hitler's Germany. Many death cards, therefore, bore slogans on this idea of a heroic death – the *Heldentod*. This was understandable, perhaps, but it was a theme that, under Goebbels's guiding hand, would reach ridiculous proportions, with soldiers being 'fulfilled' only by their own demise.[2] Nazism was beginning to resemble a death cult.

> *'For most of the bereaved, the humble death card was the only memento that they had.'*

Despite such propaganda flourishes, from 1941 onwards the growing numbers of military dead began to prove embarrassing for the Nazi regime. The response was to limit the number of obituaries that each daily newspaper could carry, and later to prescribe what text could be used in a death notice, effectively confining the message to the single phrase 'For *Führer*, People and Reich', thereby preventing any implied criticism of the regime.[3] However, crucially, the text on death cards was not controlled, and though overt opposition would not be printed, 'criticism by omission' was still possible. It is notable, for example, that mention of Hitler's name on a death card, while not uncommon in 1940, had become very rare by 1944.

For the vast majority, of course, the death of a loved one was scarcely viewed as an opportunity to criticise the Nazi regime. And a death card, far from being seen as a vehicle for that criticism, was instead a treasured memento of a life lost. In fact, given that all but a handful of the German military dead in World War II were buried on the battlefields where they fell, for most of the bereaved the humble death card was the only memento that they had.

1   Data from the US National World War II Museum: www.nationalww2museum.org/learn/education/for-students/ww2-history/ww2-by-the-numbers/world-wide-deaths.html.

2   Goebbels, quoted in Moorhouse, *Berlin at War*, p. 260.

3   Ibid., p. 257.

# 82 Gate house at Birkenau

*Known as 'The Gate of Death'*, the gate house at Birkenau extermination camp – with the railway line beneath – is one of the most grimly iconic images of the Third Reich, one that has come to symbolise the industrialised mass murder of the Jews by the Nazi regime.

The railway tracks leading to the gate house at Birkenau extermination camp.

The camp at Birkenau – formally known as 'Auschwitz II-Birkenau' – was begun in October 1941, initially as an overflow from the concentration camp at Auschwitz I, a short distance away. It was intended, at first, as a labour camp, to exploit the countless Soviet POWs who had fallen into German hands following the success of Operation Barbarossa. Constructed over the winter of 1941/2, Birkenau was huge: first designed for a capacity of 50,000 prisoners, which was swiftly raised to 200,000,[1] it spread over 175 hectares and contained over 300 buildings, mostly wooden stable blocks, which – though designed for 52 horses – could each be made to accommodate over 400 human beings.[2]

When it was decided that Soviet POWs might be more useful sent direct to the Reich as slave labourers, however, Birkenau was repurposed. Given its comparative remoteness from Auschwitz I, away from prying eyes, it was thought suitable as a killing centre for Jews and those deemed unable to work. After receiving an initial transport, of 1,000 Slovak Jews, in late March 1942, its first primitive gas chambers – bricked-up cottages, known as the 'Little Red House' and the 'Little White House' – were soon operational, and were used to 'process' around 800 prisoners at a time. By the summer, the camp's killing capacity had already been massively increased, with the construction of a further four purpose-built gas chambers and crematoria.

---

> *'Birkenau was a factory of death, in which it is estimated around a million people were killed.'*

---

By that time, the camp's basic method of operation had already been established, but in the spring of 1944, that method would be perfected with the laying of the railway line beneath the infamous gate, connecting the area known as 'the ramp', inside the camp, with the branch line beyond. Arriving transports from across occupied Europe could now be brought straight into the Birkenau camp for their human contents to be 'sorted' by SS doctors on the ramp, directly off the trains. Italian inmate Primo Levi described the scene:

> The climax of the journey came suddenly. The door opened with a crash, and the dark echoed with outlandish orders in that curt, barbaric barking of Germans in command . . . In less than ten minutes all the fit men had been collected together in a group. What happened to the others, to the women, to the children, to the old men, we could establish neither then nor later. The night swallowed them up.[3]

What Levi did not know was that, while his group was sent to the filthy barrack blocks, those who were deemed unfit for work – 82 per cent of those on board – were taken straight to their deaths.[4] Within perhaps an hour of arrival, the condemned would be stripped, herded into the gas chambers and killed using Zyklon B. Thereafter, their bodies would be processed: gold teeth would be extracted, women's hair shaved, and any prosthetic limbs removed, before the remains were cremated. Their ashes would then be washed into a nearby river, used as fertiliser, or dumped into open pits. They were but a few of the million or so who are estimated to have been killed at Birkenau.

For the remainder – rarely more than 20 per cent of any transport – a brutalised existence awaited, of hard labour, starvation, disease and maltreatment in horrific conditions, with lice-ridden, overcrowded barracks and scant access to running water. Though the prisoners were often taken out to work in nearby factories, the strongest amongst them were used in the so-called *Sonderkommando*, and had the spirit-crushing task of dragging the bodies out of the gas chambers and into the crematoria. As material witnesses of genocide, they were killed off every few months and replaced. As one of the few survivors recalled, Birkenau was notorious: 'Even experienced Auschwitz inmates were frightened of the place.'[5]

Birkenau has rightly become synonymous with the Holocaust; indeed with the highest death toll and the longest period of operation, it was *the* central camp in that murderous process. But it should not be forgotten that it was also a hideous hybrid. As well as its killing facilities, it contained a so-called 'Family Camp', a 'Women's Camp', a 'Roma Camp', as well as countless barracks housing many thousands of emaciated slave labourers, all a stone's throw away from the gas chambers and the crematoria. It was at Birkenau – beyond that infamous gate – that Nazi Germany's intertwined policies of the industrial exploitation of Jews, and their extermination, became a monstrous reality.

'Selection' on the ramp at Birkenau, with the gate in the distance.

1 Steinbacher, *Auschwitz*, p. 89.

2 K. Smoleń, *Auschwitz-Birkenau State Museum in Oświęcim* (Oświęcim, 2014), p. 23.

3 P. Levi, *Survival in Auschwitz* (New York, 1958), pp. 19–20.

4 Friedländer, *The Years of Extermination*, p. 504 & 768 fn. 115.

5 A. Burger, *The Devil's Workshop* (Barnsley, 2009), p. 49.

# 83 Treblinka Brooch

*This humble brass rose brooch, barely five centimetres across,* bent and buckled by time, is a witness to catastrophe. It was discovered in 2013 at the German extermination camp at Treblinka, north-east of the Polish capital, Warsaw. Its former owner, one must presume, was one of the hundreds of thousands – mainly Polish Jews – who were murdered at the camp.

Treblinka is much less known than the extermination camp at Auschwitz-Birkenau. Part of this is down to the circumstances of its discovery; whereas the Auschwitz complex was overrun almost intact by the Soviets in January 1945 – thereby revealing its full horror to the world – Treblinka had already been totally dismantled by the Nazis in the winter of 1943–4, so its Soviet liberators found little of substance remaining. Thus, while Auschwitz-Birkenau became the world's primary site of Holocaust commemoration, Treblinka slipped from memory; its killing fields – once strewn with bones, teeth and assorted fragments of lives[1] – were initially not even placed under legal protection.

A fragment of a life: the Treblinka rose brooch, found in 2013.

Yet, despite its comparative obscurity, Treblinka is profoundly significant. Its death toll – estimated at 900,000[2] – is second only to Auschwitz-Birkenau in magnitude. Moreover, unlike Auschwitz-Birkenau, Treblinka was solely and exclusively devoted to the Nazis' process of industrialised mass killing, with no labour function to complicate the business of extermination. Everything at the site – as at its sister camps Bełżec and Sobibór – was geared towards the rapid murder of arriving Jews and the swift, effective exploitation of their possessions.

Prisoners arrived at Treblinka by train. They stepped out into a reception area made to look like a train station, complete with fake timetables and a ticket office. They were told that they were there to be deloused before being sent on to their destination, a labour camp further east.

*'On average, over 2,000 people were killed at Treblinka every day.'*

Ordered to strip and relieved of their possessions, the prisoners were separated by sex and herded along a high-walled pathway into the interior of the camp, goaded by SS guards and spurred by snarling guard-dogs. There, before each batch could catch their breath, they found themselves in a large gas chamber. The heavy steel door slammed shut behind them, and as panic rose they would have heard an engine start outside – the engine whose exhaust fumes would kill them. After around 20–30 minutes, the doors would be opened and small teams of prisoners would begin hauling out the corpses, which would be tipped into mass graves and later cremated on vast pyres.

Meanwhile, the victims' possessions – still strewn across the reception yard – would be sorted by another team of prisoners: items of use such as clothing or bedding would be baled up for transport back to Germany, while all personal effects, photographs, passports – even the name tags in clothes – would be burnt. As one survivor recalled, the instructions boiled down to one word: 'Sort!'

> This involved scouring the mountain of objects for eyeglasses, spoons, shavers, watches, cigarette cases and other personal effects, and placing them in suitcases according to type. Our contingent also sorted clothing, shoes and bedding, which we laid on the ground in sheets of different colours. We were to search every object we picked up painstakingly – emptying the pockets, removing every indication of manufacturer or owner, and squeezing each bit of clothing in case diamonds, gold coins or paper money were sewn inside.[3]

The entire process lasted little more than an hour, and often a second or third trainload of unfortunates was idling in the nearby sidings, waiting to be 'processed'. On average – over the fifteen months that Treblinka was in operation – over 2,000 people were killed there every day.

It is not known which of Treblinka's victims owned the brooch, or indeed when he or she arrived at the camp. It is also unclear how the brooch came to be found in the

The Treblinka memorial site today.

vicinity of the gas chamber. It may be that it was of such sentimental value that it was taken into the gas chamber by its owner, and was dislodged as the bodies were being disposed of. Equally, it could be that it was moved during the chaos of the German clearing of the camp in the winter of 1943, or during the immediate post-war period in which the site was afforded little protection from looters.

However it found its way there, the brooch was discovered among the rubble from the gas chamber during an excavation by a British team from Staffordshire University's Centre for Archaeology. Today it is on display in the small museum at Treblinka, a poignant human remnant from an inhuman act.

1   Vassili Grossman, *The Years of War: 1941–1945* (Moscow, 1946), pp. 406–7.

2   Gitta Sereny, *Into that Darkness* (London, 1974), p. 21.

3   Samuel Willenberg, *Revolt in Treblinka* (Warsaw, 1992), p. 31.

# 84 Demyansk Shield

*Nazi Germany's system of military awards* was curiously eclectic. As a reward for valour, the Iron Cross (and its variants) are well known, but other awards were made with an often bizarre mixture of badges, medals and cuff bands.

In addition, arm shields – like this one, the Demyansk Shield – became a common way of commemorating a particular engagement. The Demyansk Shield was 91 mm high, made of zinc, and was worn on the left upper arm. Above the date '1942', it showed crossed swords and an approaching aircraft, beneath the Nazi eagle and swastika nestling between two pill-boxes. Across the centre was the word 'Demjansk'.

The campaign that it commemorated was an encirclement battle early in 1942, centring on the Russian town of Demyansk, approximately half-way between Moscow and Leningrad, where some 100,000 German troops had been cut off by a Red Army counter-offensive. For eleven weeks, from early February to mid-April 1942, five German Army infantry divisions, along with the SS *Totenkopf* Division and other assorted units, held out against repeated Soviet attacks in temperatures down to −40 °C. They were maintained, in a 'pocket' some 40 km wide, by a Luftwaffe airlift which brought in nearly 25,000 tons of supplies over 14,000 sorties,[1] and were relieved when neighbouring forces freed a land corridor through which they could be supplied and reinforced. Thereafter Demyansk would remain in German hands for a further ten months.

---

*'Demyansk signified the looming humbling of German military force.'*

---

Understandably perhaps, Hitler viewed the holding of Demyansk as a brilliant tactical victory, a military success that not only showcased Germany's warrior spirit but had also tied down fully five Soviet armies. In April 1943, therefore, when German morale was in dire need of a fillip following the defeat at Stalingrad, he decreed that the Demyansk Shield would be awarded to all those soldiers who had served in the pocket for sixty days, or to airmen who had flown a minimum of fifty combat or supply missions in the theatre. In a sense, therefore, Demyansk – a story of German forces encircled by the enemy, but ably supplied by the Luftwaffe, before being relieved and reinforced – was used to provide a public counter-narrative to the bloody debacle at Stalingrad, which by then had only recently unfolded.

Yet, whatever message the German High Command might have told themselves, Demyansk was certainly instructive. It was, for one thing, symptomatic of Hitler's desire to hold on to territory for reasons of prestige rather than military necessity – a tendency that would prove hugely wasteful over the remaining two years of the war. Moreover, Demyansk also signified the looming humbling of German military force. As an encirclement battle, it was the sort of engagement in which Hitler's armies had excelled in the early advances against the Red Army. But now it was the Wehrmacht that was being encircled. At Demyansk, they fought themselves free, but such successes would become increasingly rare.

Demyansk, a taste of things to come.

1   Robert Forczyk, *Demyansk 1942–43* (Oxford, 2012), p. 56; figures are for Demyansk and the smaller pocket nearby at Kholm.

# 85 Panzerfaust Anti-Tank Weapon

*The Panzerfaust, literally meaning 'tank fist'*, was a cheap, single-shot, recoilless grenade-launcher deployed by the German Army from 1943 onwards. Issued to the Wehrmacht as well as to Volkssturm – 'People's Storm' (Germany's Home Guard) – conscripts, it was the first disposable anti-tank weapon.

The armour-busting punch of the Panzerfaust came from its shaped-charge warhead, which focused its explosive power, creating a high-pressure, high-temperature jet of molten metal which would penetrate the dense steel armour of a tank. The shaped charge used the principle of the 'Munroe Effect', which had first been observed in the 1880s and was given a military application in 1935. It would see practical use in the American M1 bazooka, which debuted during the North African campaign, in November 1942. Speaking of the technology earlier that year, Hitler had proclaimed that 'the hollow charge means the death of the tank'.[1]

Combining captured American bazookas with their own research, German armourers quickly developed their own versions of the weapon – the Panzerschreck – meaning 'Tank Fright', which fired an 88mm rocket, and the smaller, disposable Panzerfaust. Intended for one man, single-shot use, the Panzerfaust was very simple, consisting of an 80cm steel tube, containing a simple firing mechanism that used black powder as a propellant. Held under the arm and aimed over a primitive steel sight, the weapon was fired by the push of a lever, with the blast of the propellant charge from the rear of the tube compensating for the recoil. Range varied – with early models restricted to 30 metres, and later versions extending that to 150 metres – but in practice the Panzerfaust was most usually fired from as close to the target as its operator dared.

The *Panzerfaust* anti-tank weapon.

211

## 'Hitler proclaimed that "the hollow charge means the death of the tank"

For all its simplicity, the Panzerfaust was remarkably effective and could penetrate the armour of any tank or armoured vehicle of the period, spraying a deadly spall of molten metal into the interior. A single shot from a Panzerfaust normally sufficed to stop a 30-ton enemy tank in its tracks. Most importantly, perhaps, it could be operated with scarcely any training: by new recruits, Hitler Youth boys, even housewives. As Soviet Marshal Ivan Koniev noted, in Berlin in April 1945, a German with a Panzerfaust was 'a dangerous opponent', as it was 'one of those weapons that lends a feeling of self-confidence to an untrained infantryman: he is scarcely a soldier, yet he is capable of achieving a feat of arms'.[2]

It is no surprise, perhaps, that some 6.5 million Panzerfausts were manufactured by the Germans in the final two years of the war, and that it became one of the most common weapons used in the dying days of the Third Reich.

No uniforms, no kit, a single Panzerfaust each: three Volkssturm men await their fate.

1   Trevor-Roper, *Hitler's Table Talk, 1941–1944* (London, 2000), p. 177.

2   Diary of Ivan Koniev, quoted in P. Gosztony, *Der Kampf um Berlin 1945 in Augenzeugenberichten* (Düsseldorf, 1970), pp. 264–5.

# 86 Reinhard Heydrich Postage Stamp

*When Reinhard Heydrich succumbed* to his wounds in early June 1942, he became the highest-ranking official of the Third Reich to fall victim to assassination.

Heydrich was born in 1904 in Halle, Saxony, and served as an officer in the German Navy in the 1920s before rising swiftly in the ranks of the SS, becoming Himmler's second-in-command and then chief of the SS Security Service – the Sicherheitsdienst (SD) – in 1936. Renowned for his ambition and his cold, humourless demeanour, he was appointed Deputy *Reichsprotektor* of Bohemia and Moravia in September 1941, responsible for the 'pacification' of the German-occupied Czech lands. Referring

A German postage stamp commemorating the death of Reinhard Heydrich.

to the Czechs as 'vermin', he had nearly 100 prisoners executed within days of his arrival.[1] Little wonder that he would become known as the 'Butcher of Prague'.

By the following summer, Heydrich's success in suppressing Czech opposition left the Czech government-in-exile in London with a problem. Facing criticism that his countrymen were working too willingly for the Germans, the exile Czech leader, Edvard Beneš was keen for a spectacular demonstration of Czech resistance and suggested striking at Heydrich himself.

## 'Even in death, Heydrich was still exploiting them.'

In due course, Czech agents – Jozef Gabčik and Jan Kubiš – who had been trained by the British Special Operations Executive, were parachuted into Bohemia to carry out 'Operation Anthropoid', the assassination of Reinhard Heydrich. They intercepted their target on 27 May 1942, while he was being driven into Prague in his open-top Mercedes. As the car slowed down to negotiate a bend in the road, Gabčik pointed a submachine gun at Heydrich, but the weapon jammed; next Kubiš threw a grenade, which exploded beneath the rear of the car. The attackers then made their escape. Suffering from splinter wounds, Heydrich was taken to hospital, where he died seven days later from blood poisoning.

In the aftermath, Heydrich – whom Hitler lauded as 'the man with the iron heart' – was commemorated with a ceremonial state funeral. In addition, a terrible retribution was visited upon the Czechs. The village of Lidice was wiped out: every man and boy over fifteen was shot – almost 200 in total – while women and children were sent to concentration camps

Reinhard Heydrich, Deputy *Reichsprotektor* of Bohemia and Moravia, assassinated in 1942.

where few survived. A few weeks later, a second village, Ležáky, was also destroyed. Kubiš and Gabčik, meanwhile, were hunted down and killed alongside other Czech resistance agents. In all, some 1,300 Czechs were murdered in reprisal for Heydrich's death.

A year after the attack, in May 1943, this postage stamp was released by the German authorities, for use in the Protectorate. It showed Heydrich's death mask, along with his life dates and the prominent SS runes, but it also carried a financial sting. Though its face value was 60 haléřů, it had a purchase price of 5 koruna, with the difference of 4 koruna and 40 haléřů being, in effect, a 700 per cent surcharge. For Berlin, it was a useful way of raising money, of squeezing the occupied lands as much as possible. For Czechs, it was another reminder of their subjugation. Even in death, Heydrich was still exploiting them.

1   C. Bryant, *Prague in Black: Nazi Rule and Czech Nationalism* (Cambridge, MA, 2007), p. 143.

# 87 Wehrmacht Mittens

*When Hitler launched his Blitzkrieg invasion* of the Soviet Union in June 1941, such was his confidence that he believed the Red Army would collapse within months and that victory over Stalin would be gained before the onset of winter. Thus, he thought, there would be no need for specialist winter wear for his soldiers. How wrong he was.

Initial German victories that summer were certainly overwhelming and hundreds of thousands of Soviet troops were captured. But October mud was followed by November snows and a concerted Soviet counter-attack. Hitler's invasion ground to a halt and his soldiers were forced to endure a horrendous Russian winter – said to be the most severe in a hundred years – for which they were ill-prepared.

At first, German soldiers improvised, wearing captured Russian garments and stuffing newspaper and straw inside their clothing. On the home front, meanwhile, the Winterhilfswerk – Winter Relief organisation – quickly collected furs and other winter clothing from civilians to donate to their soldiers at the front. But, as the temperatures plummeted, more soldiers suffered from frostbite and other winter ailments than combat wounds. One Panzer division west of Moscow in January 1942 reported 800 frostbite casualties in a day. Sentries were literally freezing to death at their posts.[1]

Wehrmacht reversible mittens and knitted gloves.

As the idea of a quick victory over Stalin evaporated, the Wehrmacht's Quartermaster-General, Eduard Wagner, was instructed to introduce a winter combat uniform. Tested in Finland, it included a padded jacket and trousers, an insulated hood, over-mittens and gloves, and a very popular scarf that could be wrapped around the head.

The reversible mittens and knitted gloves from the winter uniform are shown here. The knitted gloves were standard Army issue in field-grey wool, while the mittens, to be worn over the gloves, show the *Splittermuster* – 'splinter camouflage pattern' – characteristic of German Army troops, and could be reversed to snow white. They are linked by a white ribbon.

Though the uniform was meant for deployment in the winter of 1942–3, production and supply problems as well as the sheer size of the German Army to be equipped meant that this outfit would not become general issue until the following winter, two years after it had first been required. It is little wonder, perhaps, that Germany's Eastern Front medal was known among its recipients as 'The Order of the Frozen Flesh'.[2]

Ill-equipped German soldiers try to keep warm during the Russian winter of 1941–2.

After their failure to knock the Soviet Union out in the *Blitzkrieg* attack of 1941, German forces were never realistically going to defeat the armies – and economies – that were ranged against them. Ultimately it would be the cold statistics of industrial production that would lead to their defeat, but in the meantime the ravages of the Russian winter helped highlight their weakness and pointed the way to their demise.

---

*'One Panzer division west of Moscow in January 1942 reported 800 frostbite casualties in a day.'*

---

1  Clark, *Barbarossa*, p. 173.

2  D. T. Zabecki (ed.), *World War II in Europe* (Connecticut, 1999), p. 1053.

# 88 Hindenburg Lights

*The simple Hindenburg light was as essential* as it was ubiquitous on the German home front during World War II. Widely used in the trenches during World War I, and named after Germany's most prominent field marshal during that conflict, it was a simple candle – a larger precursor to the modern 'tea-light' – consisting of a waxed paper cup containing tallow and a supported wick made of fabric.

Ordinarily sold in rolls or boxes of a dozen, as seen here, Hindenburg lights would prove as indispensable during World War II as they had been during the First. In the cellars and bunkers of Hitler's Reich, they were kept on hand to provide light in the event of a loss of power, thereby providing a vital fillip for civilian morale during the long nights of Allied air attack.

A box of Hindenburg lights – simple but essential.

In September 1939 Hindenburg lights were included on a list of items that every cellar and shelter was obliged to provide for its inhabitants – including wooden benches, picks, shovels and a bucket of sand for extinguishing incendiaries – but given that most cellars had power and those early raids were less than immediately deadly, the need was perhaps more theoretical than urgent.

In time, however, they would come into their own. After the Allied bombing of Germany's cities intensified in 1942, and civilians spent more and more time confined to their cellars, Hindenburg lights would become an essential part of home front 'kit', not only providing light but also saving lives.

The problem for many shelters, cellars and bunkers from 1942 was that of overcrowding, which combined with longer stays below ground to heighten the risk of a lack of oxygen. In such circumstances, Hindenburg lights would be employed – like the proverbial 'canary in the coalmine' – to show when the air was growing stale: one placed on the ground, one on a table and one at head height. If the bottom light went out (stale air being heavier than oxygenated air), children would be placed on laps. If the middle lamp went out, people would stand. And, if the uppermost Hindenburg light began to flicker, they would know that – whatever the perils above ground – it was time to leave the shelter. The humble Hindenburg light thereby provided an ingenious early warning against one of the air war's invisible killers: asphyxiation.

An air-raid shelter in Emden, crowded but comfortable enough.

# 89 The Stroop Report

*On yellowing paper,* and in elaborate Gothic script, the front page proudly declares: 'The Jewish Quarter of Warsaw is no more!' The so-called 'Stroop Report', named after its SS-officer author, was compiled in 1943 as a commemorative souvenir of the German destruction of Warsaw's Jewish ghetto. It was to be presented as a personal gift to the head of the SS, Heinrich Himmler.

Established in November 1940, the Warsaw Ghetto was the largest in German-occupied Europe, spreading across some 3½ square kilometres of the city and accommodating over 400,000 people, fully 30 per cent of Warsaw's population. Ghettos were set up by the Germans across central and eastern Europe, and over 200 were established on Polish soil, including at Kraków, Łódź and Białystok. Their purpose was simple: essentially they were intended as holding pens where local Jewish populations could be concentrated – and worked – until Berlin decided what was to be done with them. In practice, conditions in the ghettos were often so bad that incarceration in them amounted to a deliberate slow death for their inhabitants. In Łódź, for instance, there was one toilet per 600 people, while food supplies were predictably meagre, with rationing levels set at a fraction of those required for survival.[1] Unsurprisingly, disease and malnutrition were rife.

> *'A document intended as a proud record of a murderous act was used as evidence to damn the perpetrators.'*

In time, the ghettos were 'liquidated' by the Germans and their surviving inhabitants deported to the death camps. Warsaw, as the largest amongst them, proved especially problematical, with German incursions into the ghetto already being met with increasing armed resistance by late 1942. In April of the following year the confrontation came to a head when SS troops were ordered to clear the ghetto and deport the remaining survivors to the death camp at Treblinka. Under the command of SS-Gruppenführer Jürgen Stroop, they succeeded in burning and razing the ghetto, block by block, driving out the survivors and murdering those who dared resist. In around a month the Warsaw ghetto was systematically destroyed and over 50,000 people were killed.

This, then, was the brutal, murderous 'action' that was to be commemorated with three identical, leather-bound volumes, as 'proof of the burdens and sacrifices endured . . . in the attempt to rid Europe and the world of the Jews'.[2] One was intended

**Es gibt keinen
jüdischen Wohnbezirk
in Warschau mehr !**

The cover page of the Stroop Report – with the text 'The Jewish Quarter of Warsaw is no more!'

as a gift for Himmler, and the other two were for Stroop himself and his superior, the SS commander in occupied Poland, Friedrich-Wilhelm Krüger. In addition, a fourth, unbound volume was prepared, which was archived at the SS headquarters in Warsaw. With only minor discrepancies, the four copies were essentially identical, consisting of 125 pages of heavy bond paper, with text by Stroop chronicling the Warsaw operation, listing the German casualties and the combat units involved, and giving a verbatim record of his own daily situation reports and dispatches. In addition, a pictorial appendix was added, with some fifty-three photographs.

Of the report's contents, the photographs are perhaps the most interesting. They give an astonishing record of the brutal battle for the Warsaw Ghetto, with many images of burning buildings, surrendering civilians and the dead. Some of the images have become well-known, such as that of Stroop himself, pictured alongside his lieutenants, or that of a column of civilians being herded down a smoke-filled street by soldiers. The most famous image, however, is that of a group of terrified women and children, who – according to the caption – had been 'pulled from the bunkers by force'. In front of the group stands a small boy of perhaps eight years of age, in short trousers, his arms aloft, an expression of uncomprehending fear etched on his face. It is one the most iconic pictures of World War II.

'Pulled from the bunkers by force' –
one of the most moving images of World War II.

Of the four copies of the Stroop Report that were created, only two survived; one of the leather-bound examples is in the Institute of National Remembrance in Warsaw, while the unbound archive copy (pictured on the previous page) is in the US National Archives in Washington, DC. The stamps of 'International Military Tribunal', as well as that of the British 'MIRS' (Military Intelligence Research Section) and 'SHAEF' (Supreme Headquarters Allied Expeditionary Force) can be seen on the cover page. Both surviving copies were used extensively as evidence at the Nuremberg Trials, where the US Chief Counsel, Justice Robert H. Jackson, referred to them as 'sickening' and evidence of 'the planned and systematic character of the Jewish persecution'.[3]

The supreme irony, of course, was that a document that was intended by its Nazi authors as a proud record of a murderous act of ethnic cleansing should have been used as evidence to damn the perpetrators. By the time that the Nuremberg Tribunal was convened, two of the report's intended recipients – Heinrich Himmler and Friedrich-Wilhelm Krüger – were already dead, having both committed suicide at the end of the war. Only Jürgen Stroop was still alive. Captured by the Americans in May 1945, he was transferred to Poland in 1947, where he stood trial for his crimes. Sentenced to death, he was hanged in Warsaw on 6 March 1952.

Jürger Stroop in the mugshot taken by his American captors
at the end of the war.

1   Isaac Trunk & Robert Shapiro, *Łódź Ghetto: A History* (Indiana, 2006), p. 117.

2   Quoted in Richard Raskin, *A Child at Gunpoint* (Aarhus, 2004), p. 26.

3   Quoted in ibid., p. 32.

# 90 July Bomb Plot Wound Badge

*This badge – among the rarest of Third Reich decorations –* commemorates the attempt on Hitler's life on 20 July 1944, when a time-bomb was detonated in the "Wolf's Lair" *Führer*-Headquarters at Rastenburg in East Prussia (now Kętrzyn, Poland). Of the twenty-four men present in the room when the bomb went off, one was killed outright, and three more died later of their wounds. Hitler suffered only superficial injuries, but it was nonetheless the most serious attempt on his life.

July 20, 1944 was a hot, sultry day and Hitler had risen earlier than usual, anticipating the arrival that afternoon of his fellow dictator, the Italian leader Benito Mussolini, and in preparation had brought forward his daily situation conference, which was to begin at 12.30.[1] Shortly before that time, Hitler walked the short distance from his bunker to the grey conference hut, its windows flung open because of the heat, where his senior officers – generals, admirals and adjutants – were gathered around a long oak map-table.

The 20 July Wound Badge posthumously awarded to Rudolf Schmundt.

A late arrival to the meeting was Colonel Claus Schenk Graf von Stauffenberg – a tall and aristocratic soldier, who was expected to present an update to the assembled dignitaries on the 'replacement army'. Gravely maimed – he had lost an eye, his right hand and two fingers of his left hand in the North African campaign – he was described by one of those present as 'the classic image of the warrior through all of history'.[2] He came not as a warrior, however, but as an assassin.

Stauffenberg entered the room during a briefing on the situation on the Eastern Front by Major-General Adolf Heusinger. Making his apologies for the interruption, he took his place to Hitler's right, and set his briefcase on the floor, approximately a metre away from his target, before muttering something about a telephone call and leaving the room again. Unknown to those present, the briefcase contained a 1 kg explosive charge on a 10-minute fuse. At 12.42 p.m., as Stauffenberg watched from a nearby building, the bomb exploded.[3]

When the smoke cleared, a chaotic scene was revealed; the floor and walls had been shattered and the oak table had been smashed to matchwood. As the wounded staggered from the briefing room, almost all had concussion and burst ear drums. Some had not been so lucky. The stenographer, Heinrich Berger, had been closest to the blast. He had lost both legs and lay in a spreading pool of his own blood. He would not last the afternoon. Three senior officers were mortally wounded. Hitler, though dazed, had received only superficial injuries; his ears were damaged, his arm and buttocks badly bruised and his legs were pitted with hundreds of splinters. As his doctor treated him, he said 'I am invulnerable, I am immortal.'[4]

---

*'Stauffenberg came not as a warrior, but as an assassin.'*

---

In fact, Hitler's survival was down to pure chance. The open windows of the conference room had helped dissipate the blast and the briefcase had unwittingly been moved behind a sturdy table leg, deflecting the explosion away from Hitler. Most importantly, the one-handed Stauffenberg had only had time to prime half of the explosives he had brought with him. Had he thought even to include the second charge of plastic explosive in his briefcase, it is likely that everyone in the hut would have been killed.

Of course, for Stauffenberg and his co-conspirators, assassinating Hitler was only part of the plan. So, while chaos reigned at the Wolf's Lair, he and his adjutant, Werner von Haeften, made good their escape, bluffing their way past two check-points and taking their flight back to Berlin. As far as they were concerned, Hitler was dead and on arrival they set in train the wider military coup against Nazi rule, by attempting to seize key points in the capital. When that attempt failed – primarily because word of Hitler's survival fatally undermined the plot – Stauffenberg and the other key plotters were arrested. Around midnight that same day, they were taken out to the courtyard of the Defence Ministry, and executed by firing squad.

In the aftermath, Nazi security services set about rounding up and interrogating all those with any connection to the plot, however tenuous. In total, some 5,000 were arrested; hundreds were executed, countless more consigned to the concentration camps; among the former were Admiral Wilhelm Canaris, head of the Abwehr military intelligence service, and among the latter the former governor of the Reichsbank, Hjalmar Schacht. Others escaped Hitler's vengeance through suicide, among them Field Marshal Günther von Kluge, and the former resistance lynchpin Major-General Henning von Tresckow.

As the bloodletting continued, and his regime raged towards its end, Hitler ordered that a commemorative badge should be instituted to be presented to the survivors of the assassination attempt, and posthumously awarded to those who were killed. It was modelled on the existing wound badge, which had been founded by Kaiser Wilhelm II in 1918 and, like the original, it featured a *Stahlhelm* on a background of crossed swords. However, the new version was cast in solid silver and hand-finished, bearing the date '20. Juli 1944' with a facsimile of Hitler's signature in relief below the helmet. It was awarded in three grades according to the severity of the injuries incurred –

black for superficial wounds, silver for multiple wounds or maiming, and gold for severe injuries, disability, blindness or death. Each of the twenty-four recipients was given two identical badges – one to be worn and one to be kept – and an elaborate vellum award document, bearing a swastika in gold leaf as well as Hitler's signature and seal. This example, one of only five made in gold, was awarded on 19 September to Colonel-General Rudolf

The wreckage of Hitler's conference room, as photographed by Heinrich Hoffmann immediately after Stauffenberg's bomb exploded.

Schmundt, Hitler's chief adjutant, who had lost a leg and an eye in the attack. Schmundt succumbed to septicaemia and died from his wounds ten days later on 1 October 1944.

1   Peter Hoffmann, *Stauffenberg: A Family History, 1905–1944* (Cambridge, 1995), p. 264.

2   Walter Warlimont, *Inside Hitler's Headquarters* (London, 1964), p. 441.

3   Moorhouse, *Killing Hitler*, p. 203.

4   M. C. Thomsett, *The German Opposition to Hitler* (Jefferson, 1997), p. 204.

# 91 The *Schattenmann*

*All combatant nations in World War II* went to great lengths to dissuade their populations from inadvertently sharing information which might have been of value to their enemies. In Britain, there were the slogans 'Careless Talk Costs Lives' and 'Keep Mum'; in the USA, there was 'Loose Lips Sink Ships'. Nazi Germany had the mysterious *Schattenmann* – the 'shadow man'.

Germany's campaign to prevent 'loose talk' began immediately upon the outbreak of war in September 1939, and revived a very effective slogan from World War I: '*Feind hört mit*': 'The Enemy is Listening'. The slogan featured on posters, as well as on

'Hans tells me his division is going to . . .': The *Schattenmann* looms over an indiscreet conversation.

enamelled signs, which were placed beside public telephones. It was even used for a propaganda film: *Achtung! Feind hört mit!* was a cautionary tale from 1940 outlining the perils of enemy espionage and the merits of tight-lipped vigilance.

In due course, the message was simplified still further and '*Pst!*' was used as an admonishing reminder, often with the slogan appended. Another addition was the shadow of a man wearing a distinctive Homburg hat – known naturally as the *Schattenmann* – whose looming figure would suggest a sinister presence, eavesdropping on careless conversations. From 1944, he featured on a series of posters and placards, overshadowing everyday situations, such as women chatting about the movements of their husbands' regiments, or men discussing nearby building projects.

The beauty of the '*Pst!*' and the *Schattenmann* figure was that they could be employed as shorthand for the wider campaign – so a tiny newspaper advertisement using just the roughly drawn shadow and the word '*Pst!*' would effectively remind readers of the need for secrecy, without lengthy text or expensive illustrations. The *Schattenmann* was even printed on matchboxes, or daubed on walls by enthusiastic Hitler Youths and the Party faithful.

*'A sinister presence, eavesdropping on careless conversations.'*

The irony was, of course, that it was the Nazis and their organisations that were much more likely to be spying on the German people than the imaginary legions of foreign agents in their midst. Some Germans at least saw the dark humour in the situation. One diarist recalled that a '*Pst! Feind hört mit!*' poster in Berlin had been defaced so that it was no longer the enemy that was listening, but the SS.[1] The *Schattenmann*, it seems, was just as likely to be one of their own.

1   Howard Smith, *Last Train from Berlin* (London, 1942), p. 199.

# 92 Forced Labourer's 'Work Card'

*Of all the groups persecuted and exploited* by the Third Reich, *Zwangsarbeiter*, or forced labourers, are among the least acknowledged. Though unseen and unknown, they were ubiquitous in Germany during the war, filling jobs in armaments, industry and agriculture in their millions. They were present in almost every business and enterprise – from the local butcher to the largest industrial concern – and their barrack blocks and camps, 3,000 in Berlin alone, would have filled the open spaces. Making up over a third of the total German workforce, they were essential to the Nazi war effort.

About one in five forced labourers – some 2 million in total – were Poles, the vasy majority of whom had been conscripted and deported often with little knowledge even of where they were going.[1] The holder of this *Arbeitskarte* – or 'work card' – was one of them. Aleksandra M. was twenty-eight when this card was issued to her in October 1944. Born near Sosnowiec in Upper Silesia, she was registered as married and living in Warsaw in what the Germans called the General Gouvernement. This card, which bore both her photograph and index fingerprints, served as an ID document as well as a work pass. To lose it was to court serious trouble.

It is not clear from the card when Aleksandra was brought to Germany – she may have been among the cohort of women deported from Warsaw following the crushing of that city's uprising that autumn. But the card states that she worked as a labourer in Berlin, at 'Gasag', the city's natural gas supplier, most probably at a gasworks. It is also stamped with the word *Kennzeichenpflichtig* – meaning that Aleksandra was required by law to wear a fabric badge bearing a purple P on a yellow background, which clearly identified her as a Polish forced labourer. Those who dared to defy the regulation were subject to a 150 RM fine and up to six months in punitive detention.

---

*'East Europeans were treated more as prisoners than employees.'*

---

In addition to that petty humiliation, Aleksandra would have been subject to a raft of rules and restrictions. Conditions for forced labourers varied enormously, depending primarily on where they came from. West Europeans – including French, Dutch or Danes – generally enjoyed far superior treatment, with regular pay, food and even some leisure time. East Europeans, meanwhile, were treated more as prisoners than employees, with limitations imposed on their movement, their pay, and the quality and quantity of their food. According to the 'Polish Decrees' of March 1940, Polish

The *Arbeitskarte* of Aleksandra M.

labourers were to be kept away from German cultural life, as well as churches and restaurants; they were banned from public transport, subjected to a strict curfew and obliged to work seven days a week.[2] As one of their number recalled: 'For us, everything was forbidden.'[3]

Aleksandra's existence in Berlin – like that of her fellows – would most likely have been a bleak one, therefore. Confined to a chilly, lice-infested barrack block, surrounded by barbed wire, she would have endured poor sanitary conditions, insufficient food and almost non-existent medical care. To defy one's employers was to risk a spell in a punishment camp. To fall ill was akin to a death sentence. Only a benign employer could make life bearable, by supplying hot canteen food, for instance, or a modicum of care. Not many obliged.

Aleksandra's fate is unknown. She may have returned to the ruins of Warsaw at war's end, to rebuild her life under communism, forever tight-lipped about her experiences, terrified of revealing that she had worked for the Germans. Or she may have been among the countless thousands of forced labourers who died under Nazi rule, to be buried in mass graves and forgotten, collateral damage in Germany's race war.

---

1   See Moorhouse, *Berlin at War*, pp. 117–35.

2   Ulrich Herbert, *Hitler's Foreign Workers: Enforced Foreign Labour in Germany under the Third Reich* (Cambridge, 1997), p. 72

3   Quoted in Moorhouse, *Berlin at War*, p. 124.

# 93 Feldgendarmerie Gorget

*There were few sights during World War II* that could make a battle-hardened Wehrmacht infantryman stop in his tracks, but this was certainly one of them. This is the *Ringkragen* – gorget – of the German Feldgendarmerie military police, an organisation which – by the end of the war – effectively held the power of life and death over every German soldier.

Worn around the neck, over a field service uniform, the gorget was historically intended as a symbol of authority, marking its wearer out as being set apart from the ordinary soldiers around him. During the Third Reich, a police badge on the arm sleeve and orange piping on the collar tabs would also make the Feldgendarmerie uniform distinctive, but it was the gorget that would first catch the eye. This was true even in low light: both its lettering and Nazi eagle were picked out with luminescent paint – now a dull beige – to ensure optimum visibility. The gorget also gave the men of the Feldgendarmerie their nickname of *Kettenhunde* – or 'chained dogs'.

The Feldgendarmerie was reconstituted in 1933 and its recruits – many of whom were ex-policemen – combined full infantry training with extensive police powers. With the outbreak of war in 1939, they were responsible primarily for the maintenance of order behind the front line, their duties ranging from simple traffic control to rounding up prisoners of war and 'pacifying' the local population.

It would be in this last capacity that the Feldgendarmerie would first earn a dark reputation. 'Pacification' in Nazi parlance often involved atrocities, massacres and war crimes in occupied areas, and the participation of military police units in the preparation of such actions on the Eastern Front is well documented. One captured officer confirmed that his unit's routine tasks had included the selection of suitable civilians for forced labour in Germany, as well as of Jews and suspected communists who were slated for execution.

---

*'The gorget gave the men of the Feldgendarmerie their nickname of Kettenhunde – or "chained dogs".'*

---

In time, as the war turned against Germany, the Feldgendarmerie were increasingly involved in policing – and terrorising – their own side, checking for deserters, and screening refugee columns for malingerers and military personnel without permission to be away from the front. In carrying out these tasks, they had the authority to detain anyone they suspected of being a deserter, and suspects were often dispatched for even the slightest infraction to a punishment battalion, where they might find themselves clearing minefields by hand.

In the last months of the war, the Feldgendarmerie increasingly resorted to the execution of suspects, so as to galvanise failing martial spirit, and in this way some 8,000 Wehrmacht soldiers were executed.[1] Little wonder, perhaps, that the Feldgendarmerie gained a deserved reputation for brutality, and that the sight of this gorget could strike fear into many a soldier's heart.

A fearsome sight: a Feldgendarmerie gorget.

1   Stephen Fritz, *Frontsoldaten: The German Soldier in World War II* (Kentucky, 1997), p. 93.

# 94 V-1 Flying Bomb

*The V-1 flying bomb – or Doodlebug* as it was known in Britain – was one of Hitler's notorious 'Vengeance' weapons, designed as a riposte to the Anglo-American bomber offensive against Nazi Germany. An early form of cruise missile, it was intended to deliver Hitler a miraculous victory towards the end of World War II, and – though it failed – was an exemplar of the technical brilliance of his military scientists.

The concept of a pre-set guided missile was developed from 1936 by Fritz Gosslau at the Berlin engine manufacturer Argus. Turned down by the German Air Ministry in 1940, Gosslau persisted with the project, later bringing in engineer Robert Lusser of Heinkel, who helped simplify the design, reducing its two engines to just one. The revised weapon was given the go-ahead in June 1942 and aircraft maker Fieseler in Kassel was contracted to produce it. At the time it was called the Fi 103.

---

*On the morning of 18 June 1944, a V-1 destroyed the Guards Chapel in St James's; 121 civilians and military personnel were killed.'*

---

Code-named *Kirschkern* ('Cherry Stone') or *Maikäfer* ('Maybug'), the prototype was test-flown at Peenemünde, the home of Nazi rocket research, with the first successful powered flight taking place in December 1942. Consisting of an 8-metre steel fuselage, with 5-metre plywood wings and an 850 kg Amatol explosive charge, it was powered by an Argus pulse-jet engine – giving the trademark 'buzz' – mounted at the rear. After an assisted launch, usually from fixed ramps with steam-powered catapults, the pulse-jet would take over and power the Fi 103 to a maximum speed of over 500 kmh and a service altitude of 3,000 m, giving it a range of around 275 km.

Contrary to popular belief, the Fi 103 did not simply fly until its fuel ran out; rather it contained a primitive gyroscopic guidance system, which regulated altitude and airspeed, while a wind-driven odometer in the nose controlled the range. When the preset distance had been flown, the Fi 103 was tipped into a dive, the engine cut, and it fell earthward. Remarkably, by the end of the war, its accuracy had been improved to a 10 km radius of a target.[1]

After extensive testing, the Fi 103 was ready for deployment in the summer of 1944. Re-named the V-1 – as part of Hitler's *Vergeltungswaffen* 'vengeance weapons' programme – it was first launched from the Pas de Calais, towards London, on 13 June. Of the ten launched that day, four successfully detonated – landing in Kent, East

Sussex and East London. From then on, some 10,000 would follow – at their peak over 100 per day – mostly aimed at London, with Antwerp and Brussels as secondary targets. A new chapter in the air war had begun.

Given their constant speed, trajectory and altitude, V-1s were relatively easy to intercept and various methods were soon developed, most usually through shooting down with ack-ack, or by interception with Tempests or Spitfires. The most intriguing countermeasure was the use of double agents to mislead the Germans about where their V-1s were landing. Aware that most V-1 strikes seemed to cluster to the south-east of the capital, around Dulwich, British intelligence instructed its agents to tell the Germans that they were landing predominantly in the north-west, so that the resulting adjustment might leave them falling harmlessly to earth over the Kent countryside. The deception was, its originator crowed, 'a triumph' which saved 'thousands of lives'.[2] In all, Allied countermeasures were so successful that only around one in four V-1s actually reached their target.

Nonetheless, those that managed to get through the defences could cause chaos. On 30 June, 46 people were killed by a V-1 strike close to the Air Ministry on the Aldwych; a month later a further 59 were killed when a V-1 landed in a crowded market in Lewisham. The worst single incident was on the morning of 18 June 1944, when a V-1

A V-1 flying bomb blasts away from its launch ramp.

A preserved V-1 flying bomb on a launch ramp at Ardouval, Normandy.

destroyed the Guards Chapel in St James's, while it was packed with servicemen and their families; 121 civilians and military personnel were killed. In total, around 6,000 lives were lost to V-1s in London alone.[3]

Eventually, following D-Day, as the Allies gradually overran the launch sites, the V-1 Blitz on Britain drew to an end, with the last 'Doodlebug' coming to earth on 28 March 1945, at Swanscombe in Kent – some 30 km east of central London.

Like its cousin the V-2, the V-1 was a brilliant failure. For all the genius of its conception and development, it bears the ignominy that its construction – carried out by half-starved concentration camp inmates, living in horrific conditions – cost many more lives than its deployment. It is an example, not only of the ingenuity of Germany's wartime engineers, but also of their amorality.

1   K. M. Kloeppel, *The Military Utility of German Rocketry During World War II* (Air Command and Staff College, 1997).

2   John Masterman, quoted in Ben Macintyre, *Agent Zigzag* (London, 2007), p. 282.

3   See the excellent website www.flyingbombsandrockets.com/index.html.

# 95 Messerschmitt Me 262 Fighter

Even as Hitler's Third Reich was heading towards defeat, it could still spring some deadly surprises. One of these occurred on 26 July 1944, over Bavaria, when a photo-reconnaissance RAF Mosquito of 544 Squadron was approached by a very fast-moving German fighter plane and engaged in a brief dog-fight. The Messerschmitt Me 262 had arrived.

Jet-technology had been in development in the Third Reich from the 1930s after Hans Joachim Pabst von Ohain ran the first jet engine in 1937. Two years later, a turbojet engine was installed in the primitive Heinkel He 178, which made the first jet-powered flight on 27 August 1939, a week before the outbreak of war. Amazingly, however, despite its achievement, the prototype aroused little interest from the Air Ministry and was consigned to the Berlin Air Museum, where it was destroyed during an air raid in 1943.

Me 262 – the world's first jet fighter to shoot down a manned enemy aircraft.

In the meantime, however, the Me 262 project was already under way, overseen by Messerschmitt, with Hans Mauch and Helmut Schlep developing turbojets with Junkers and BMW, while Hans Antz worked on an airframe to carry the powerful engines. Mindful of the technical problems encountered by the single-engine He 178, they chose twin jet engines, one fixed beneath each wing to facilitate maintenance. The result was a sleek single-seater, with a slightly swept wing and a bubble-canopy.

In 1940 Messerschmitt was granted the contract to build three test prototypes of the Me 262, one of which made its maiden flight on 18 July 1942, powered by the Junkers Jumo 004 jet engine. Orders for sixty aircraft followed and on 22 April 1943, Adolf Galland, famed air ace and head of the Luftwaffe fighter arm, test-flew the aircraft, reporting that it felt 'as if an angel were pushing me'.[1] Galland's blessing convinced the German Air Ministry to demand that Messerschmitt switch production from the successful but conventional Bf 109 fighter to the Me 262. Further progress was hampered, however, when a US air raid struck the Messerschmitt factory at Regensburg in August 1943, destroying vital tooling, and – ironically – underlining Germany's urgent need for a fast, jet-powered interceptor.

---

*'One Nazi minister complained that "any child could see it was a fighter"'.*

---

When Hitler was shown the aircraft, however, in 1943, he foresaw a rather different role for it. Still convinced he could win the war by intensifying the bombing offensive against the Allies, he wanted the Me 262 to be his bomber of choice. Though Galland and others furiously disagreed – one minister complained that 'any child could see it was a fighter'[2] – Hitler's orders prevailed, and the Me 262 was reconfigured as a fast bomber, with a 500 kg external payload which considerably reduced its top speed. This decision, combined with delays in engine development, meant that by the time that Hitler relented, in November 1944, and fighter production was resumed, precious time had been lost. By then, Allied armies were sweeping into Germany in the wake of D-Day and Allied air superiority was already all but assured. Whatever advantage the Me 262 might have offered to Nazi Germany had been squandered.

By the spring of 1945, then, some 1,430 Me 262s had been built, although technical difficulties meant that it was rare for more than 100 to be ready for action at any one time. Armed with four 30 mm cannon grouped in the nose, and a speed of over 800 kmh, the Me 262 had an advantage in aerial combat and could be deadly when engaging US bomber formations, especially as it proved too fast for Allied turret gunners to follow. The most concerted attack using the new aircraft occurred on 18 March 1945, when 37 Me 262s engaged an 1,800-strong USAAF force, en route to Berlin, shooting down 12 enemy bombers at the cost of 3 Messerschmitts. It was a success, of a sort, but one that showed the horrific odds that German pilots faced in the final months of the war.

In total, some 735 Allied aircraft are believed to have been shot down by the Me 262, including the last air victory of the war: a Red Air Force P-39 Airacobra, downed on the afternoon of 8 May 1945 over the Erzgebirge, south of Berlin. As the first jet fighter to enter combat, and the most advanced aircraft of the period, the Me 262 was certainly revolutionary, but it was too little, too late, and was symptomatic of the Nazi regime's bizarre faith in 'wonder weapons'. Had it taken to the air a year earlier and in sufficient numbers, the overall outcome might have been different, but development problems, fuel shortages and political meddling conspired to negate its impact.

Allied fighter pilots aimed to catch Me 262s when they were easier, slower targets, just after take-off or just before landing, as in this image taken by a fighter's gun camera.

1   R. Ford, *Germany's Secret Weapons in World War II* (Staplehurst, 2000), p. 14.

2   Quoted in H. E. Ziegler, *Turbinenjäger Me 262* (Stuttgart, 1977), p. 86.

# 96 Volkssturm Armband

*The idea of the levée en masse* – a mass popular conscription in time of emergency – is one that has a long pedigree. In Nazi Germany, military conscription had been in place since 1935 and ever-younger categories of recruit had been called up after 1941, but it took until October 1944 before a genuine *levée en masse* was carried out – and it took the form of the Volkssturm.

The Volkssturm – or 'People's Storm' – was a national militia which called up all German males between the ages of sixteen and sixty who were not already serving in military organisations, including the injured as well as those who were previously deemed too old, too young, or otherwise unfit for service. With the Soviets encroaching on Germany's eastern frontier and the Western Allies poised to invade the Reich from the west, the Volkssturm represented a last desperate throw of the dice by a regime that was hastening towards its ignominious end.

> *'They were little more than a disparate rabble, a collection of pale boys and old men, in raincoats and tunics.'*

Training for the Volkssturm was rudimentary. Most of those who registered took an oath of loyalty to Hitler personally – swearing that they would rather die than surrender – and then attended a four-day training period, in which they might undertake some elementary map-reading, and be instructed about tactics and fortification. They might also receive weapons, particularly the ubiquitous Panzerfaust single-shot bazooka, or an elderly rifle. The most fortunate might receive a primitive Volkssturmgewehr machine gun. Many received nothing at all.[1] One veteran recalled:

> When I registered with my company, I saw what a motley mob it was. I received an old Italian rifle and ten bullets, but I didn't know what to do with them. Everything looked so disorganised . . . In the state we were in, the Russians would simply walk all over us.[2]

Uniforms were also non-existent. Recruits were simply ordered to avoid brightly coloured clothing, and advised that items were ideally to be dyed 'field-service brown'. In addition, a nationwide initiative was mounted to collect suitable garments from the general public. The only formal indicator of membership of the Volkssturm,

A Volkssturm armband, an invitation to the slaughter.

therefore, was an armband, such as the one above, which would be worn on the upper left arm. It was this – fatally for many – that identified them as combatants.

In November 1944, Propaganda Minister Joseph Goebbels held a ceremonial mass oath-taking for the new cadres of the Volkssturm, on the Wilhelmplatz in central Berlin. There, after a short speech from their host, the thousands of new recruits marched out in close order, through the drizzle and past the newsreel cameras. Though Goebbels considered that they made 'an excellent impression',[3] less blinkered eyes would not have been so sure. They were little more than a disparate rabble, a collection of pale boys and old men, in raincoats and tunics, vintage steel helmets and flat caps, carrying weapons of all shapes and sizes. They could hardly have looked less like an army.

The Volkssturm was intended to have a dual purpose – a public one and a military one. In Nazi propaganda, it was meant to inspire a new confidence and will to resist among the German people who, though they were tiring of war, were in most cases yet to witness its horrors at first hand. In this regard it was perhaps momentarily successful, but for many Germans the Volkssturm was considered to be merely ridiculous, and darkly symbolic of how badly the war was going. One Berlin ditty summed up the public mood:

> *Lieb Vaterland, magst ruhig sein*  Dear Fatherland, set your mind at rest,
> *Der Führer zieht die Opas ein.*  The *Führer* has called the Grandpas up.[4]

The other purpose was military. It was expected that the zeal – or desperation – of Volkssturm men defending their own towns and villages would galvanise the German Army, providing a necessary human focus to its efforts. In this too, however, its value was dubious. Though the Volkssturm represented a welcome numerical boost to German armed forces at the end of the war, its military utility was very limited.

Volkssturm men fought and died across Germany in that last winter of the war – indeed the defence of besieged cities like Breslau would have been almost impossible

'A motley mob'. Volkssturm, Berlin 1944.

without them – but they were nonetheless unable to halt their enemies' advance. For all their fanaticism and bravery, old men and boys were no match for the trained, battle-hardened soldiers of the Grand Alliance. At Ostrowo in occupied Poland, for instance, only two Volkssturm men survived out of the 200 sent to defend the town against the Red Army in January 1945.[5] Those who died there were but a tiny fraction of the estimated 175,000 members of the Volkssturm who were killed in the last six months of the war. For all the propaganda and hyperbole, therefore, the Volkssturm must be judged as a grievous and wasteful failure.

1   Moorhouse, *Berlin at War*, pp. 352–3.

2   Quoted in Gleiss, *Breslauer Apokalypse*, Vol. V, p. 279.

3   Elke Fröhlich (ed.), *Die Tagebücher von Joseph Goebbels*, Vol. XIV (Munich, 2006), p. 208.

4   Quoted in Moorhouse, *Berlin at War*, p. 351.

5   Richard Hargreaves, *Hitler's Final Fortress – Breslau 1945* (Barnsley, 2011), p. 69.

# 97 V-2 Missile

*The V-2 ballistic missile exemplified* the amoral insanity of the Third Reich as well as the scientific ingenuity of its scientists. Not only was it the first man-made object to reach space, it was also a spectacular waste of resources and human lives.

A V-2 missile at Peenemünde Historical Technical Museum, Germany.

German scientists were among the pioneers of guided rockets. As early as 1923, Hermann Oberth published a book entitled *The Rocket into Planetary Space*, and he and fellow far-seeing scientists formed the Society for Space Travel in 1927. The society was joined by the brilliant but unscrupulous Wernher von Braun in 1930, and the following year they successfully launched a small rocket, fuelled by liquid oxygen and petrol. The rocket age had begun.

With Hitler in power, the German Army increased its interest in rocketry, seeing it as a possible alternative to long-range artillery. In 1936, it joined forces with Braun's researchers to buy land to test their rockets at Peenemünde, on the island of Usedom, on Germany's Baltic coast. There, test launches could be made over the sea, with the results visible from the nearby coast. Braun was appointed as technical director, under the leadership of Captain Walter Dornberger, who had headed the Army's ballistic missile research since 1930.

Test launches continued at Peenemünde, with a number of designs and configurations being assessed. The most promising was the A-4 prototype. Standing over 14 metres tall, with a total weight of 13 tonnes, including 9 tonnes of fuel and a 750 kg Amatol warhead, it was powered by combining an explosive mixture of ethanol and liquid oxygen and controlled using three-axis gyroscopes that operated small rudders set into fins in its tail, and vanes in the exhaust of its engine. On its first successful launch, on 3 October 1942, it flew over 200 km, reaching Mach 5 and an altitude of 85 km, higher than any rocket previously tested, before landing within 4 km of its target. The A-4 would later be redesignated as the V-2: *Vergeltungswaffe 2*, one of Hitler's so-called 'Revenge Weapons'.

After this initial success, though, the V-2 struggled with reliability, not least because the slightest malfunction from any one of its 20,000 components usually proved catastrophic, and left little evidence through

A V-2 missile lifts off during a test flight.

which to examine the cause. Nonetheless, Hitler was impressed enough to place an order for the manufacture of 250 V-2s per month, and in July 1943 described it as the weapon that would determine the outcome of the war.[1]

By that time, however, the V-2 programme had already come to the attention of the Royal Air Force, and, on the night of 17 August 1943, the research station at Peenemünde was raided by over 500 aircraft, targeting the test stands and the workers' quarters. In the aftermath, with over 700 dead on the ground, and progress on the V-2 halted for seven weeks, the German authorities decided to shift production underground, to the concentration camp of Mittelbau-Dora near Nordhausen in Thuringia, where thousands of slave labourers would toil in the most appalling conditions. One third of approximately 60,000 workers deployed on the project did not survive.[2]

With mass production under way at Mittelbau-Dora, the V-2s were soon ready for combat deployment and, on 8 September 1944, the first one was launched towards London, where it killed three civilians in Chiswick. Over the months that followed, some 3,200 V-2s were fired from mobile launchers in Holland and France, mainly targeting London and the Belgian port of Antwerp, which was strategically vital to the Allied land advance into Germany. The V-2s proved effective; reaching an altitude of over 80 km and a speed of 2,900 kmh, their maximum range of 330 km was covered in less than four minutes, and there was nothing that could be done to stop them as they returned to earth.

---

*'The V-2 was certainly a "wonder weapon", but it is a wonder that it was ever produced at all.'*

---

Such was their alarming impact that British authorities at first claimed that the mysterious explosions were caused by gas leaks, and only acknowledged the true nature of the attacks some eight weeks later. It was the start of a second Blitz, with some 2,700 killed in London, and a further 2,200 fatalities in Antwerp – the worst single incident being the strike on the Rex Cinema in Antwerp on 16 December, which claimed 567 lives. Fortunately, the V-2 assault proved short-lived, as the advance of Allied armies across western Europe captured the missile launch sites and brought the rocket attacks to a halt. The era of missile warfare was thereby postponed.

The V-2 was undoubtedly a spectacular technological achievement, and one that pointed the way to one of the most remarkable feats of the Cold War. It was Wernher von Braun, of course, who masterminded NASA's Apollo space programme that in 1969 put the first man on the moon. But, for all that, it must not be forgotten that the V-2 was spectacularly wasteful. Quite apart from the countless lives lost in its development and manufacture, it must be remembered that every single V-2 cost 100,000 Reichsmarks and the total budget for the programme was estimated at $2bn,[3] for which Germany could have produced 20,000 Tiger Tanks or 800 Type VII U-boats. In addition, every V-2 launch required the ethanol distilled from nearly 30 tonnes of potatoes, yet delivered less than a ton of explosives to its target.

In technological terms, therefore, the V-2 was certainly a 'wonder weapon', but in most other respects, it is a wonder that it was ever produced at all.

---

1   Volkhard Bode & Gerhard Kaiser, *Building Hitler's Missiles* (Berlin, 2008), p. 40.

2   Bode & Kaiser, p. 79.

3   Quoted in Frederick I. Ordway III & Mitchell R. Sharpe, *The Rocket Team* (New York, 1979), p. 32.

# 98 Göring's Telegram

*Ever since they first met, in Munich in 1922*, Hermann Göring had been a key ally for Adolf Hitler, a vital collaborator in the Nazi movement's rise to power. Göring was at Hitler's side during the Beer Hall *Putsch* in 1923, and was a member of his first cabinet a decade later. In power, he would serve variously as the Commander-in-Chief of the Luftwaffe, President of the Reichstag, Vice-Chancellor of Germany, Minister-President of Prussia, Minister of Aviation and Plenipotentiary of the Four-Year Plan.

Yet, like most of his Nazi fellows, Göring would fall from grace, brought down by the failings of his Luftwaffe, the vicious in-fighting that was endemic in the Third Reich, and by his own sybaritic, self-indulgent lifestyle: a world of pastel-coloured uniforms, vast train sets and pet lions. Nonetheless, as the Third Reich entered its death-throes in April 1945, Göring – though much diminished politically – still held high office, and, most crucially, was still formally designated as Hitler's deputy and successor.

> *'One of the most powerful and most prominent figures of the Third Reich was reduced to impotence.'*

It was with this position in mind that Göring, who was in Berchtesgaden as the end of the war approached, sent this telegram to Hitler on 23 April 1945 requesting permission – on the assumption that Hitler had been incapacitated by the Soviet advance on Berlin – that he might assume control of what was left of the Reich. '*Mein Führer*' he wrote:

> General Koller today gave me a briefing on the basis of communications given him by Colonel-General Jodl and General Christian, according to which you had referred certain decisions to me and emphasised that I, in case negotiations would become necessary, would be in an easier position than you in Berlin. These views were so surprising and serious to me that I felt obligated to assume, in case by 2200 hours no answer is forthcoming, that you have lost your freedom of action. I shall then view the conditions of your decree as fulfilled and take action for the wellbeing of Nation and Fatherland. You know what I feel for you in these most difficult hours of my life and I cannot express this in words. God protect you and allow you despite everything to come here as soon as possible.
>
> Your faithful Hermann Göring.

Nr. / **Marinenachrichtendienst** Ltg.-Nr. ___

| Aufgen., den 23.4. 19 45 | Weiter an | Tag | Uhrzeit | Ltg. | durch | |
|---|---|---|---|---|---|---|
| um 0056 Uhr | | | | | | Uhrzeitgruppen |
| von Ltg. | | | | | | 1811/11 frr |
| durch Schl | | | | | | 2352/14 frr |
| Verzögerungsverm. | | | | | | |

Geheim!

| Fernspruch | Funkspruch | | |
|---|---|---|---|
| Fernschreiben | Posttelegramm | von | Obersalzberg |

Mein Führer:

    General Koller hat mir heute auf Grund von Mitteilungen, die ihm
Generaloberst Jodl und General Christian gemacht hatten, eine Darstel=
lung gegeben, wonach Sie in gewissen Entscheidungen auf mich verwie=
sen hätten und dabei betont^n, ^ass ich, falls Verhandlungen notwen=
dig würden, dazu leichter i. ler Lage wäre als Sie in Berlin. Die Aus=
serungen waren für mich derart überraschend und ernst, dass ich mich
verpflichtet fühlte, falls bis 2200 Uhr keine Antwort erfolgt, nehme
ich an, dass Sie Ihrer Handlungsfreiheit beraubt sind. Ich werde dann
die Voraussetzungen Ihres Erlasses als gegeben ansehen und zum Wohle
von Volk und Vaterland handeln. Was ich in diesen schwersten Stunden
meines Lebens für Sie empfinde, das wissen Sie und kann ich durch
Worte nicht ausdrücken. Gott schütze Sie und lasse Sie trotz alledem
baldmöglichst hierher kommen.

                       Ihr getreuer Hermann Göring

Göring's telegram to Hitler, the cause of his demise.

It was not an unreasonable request. The subtext was that Göring had heard about Hitler's infamous rant in the Chancellery bunker the day before, in which he had raged at his generals, declaring that the war was lost and that he would remain in Berlin and commit suicide. In such circumstances, Göring said he felt duty-bound – as Hitler's designated successor – to act for the benefit of the Fatherland and asked that Hitler reply by 22.00 hours that evening to confirm that he had not been deprived of his freedom of action.

The telegram was clearly carefully worded so that it could not be misconstrued as an attempted power-grab, yet once it fell into the hands of Göring's arch-enemy, Martin Bormann, that is precisely what happened. Armed with this text, and a later telegram that Göring sent to Ribbentrop, Bormann persuaded Hitler that Göring's actions amounted to an attempted coup d'état. As Albert Speer recalled, Bormann exclaimed excitedly to Hitler that 'Göring is engaged in treason! . . . He will assume your office at twelve o'clock tonight, *mein Führer!*'[1]

Hitler, who was swinging between impotent rage and suicidal dejection, did not need much persuading. For months, senior Nazis had been rounding on Göring as one of the causes of Germany's malaise, deriding him as a morphine addict, a hedonist and an incompetent. This apparent betrayal was the final straw. Hitler flew into a tantrum, raging that Göring had failed, that he was lazy, corrupt and had been a drug addict 'for years'. When he calmed down he agreed a draft telegram, drawn up by Bormann, which stated that though Göring's actions amounted to treason – for which the penalty was death – in view of his former services to the Party, he would merely be stripped of all his offices and placed under arrest. Göring was requested to reply within thirty minutes.[2] His response, some days later, was merely to plead that the matter be reviewed, and to state that Hitler's doubt of his loyalty had caused him the 'worst hour of his life'.[3]

So it was that Hermann Göring's fall was complete. One of the most powerful and most prominent figures of the Third Reich was reduced to impotence, a prisoner in his own home. There was certainly much to criticise the bloated *Reichsmarschall* for, but in the end his demise was engineered by his rivals in a final round of the futile bloodletting and backbiting that had so characterised the Nazis in power. He would soon be followed into disgrace by Heinrich Himmler, deposed for his tentative negotiations with the Western powers behind Hitler's back. In the fetid, unreal atmosphere of the Reich Chancellery bunker, it was not just phantom armies that were commanded; the final death throes of Nazism itself were being directed.

Göring in pastel, and in happier times.

1  Speer, *Inside the Third Reich*, p. 644.

2  Ian Kershaw, *Hitler: Nemesis, 1936–1945* (London, 2000), p. 808.

3  Göring telegram, 27 April 1945, courtesy of Hermann Historica Auctions, Munich.

# 99 Admiral Dönitz's Baton

*When Karl Dönitz was appointed* to the rank of *Grossadmiral* (grand admiral) by Adolf Hitler on 30 January 1943, he would have been forgiven for feeling rather pleased with himself. Aged fifty-one, he was Commander-in-Chief of the German Navy; his two sons served in the U-boat arm, and – despite the minor problem of Stalingrad, then reaching its grim dénouement – the regime he served still bestrode Europe, occupying the continent from Bordeaux to the Volga, the North Cape to Libya.

Dönitz was an enthusiastic servant of Nazism, which he tended to see as synonymous with Germany. A veteran of the Imperial Navy U-boat arm in World War I, he emerged as the primary advocate of submarine warfare, specifically of the idea of targeting merchant vessels to cripple an opponent's economy.[1] He also gained a reputation, perhaps unfairly, of being a keen supporter of the Nazis and a convinced anti-Marxist and anti-Semite. At best, he was scrupulously loyal to his commander-in-chief, declaring on one occasion: 'Anyone who thinks he can do better than the *Führer* is stupid.'[2]

So, Dönitz would certainly have welcomed his promotion to grand admiral. As was customary, some time after his appointment he was presented with this admiral's baton, a ceremonial symbol of his authority. Twenty-six batons were issued by the Nazi regime: twenty-four to Army or Luftwaffe field marshals and two to Navy grand admirals – the other being Erich Raeder.

In Dönitz's case, he had insisted on having a hand in the design, rejecting a silver prototype as too heavy, and required the inclusion of both a swastika and a

To the Victor the Spoils . . .

247

submarine in the baton's two elaborate finials. The final version – created by jeweller H. J. Wilm of Berlin – weighed 900 grams and comprised a hollow aluminium shaft, wrapped in marine blue velvet, adorned with fouled anchors and German eagles in solid gold, interspersed with Iron Cross emblems in platinum. The finials featured a chain-link design in gold, and the date of Dönitz's elevation. It was all rather grand.

Such grandeur was to prove transient, however. Fast-forward some thirty months to May 1945, and the world in which Dönitz had exulted in 1943 lay in ruins. Hitler had committed suicide beneath a conquered Berlin; German forces were prostrate before their vengeful enemies and the pride of the U-boat arm had mostly been scuttled or sunk. Even Dönitz's sons had both been killed in the interim.

---

'Dönitz went into captivity, as his baton became a spoil of war.'

---

But, for Dönitz, the war had still not come to an end. By virtue of his blind loyalty to his *Führer*, he had been appointed as Hitler's successor, and now headed a phantom government – as President of the Greater German Reich and commander-in-chief of German armed forces – from the relative safety of Flensburg, close to the Danish border. Tolerated by British forces, who were well aware of its impotence, the 'Flensburg government' was a rather farcical administration, established in the Naval Academy building at Mürwik, which enjoyed vanishingly small authority, endemic factional squabbling and store rooms set aside for ministries that didn't exist.[3]

On 21 May 1945, the British authorities decided – at Soviet insistence – to bring this anomalous situation to an end. Dönitz and his senior lieutenants were called to a meeting at the local Allied headquarters, aboard the *Patria* in Flensburg harbour, on the morning of 23 May. There, they were curtly informed that 'the German government is dissolved', before being returned under armed guard to Mürwik, where some 6,000 of their fellows were already being rounded up for processing.[4] 'Operation Blackout' was deemed a complete success, the only casualties being Admiral Hans-Georg von Friedeburg, who managed to steal away from the 'circus' to commit suicide in a bathroom, and General Eberhard Kinzel, who shot his girlfriend and then turned his pistol on himself.[5]

It was during this processing that Dönitz was 'relieved' of his admiral's baton. Ordered to stand in a courtyard, while they were searched for poison vials, the admiral and the other prisoners were then told that they could pack a single bag to take with them. Dönitz's effects were thoroughly searched and his baton was handed to Brigadier John Churcher, commander of the 159th Infantry Brigade. Tight-lipped and scowling, Dönitz went into captivity, as his baton became a spoil of war. It was a potent symbol of Nazism's fall.

In time, Dönitz would be taken to Nuremberg, where he would stand trial from November 1945 on charges of crimes against peace, planning wars of aggression and war crimes. Found guilty on the latter two counts, he would be sentenced to ten years' imprisonment and released in 1956. He died in 1980, aged eighty-nine.

The baton, meanwhile, remained in Brigadier (later General) Churcher's possession until 1964, when it was donated to the regimental museum of the King's Shropshire Light Infantry (the regiment's 4th Battalion had been part of the 159th Infantry Brigade). It remains there to this day.

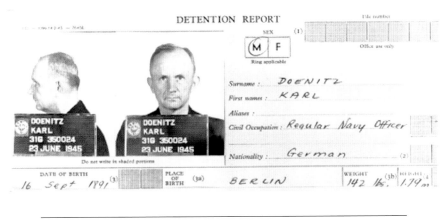

Dönitz in American detention: his fall is complete.

1  See Karl Dönitz, *Memoirs: Ten Years and Twenty Days* (Cleveland, 1959).

2  Alan Steinweis & Daniel Rogers (eds), *The Impact of Nazism: New Perspectives on the Third Reich and its Legacy* (Nebraska, 2003), pp. 186–8.

3  Michael Jones, *After Hitler* (London, 2015), p. 323.

4  Major 'Ned' Thornburn, *After Antwerp: The Long Haul to Victory*, Vol. III (Shrewsbury, 1993), p. 135.

5  Peter Padfield, *Dönitz: The Last Führer* (London, 1984), p. 434.

# 100 Göring's Cyanide Capsule

*When Hermann Göring broke this glass vial* of cyanide between his teeth on the night of 15 October 1946, he was following the lead of most of his fellow Nazi leaders in cheating justice by committing suicide.

At 10.44 p.m. the guard outside Göring's door glanced through the hatch and noticed that the prisoner was twitching and moaning. By the time that help arrived, Göring was having convulsions and turning blue, with froth forming at his lips and his fists clenched tight. Before any medical aid could be administered, he gave a rattle in his throat and sank into the bed. He was dead.

Upon examination of the corpse, the prison doctor discovered this broken glass vial on Göring's tongue and the empty brass container clutched in his fist. Due to the presence of cyanosis discolouration on the skin and the smell of bitter almonds in the cell, his conclusion was that Göring had taken cyanide.[1]

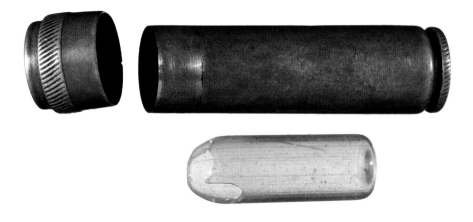

The cyanide vial and brass container retrieved from Göring's body.

Göring, along with a further fifteen defendants tried by the Nuremberg Tribunal, had been sentenced to death two weeks earlier, on 1 October. He had been found guilty on all four counts of crimes against peace, planning wars of aggression, war crimes and crimes against humanity. His guilt, the judgment stated, 'was unique in its enormity'.[2]

Göring had, perhaps, expected the death sentence, but when told that he would be hanged he was indignant, complaining to a prison psychologist that he 'should be spared the ignominy of the noose'.[3] Though his petition to the tribunal, asking to be shot as a soldier, had been rejected, he was adamant. He told his wife in his last meeting with her, a week before his death: 'You can be sure of one thing. They won't hang me.'[4]

---

*'Göring told his wife: "You can be sure of one thing. They won't hang me."'*

---

For a year or so before that, Göring – who was the most senior Nazi to stand trial at Nuremberg – had been something of a talisman for the accused, leading their defence and dominating proceedings, much to the frustration of the prosecutors. Clean from morphine for the first time in years, he was alert, shrewd and resourceful, swiftly mastering the documents placed before the court. 'Nobody' the British judge Norman Birkett noted, 'seems to have been prepared for his immense ability and knowledge.'[5]

Göring had been determined to be the master of his own fate, to have the last word. It is still unclear precisely how he came into possession of the cyanide capsule; some accounts maintain that he smuggled it into the cell himself and concealed it for a year; others suggest that a prison guard, Lieutenant Jack Wheelis, was charmed and bribed by Göring to deliver the poison to him unwittingly. Another account states that Obergruppenführer Erich von dem Bach-Zelewski – who was at Nuremberg as a prosecution witness – managed to hand the cyanide capsule to Göring personally, concealed in a bar of soap.[6]

Whatever its precise origins, Göring's use of cyanide in his cell in October 1946 was only a belated example of a much wider phenomenon, that of suicide in the Third Reich. Suicide was very widespread in 1945, as a generation of Germans were forced to confront the harsh realities of the collapse of Nazi Germany and the prospect of justice or vicious reprisals at the hands of their enemies. Over 7,000 suicides were reported in Berlin alone in 1945, while the town of Demmin in Pomerania saw a mass suicide of some 1,000 inhabitants after the arrival of the Red Army.[7] The total number of suicides amongst ordinary Germans in 1945 will never be known for sure, but must range well into the tens of thousands.

It was a course of action that even had the official sanction of the Nazi regime. Over 3,000 cyanide vials, complete with brass containers made from spent rifle cartridges, were made by the SS, using laboratories in Sachsenhausen concentration camp. Each one – 9 mm × 35 mm – contained a cubic centimetre of hydrocyanic acid, enough to

Nazi family suicide in Leipzig, 1945.

kill an adult within a couple of minutes. Around 1,000 of them were delivered to the Reich Chancellery in Berlin, for distribution to the Nazi elite. It was one of these that Göring used in 1946.[8]

Of course, by the time that Göring took his own life, many of his fellow senior Nazis had already shown the way; Hitler and Goebbels had killed themselves in the Berlin bunker, and Himmler had taken cyanide in Lüneburg after he fell into British hands in May 1945. At least a hundred other top Nazis committed suicide.[9]

1  Original documentation, including the report of the prison doctor, Dr Charles J. Roska, courtesy of Hermann Historica Auctions, Munich.

2  International Military Tribunal, Nuremberg, proceedings (courtesy of the Avalon Project). Göring judgment is available at http://avalon.law.yale.edu/imt/judgoeri.asp.

3  Quoted in Anthony Read, *The Devil's Disciples* (London, 2003), p. 922.

4  Ibid.

5  Ibid.

6  For a summary, see Ann Tusa & John Tusa, *The Nuremberg Trial* (London, 1983), pp. 483–4.

7  See Christian Goeschel, *Suicide in Nazi Germany* (Oxford, 2009), and Florian Huber, *Kind versprich mir, dass du dich erschießt: Der Untergang der kleinen Leute 1945* (Berlin, 2015).

8  Anton Joachimsthaler, *The Last Days of Hitler* (London, 1996), p. 169, and related documentation (see note 1).

9  Goeschel, p. 152.

# ACKNOWLEDGEMENTS

By its nature, a book of this sort involves asking more favours of more people than a straightforward history does. As well as the advice and expertise sought of fellow historians and academics, there are numerous pictures to be sourced, from archives, museums and auction houses. I had imagined at the outset that finding the pictures to illustrate the book would prove the most difficult and costly part of the process; however – thanks to the kind help of many of those listed below – it has been a pleasure.

For their specialist and technical knowledge, I would like to thank Lucy Adlington, Chris Evans, Ed van Engeland, Robert Forczyk, Johannes Gelsius, Richard Goldstein, Chris Goss, Joel Greenberg, Peter Jacobs, Nigel Jones, Charles Messenger, James Opie, Lawrence Paterson, Robin Schäfer, Jak Showell, Professor Caroline Sturdy Colls, Professor Nikolaus Wachsmann, John Walter and Martin Winstone. Matthew James helped with ancillary research; Donald Sommerville mastered the editing, and Jem Butcher did the excellent design. Special thanks must go to Tim Newark for all his hard work and expertise in preparing the text.

The seemingly Sisyphean task of sourcing pictures was eased massively by the wonderfully helpful Sina Nickoleit at Hermann Historica Auctions in Munich, also by the generous assistance of Peter Newark Historical Pictures, Ian Sayer, Gunnar Hansen, Norbert Podlesny at 3reich-collector.com, Edward Petruskevich at the Wilhelm Gustloff Museum, Jim Kreunen at militariaplaza.nl, Kenneth Rendell at the International Museum of World War Two, Michael Foedrowitz, Auktion Team Breker in Cologne, Christine Bernáth at the Shropshire Regimental Museum, the Gedenkstätte Deutscher Widerstand in Berlin, the Imperial War Museum in London, United States Holocaust Memorial Museum in Washington, DC, and Alexander Historical Auctions in Chesapeake City.

Thanks are also due to Professor Richard Overy – Britain's leading authority on the Third Reich – for his kind foreword, and to my publisher, the indomitable Michael Leventhal, without whose vision and drive the project would scarcely have achieved lift-off at all.

Lastly I would like to thank my family for their continued good-humoured tolerance of their 'author-in-residence', and in particular my parents-in-law, Nic and Eve Smellie, for being so consistently wonderful and redefining the role of 'in-laws'. This book is dedicated to them.

# PICTURE CREDITS

# BIBLIOGRAPHY

J. W. Baird, *To Die for Germany* (Bloomington, 1992)

H. Baur, *Hitler at my Side* (Houston, 1986)

Wolfgang Benz, *Die 101 wichtigsten Fragen – Das Dritte Reich* (Munich, 2006)

Wolfgang Benz & W. Pehle (eds), *Encyclopedia of German Resistance to the Nazi Movement* (New York, 1997)

Volker Berghahn, *Modern Germany* (Cambridge, 1982)

R. T. Bickers, *The Battle of Britain* (London, 1990)

Heinz Boberach (ed.), *Meldungen aus dem Reich*, Vol. VI (Herrsching, 1984)

Volkhard Bode & Gerhard Kaiser, *Building Hitler's Missiles* (Berlin, 2008)

G. Boeck & H.-U. Lammel (eds), *Die Universität Rostock in den Jahren 1933–1945* (Rostock, 2012)

Horst Boog, *The Global War: Germany and the Second World War* (Oxford, 2001)

Christopher Browning, *The Origins of the Final Solution: The Evolution of Nazi Jewish Policy, 1939–1942* (London, 2004)

C. Bryant, *Prague in Black: Nazi Rule and Czech Nationalism* (Cambridge, MA, 2007)

Alan Bullock, *Hitler: A Study in Tyranny* (London, 1962)

A. Burger, *The Devil's Workshop* (Barnsley, 2009)

Michael Burleigh, *Death and Deliverance: Euthanasia in Germany, c. 1900–1945* (Cambridge, 1994)

———, *The Third Reich: A New History* (London, 2000)

Terry Charman, *The German Home Front 1939–1945* (London, 1989)

———, *Outbreak 1939* (London, 2009)

Winston Churchill, *The Second World War* (London, 1959)

A. Clark, *Barbarossa: The Russian–German Conflict, 1941–1945* (London, 1995)

L. Clark, *Kursk* (London, 2011)

S. Cook & J. Bender, *Leibstandarte SS Adolf Hitler: Uniforms, Organization, & History* (San José, 1994)

Robin Cross, *The Battle of Kursk* (London, 1993)

*Deutschland-Berichte der Sozialdemokratischen Partei Deutschlands (SOPADE), 1934–1940* (Salzhausen 1980)

Herbert Döhring, *Hitlers Hausverwalter* (Bochum, 2013)

M. Domarus (ed.), *Adolf Hitler: Speeches and Proclamations, 1932–1945*, Vol. 2 (London, 1992)

Karl Dönitz, *Memoirs: Ten Years and Twenty Days* (Cleveland, 1959)

Angelika Ebbinghaus, 'Der Prozeß gegen Tesch & Stabenow', in *Zeitschrift für Sozialgeschichte*, Vol. 13 (1998)

John Ellis, *The World War Two Data Book* (London, 2003)

U. Feist, *The Fighting Me 109* (London, 1993)

A. Fergusson, *When Money Dies* (London, 2010)

Joachim Fest, *Hitler* (London, 2002)

———, *Inside Hitler's Bunker* (London, 2004)

Michael Foedrowitz, *The Flak Towers* (Berlin, 2007)

M. R. D. Foot (ed.), *The Oxford Companion to the Second World War* (Oxford, 1995)

Robert Forczyk, *Demyansk 1942–43* (Oxford, 2012)

R. Ford, *Germany's Secret Weapons in World War II* (Staplehurst, 2000)

Saul Friedländer, *The Years of Extermination: Nazi Germany and the Jews, 1939–1945* (London, 2007)

Karl-Heinz Frieser, *The Blitzkrieg Legend* (Annapolis, 2013)

Stephen Fritz, *Frontsoldaten: The German Soldier in World War Two* (Kentucky, 1997)

Elke Fröhlich (ed.), *Die Tagebücher von Joseph Goebbels*, Vol. XIV (Munich, 2006)

T. Gander, *German 88: The Most Famous Gun of the Second World War* (Barnsley, 2009)

R. Gellately, *The Gestapo and German Society: Enforcing Racial Policy, 1933–1945* (Oxford, 1992)

B. Gilmour, 'The KdF Brochure', *VW Trends*, 4/85

Horst Gleiss, *Breslauer Apokalypse 1945* (Wedel, 1986)

Joseph Goebbels, *Signale der neuen Zeit: 25 ausgewählte Reden von Dr. Joseph Goebbels* (Munich, 1938)

Christian Goeschel, *Suicide in Nazi Germany* (Oxford, 2009)

Heike Görtemaker, *Eva Braun: Life with Hitler* (London, 2011)

Vassili Grossman, *The Years of War: 1941–1945* (Moscow, 1946)

Lothar Gruchmann, *Justiz im Dritten Reich 1933–40* (Munich, 1988)

Richard Grunberger, *A Social History of the Third Reich* (London, 1970)

Michael Grüttner, *Das Dritte Reich. 1933–1939* (Stuttgart, 2014)

Heinz Guderian, *Panzer Leader* (London, 1952)

Ernst Hanfstaengl, *15 Jahre mit Hitler* (Munich, 1980)

Richard Hargreaves, *Hitler's Final Fortress – Breslau 1945* (Barnsley, 2011)

Christian Hartmann et al. (eds), *Hitler, Mein Kampf: Eine kritische Edition*, Vol. 1 (Munich, 2016)

Peter Hayes, *From Cooperation to Complicity: Degussa in the Third Reich* (Cambridge, 2004)

Ulrich Herbert, *Hitler's Foreign Workers: Enforced Foreign Labour in Germany under the Third Reich* (Cambridge, 1997)

A. Hitler, *Mein Kampf* (London, 1939)

Peter Hoffmann, *Stauffenberg: A Family History, 1905–1944* (Cambridge, 1995)

———, *Hitler's Personal Security* (Boston, 2000)

Florian Huber, *Kind versprich mir, dass du dich erschießt: Der Untergang der kleinen Leute 1945* (Berlin, 2015)

Keith Jeffery, *MI6: The History of the Secret Intelligence Service, 1909–1949* (London, 2011)

T. Jentz, *Panzertruppen 2: The Complete Guide to the Creation & Combat Employment of Germany's Tank Force 1943–1945* (Atglen, PA, 1998)

T. Jentz & H. Doyle, *Tiger I Heavy Tank: 1942–45* (Oxford, 1993)

Anton Joachimsthaler, *The Last Days of Hitler* (London, 1996)

E. Johnson & K.-H. Reuband, *What We Knew: Terror, Mass Murder and Everyday Life in Nazi Germany* (London, 2005)

Michael Jones, *After Hitler* (London, 2015)

Nigel Jones, 'A Song for Hitler', *History Today*, October 2007

Traudl Junge, *Until the Final Hour* (London, 2003)

Sven Felix Kellerhoff, *Berlin im Krieg: Eine Generation erinnert sich* (Berlin, 2011)

———, *The Reichstag Fire* (Stroud, 2016)

Erich Kempka, *I was Hitler's Chauffeur* (London, 2010)

Ian Kershaw, *Hitler: Hubris 1889–1936* (London, 1998)

———, *Hitler: Nemesis, 1936–1945* (London, 2000)

Victor Klemperer, *I Shall Bear Witness* (London, 1998)

K. M. Kloeppel, *The Military Utility of German Rocketry During World War II* (Air Command and Staff College, 1997)

Maik Kopleck, *München, 1933–1945* (Berlin, 2005)

Hanns von Krannhals, *Der Warschauer Aufstand 1944* (Frankfurt am Main, 1964)

R. Kriebel, *Inside the Afrika Korps* (London, 1999)

A. Kubizek, *The Young Hitler I Knew* (London, 2006)

P. Levi, *Survival in Auschwitz* (New York, 1958)

Peter Longerich, *Goebbels* (London, 2015)

S. P. Lovell, *Of Spies & Strategems* (New Jersey, 1963)

Robin Lumsden, *SS: Himmler's Black Order, 1923–45* (Stroud, 1997)

Frank McDonough, *The Gestapo: The Myth and Reality of Hitler's Secret Police* (London, 2015)
———, *Hitler and the Rise of the Nazi Party* (London, 2003)
Ben Macintyre, *Agent Zigzag* (London, 2007)
Mark Mazower, *Dark Continent* (London, 1998)
H. Metelmann, *A Hitler Youth* (Staplehurst, 2004)
Roger Moorhouse, *Killing Hitler: The Third Reich and the Plots against the Führer* (London, 2006)
———, *Berlin at War: Life and Death in Hitler's Capital, 1939–1945* (London, 2010)
———, *The Devils' Alliance: Hitler's Pact with Stalin, 1939–1941* (London, 2014)
———, *Ship of Fate: The Story of the MV Wilhelm Gustloff* (London, 2016)
C. Mulley, *The Women Who Flew for Hitler* (London, 2017)

T. Newark, *Brassey's Book of Camouflage* (London, 1996)
———, *Camouflage* (London, 2007)
Jeremy Noakes (ed.), *Nazism 1919–1945*, Vol. 4: *The German Home Front in World War II* (Exeter, 1998)
J. Norris, *88mm Flak 18/36/37/41 & PaK 43, 1936–45* (Oxford, 2002)

Norman Ohler, *Blitzed: Drugs in Nazi Germany* (London, 2016)
Frederick I. Ordway III & Mitchell R. Sharpe, *The Rocket Team* (New York, 1979)
G. Orwell, *The Orwell Reader* (London, 1956)

Peter Padfield, *Dönitz: The Last Führer* (London, 1984)
———, *Hess: The Führer's Disciple* (London, 1991)
S. Parkinson, *Volkswagen Beetle* (Dorchester, 1996)
Henry Picker, *Tischgespräche im Führerhauptquartier: 1941–1942* (Bonn, 1951)
Anna Plaim, *Bei Hitlers* (Munich, 2005)
Othmar Plöckinger, *Geschichte eines Buches: Adolf Hitlers 'Mein Kampf': 1922–1945* (Munich, 2006)

Richard Raskin, *A Child at Gunpoint* (Aarhus, 2004)
Nicolas Rasmussen, *On Speed: The Many Lives of Amphetamine* (New York, 2009)
Anthony Read, *The Devil's Disciples* (London, 2003)
Laurence Rees, *World War II Behind Closed Doors* (London, 2009)
———, *The Holocaust* (London, 2017)
David Rolf, *The Bloody Road to Tunis: The Destruction of Axis Forces in North Africa* (London, 2001)
Mark Roseman, *The Lake, The Villa, The Meeting: Wannsee and the Final Solution* (London, 2002)
Ron Rosenbaum, *Explaining Hitler* (New York, 1998
G. Rottman, *World War II Axis Booby Traps and Sabotage Tactics* (Oxford, 2011)
Timothy Ryback, *Hitler's Private Library* (London, 2009)

B. Sax & D. Kuntz (eds), *Inside Hitler's Germany: A Documentary History of Life in the Third Reich* (Lexington, 1992)
Wolfgang Schäche, Norbert Szymanski, *Das Reichssportfeld. Architektur im Spannungsfeld von Sport und Macht* (Berlin, 2001), p. 57.
Christa Schikora et al., *Die Wannsee-Konferenz und der Völkermord an den europäischen Juden* (Berlin, 2006)
A. Schmidt & M. Urban, *Das Reichsparteitagsgelände* (Nuremberg, 2009)
Detlef Schmiechen-Ackermann: '"Der Blockwart". Die unteren Parteifunktionäre im nationalsozialistischen Terror- und Überwachungsapparat', *Vierteljahrshefte für Zeitgeschichte*, No. 48 (2000)
Christa Schroeder, *He Was My Chief* (London, 2009)
G. Schulze-Wegener, *Das Eiserne Kreuz in der deutschen Geschichte* (Graz, 2012)
Gitta Sereny, *Into that Darkness* (London, 1974)
William L. Shirer, *The Rise and Fall of the Third Reich* (London, 1959)
Daniel Siemens, *The Making of a Nazi Hero: The Murder and Myth of Horst Wessel* (London, 2013)
Anna Maria Sigmund, *Die Frauen der Nazis* (Vienna, 1998
Denis Mack Smith, *Mussolini* (London, 1981)

Howard Smith, *Last Train from Berlin* (London, 1942)

K. Smoleń, *Auschwitz-Birkenau State Museum in Oświęcim* (Oświęcim, 2014)

Albert Speer, *Inside the Third Reich* (London, 1970)

W. Spielberger, *Der Panzerkampfwagen Tiger und seine Abarten* (Stuttgart, 1997)

Alfred Spieß, *Heiner Lichtenstein, Das Unternehmen Tannenberg* (Wiesbaden, 1979

F. Spotts, *Hitler and the Power of Aesthetics* (London, 2003)

S. Steinbacher, *Auschwitz: A History* (London, 2005)

Alan Steinweis & Daniel Rogers (eds), *The Impact of Nazism: New Perspectives on the Third Reich and its Legacy* (Nebraska, 2003)

Stiftung Topographie des Terrors (ed.), *Topography of Terror – Documentation* (Berlin, 2014)

Despina Stratigakos, *Hitler at Home* (New Haven & London, 2015)

Teddy Suhren, *Ace of Aces: Memoirs of a U-Boat Rebel* (London, 2011)

C. G. Sweeting, *Hitler's Squadron* (Dulles, 2001)

B. Taylor, *Volkswagen Military Vehicles of the Third Reich* (Cambridge, 2004)

F. Taylor, *The Downfall of Money* (London, 2013)

T. Thacker, *Joseph Goebbels: Life and Death* (London, 2009)

M. C. Thomsett, *The German Opposition to Hitler* (Jefferson, 1997)

Major 'Ned' Thornburn, *After Antwerp: The Long Haul to Victory*, Vol. III (Shrewsbury, 1993)

A. Tooze, *The Wages of Destruction* (London, 2006)

Hugh Trevor-Roper (ed.), *Hitler's Table Talk: 1941–1944* (New York, 2000)

Isaac Trunk & Robert Shapiro, *Łódz· Ghetto: A History* (Indiana, 2006)

F. Tubbs & R. Clawson, *Stahlhelm: Evolution of the German Steel Helmet* (Kent, Ohio, 2000)

Ann Tusa & John Tusa, *The Nuremberg Trial* (London, 1983)

Volker Ullrich, *Adolf Hitler* (Frankfurt am Main, 2013)

———, *Hitler: Ascent 1889–1939* (London, 2016)

Herwart Vorländer, 'NS-Volkswohlfahrt und Winterhilfswerk des Deutschen Volkes', *Vierteljahrshefte für Zeitgeschichte*, No. 34 (1986)

Nikolaus Wachsmann, *KL: A History of the Nazi Concentration Camps* (London, 2015)

Robert G. L. Waite, *The Psychopathic God: Adolf Hitler* (New York, 1993)

Walter Warlimont, *Inside Hitler's Headquarters* (London, 1964)

J. Weingartner, *Hitler's Guard* (Nashville, 1974)

David Welch, *The Third Reich: Politics and Propaganda* (London, 1993)

Samuel Willenberg, *Revolt in Treblinka* (Warsaw, 1992)

Gordon Williamson, *Aces of the Reich* (London, 1989)

T. Zabecki (ed.), *World War II in Europe* (Connecticut, 1999)

Stanislav Záměcník, *That was Dachau: 1933–1945* (Brussels, 2003)

H. E. Ziegler, *Turbinenjäger Me 262* (Stuttgart, 1977)